The Contingency of Theory

THE CONTINGENCY OF THEORY

Yale University Press New Haven and London

Pragmatism, Expressivism, and Deconstruction **Gary Wihl**

Grateful acknowledgment is given to the following for permission to reprint in substantially revised form: "Marxism," in *The Johns Hopkins Guide to Literary Theory and Criticism,* ed. Martin Kreiswirth and Michael Groden (Baltimore: Johns Hopkins Univ. Press, 1993), 495–99; "Empsonian Honesty and the Beginnings of Individualism," in *William Empson: The Critical Achievement,* ed. Christopher Norris and Nigel Mapp (Cambridge: Cambridge Univ. Press, 1993), 121–42; "Aesthetic Ideology: Paul de Man's Final Phase," in *Theory between the Disciplines,* ed. Martin Kreiswirth and Mark Cheetham (Ann Arbor: Univ. of Michigan Press, 1990), 35–57; "Why the Interpretive Community Has Banished Literary Theory," *Philosophy and Literature* 11 (1987): 272–81.

Designed by Deborah Dutton
Set in Sabon type by The Composing Room of Michigan, Inc., Grand Rapids, Michigan

Printed in the United States of America by Edwards Brothers, Ann Arbor, Michigan

Library of Congress Cataloging-in-Publication Data

Wihl, Gary, 1953–
    The contingency of theory : pragmatism, expressivism, and deconstruction / Gary Wihl.
        p.   cm.
    Includes index.
    ISBN 0-300-05798-9
    1. Literature—Philosophy.   2. Pragmatism.
    3. Deconstruction.   I. Title.
PN45.W467   1994
801—dc20   93-36108
                                                     CIP

A catalogue record for this book is available from the British Library.
The paper in this book meets the guidelines for permanence and durability of the Committee on Production Guidelines for Book Longevity of the Council on Library Resources.

10 9 8 7 6 5 4 3 2 1

CONTENTS

PREFACE

This book provides a detailed examination of some contemporary theoretical discourse about literary texts in order to strengthen and represent some central features of a pluralist, democratic culture, which is the sort of culture I assume for my readers.

Critics and students of literature commonly exchange the words *text* or *textuality* for almost any traditionally understood feature of a work of literature: its genre, rhetorical structure, aesthetic status, or the psychology of its author. At a general level of discussion the term *textuality* now encompasses entire schools or periods of literature and makes it possible to compare directly features of novels, poems, plays, prose tracts, autobiography, or practically any written form of documentation within a specified period of history. Texts rather than works of literature are now seen as part of the symbolic production of complex modern societies, for the concept of the "text," as opposed to "the work," seems to be better adapted to modernist and postmodernist theories about the way societies organize values and enrich or diminish the everyday quality of life. In many ways, the whole discourse about texts seems to be gradually replacing the discourse about aesthetics that we have inherited from the great Enlightenment and Romantic traditions, although it is presently unclear what exactly is being exchanged, in the name of the text, for the aesthetics of beauty, feeling, and the use of art and literature as a measure of social harmony.

Curiously, the widespread discourse about texts seems to be occurring without any point of agreement or central definition of *text*. Counter to some of the positive tendencies I have just sketched, there is a great deal of hostility toward the literary theories which gave the word its currency, namely, New Criticism, Structuralism, and Deconstruction. A few oft-cited quotations have become the clichés of antiformalists who see themselves as resisting currents of nihilism and skepticism in literary studies. These quotations include Jacques Derrida's "Il n'y a pas de hors-texte," Paul de Man's "Texts masquerade in the guise of wars or revolutions," and Roland Barthes's "The Text is plural . . . thus it answers not to an interpretation, liberal though it may be, but to an explosion, a dissemination." The time has surely come for a patient reflection upon the meaning of these phrases, which have been in circulation for more than twenty years. Part of this reflection must incorporate some of the very pressing issues about the nonfoundationalism of literary studies within deeply plural societies that seem to lie behind the adoption and circulation of the vocabulary about texts. The undercurrent of nonfoundationalism cannot be easily shrugged off as the same thing as skepticism and nihilism. The discourse about texts has put the issue of nonfoundationalism on the table of literary studies, even if many of these issues need to achieve a much greater degree of clarity.

The philosophical movement that most clearly supports a nonfoundationalist approach to literary studies and links the study of literary texts to the plural nature of modern society is pragmatism. Pragmatists do not worry about foundations that would justify or legitimate the study of literature. They eschew topics like the intrinsic meaning of a literary work, the epistemology of literature as mimesis, and the hermeneutical essence of literature in a tradition of logos. But pragmatists do believe that the current theorizing about texts offers some very important insights into what knits together the plural interests of contemporary democratic societies. Richard Rorty says that texts induce us to tell "a story about their relation to other texts, or the intentions of its author, or what makes life

"storytelling"

One story linked to the next.

worth living, or the events of the century in which the poem was written, or the events of our own century, or the incidents of our own lives, or whatever else seems appropriate in a given situation." None of this weaving and reweaving of texts is upheld by a singular, predetermined language of foundationalism. Which is not to say that anything goes, but that the contact between texts will not be secured in the vocabulary of objectivity or subjectivity, which textuality has been gradually replacing. The discovery of textuality is part of the discovery that the coherence and values of the lives of readers and writers are a product of certain forms of relatedness rather than a neutral mirroring of a preestablished set of social and cultural foundations.

Rorty's statement about texts provides the loftiest claims that can be attached to the study of literature and also points to what sort of analysis remains to be done. If the literary theories of the last twenty years have taught us anything in pushing a term like *text* to the forefront, it is that we must respect the tensions and possible incompatibilities between the different components of language that make up texts, in the same way that we have come to respect a greater degree of difference among the interests of members of a pluralist society. The term *text* achieves specificity precisely to the degree that it allows for multiple strands of language to become a central feature of the utterances that have the greatest claim to be considered literary. In this book, I make a strong effort to respect that insight and to credit that insight to the work of literary theorists who study the language of those texts that are commonly acknowledged to be literature. One of the most important insights of deconstruction is the location of linguistic *cruces* that make up literary texts, say the crux between rhetoric and grammar or between performatives and mimetic tropes or between written, materially inscribed features of texts and their aesthetic status as symbols. Opponents of deconstruction characterize it as a form of relativism and nihilism. But I have found practically no engagement whatsoever with the rigorous precision and focus of deconstructive readings, which cannot be seen beneath its opponents' broad brushstrokes. Rorty's discourse about texts actually reaches a higher level of fulfillment not as a broad-based attack on the primacy of realist epistemology, but as a reminder to notice and identify those cruces, characteristic of texts, where metaphors and ironies sharpen into what can and cannot be commensurated in the language that agents use to tell their various stories. Admittedly, there remains a high degree of frustration with the concrete implications of deconstruction, but this book will try to show that the pragmatist application of texts to situations is greatly enhanced

and confirmed by the use of texts as cruces of linguistic embodiment and engagement. Once grasped and seen for what they are, these linguistic cruces, which
emerge through our discourse about texts, lend a great deal of support and coherence to the pragmatist's nonfoundationalist view of persons and societies.

My effort in this direction explains the surface structure of this book, which is
divided between philosophers and literary critics and, moreover, does not attempt
to systematize or evaluate them according to schools, methods, doctrines, ruling
principles, or with attention to each philosopher or critic's entire oeuvre. Right
from the outset, this book's commitment to the central importance of a linguistic
crux as the creation of a situation and relation places the burden of demonstrating
my philosophical position, vis-à-vis pragmatist nonfoundationalism, upon a key,
decisive passage from each of the critics and philosophers considered. That is why
I do not discuss the general approach of Stanley Fish or William Empson or
Fredric Jameson or Paul de Man, but rather a core issue which concerns their
construction of text and which may be found in a core essay of theirs, and most
probably in one core passage from that essay. To the degree this effort at precision
actually works, I am pleased to call it a deconstructive approach.

If texts can serve to point us to the most crucial instances of linguistic usage,
and if these cruces can be seen as enabling a high level of nonfoundationalist
understanding about the plural nature of our society, the nature of its coherence,
the degree to which its various interests can be commensurated, then it may not be
possible to generalize about them in the normal manner of philosophical inquiry.
Their philosophical implications will have to be realized in a way that respects
their local difference and complexity. Because so much of this book is concerned
with articulating the philosophical issue of nonfoundationalism through a textual
crux, I feel the need to caution the reader that the task of pinpointing the crux and
finding its philosophical implications cannot be dissociated. There have been
many recent attempts to give a philosophical dimension to literary studies. I refer
to the superb writings of Anthony Cascardi, Richard Eldridge, Alexander
Nehamas, and Martha Nussbaum. In each case, works of literature become what
Peter McCormick would call a "personal language of ethical resonance." These
writers do not treat literature as an empty vessel for philosophical issues but
rearticulate literature with a depth of insight that we associate with philosophical
treatises. Nevertheless, I feel a certain degree of frustration as I read them precisely
because there is a palpable absence of any reflection upon the actual construction
of a text. The overlap between literature and philosophy continues to take the

cf. Leroy on phronesis!

form of large expressions, like the narration of the self, the advent of a new Kantian aesthetic liberalism, and a reconstruction of the traditional language of Aristotelean phronesis. What would happen if these issues were subjected to analysis of the sort I tend to find in the critics I focus upon in this book? Two outcomes are likely. One is that the richly articulated views of literature among these philosophers would reveal a tendency to ignore the best insights of those people working very closely with the language of literature. Second, these philosophers tend to move backward into the great terminology of aesthetics and modernity which we have inherited from our philosophical tradition. That movement seems to me to fail to capitalize on many of the fresh insights, as yet undeveloped, of what we are discovering about the personal use of language in the name of textuality. If we do not make this effort, I believe that controversies and debates about deconstruction, pragmatism, modernity, historicism, and skepticism will continue to be fought out at a nonproductive level of inaccurate, occasionally superficial, expression. In order to settle or refine these debates, principles of textuality have to be allowed into the vocabulary of the different perspectives. How can this be done?

My approach in this book has been to rely heavily on certain writings by the philosopher Charles Taylor. In many ways, Taylor's writings bridge the issues that arise from a theory of textuality and philosophical concerns. But to date his work has received scant attention within the literary disciplines. An indirect contribution of this book, therefore, is simply to present for the first time in detail some aspects of his work outside the disciplines of philosophy and political science. Taylor's writing is indebted to Hegelian philosophy and hermeneutics; his writings typically address the problem of historical change, situatedness, and the importance of language to the realization of human identity. There are also ontological and ethical aspects of his work which run quite counter to my interest in a nonfoundationalist approach to the problem of modernity and literary theory. What stands out as a central topic in Taylor's work, however, is a very special definition of choice as the mode by which persons become embedded in the fabric of their society and in turn shape its highest values and meanings. For Taylor, choice involves interpreting contrasting articulations, and these articulations are drawn from an intense engagement with forms of language that approach the literary end of the spectrum. Taylor examines language in terms that are noninstrumental, nondesignative, and, most subtly, nonaesthetic. Here is not the place to try to summarize Taylor. What I want to note, at the outset, is a connection between an act of decision making and a particular philosophy of language. One large goal of my book is to attempt a mutual modification between the cruces that make up a theory of a text, in all their detail and local meaning, and the linguistic contrasts and incommensurables that make up Taylor's analysis of the language of choice. If these two can be brought together, then textuality gains philosophical substance by being able to incorporate choices that Taylor would see as situating agents within modernist societies.

One of the immediate implications of my approach is to see the crucial decisions enacted with the complex language of texts as having a direct bearing on human identity and personhood. That is to say, literary texts become important philosophical sources for situating selves and defining ethical positions, but not through the occurrence of normal literary practices. Texts do not need to be interpreted first and then applied to real life or grounded in universal principles or turned into aesthetic conceptions of the social world. Furthermore, critics of literature, like the ones on whom I focus, do not need to be corrected or refuted. What comes to matter is the location of textual patterns that shape a language of personhood, the language that Peter McCormick calls resonant. My approach dispenses, in pragmatic fashion, from seeking that resonance in an independent theory of textual structure or mimesis or validity.

In this sort of literary architecture, the goal of a chapter on Stanley Fish or William Empson is not to judge the critic against the primary work, but to see in their actual construction of a text an effort to situate a reader deeply in a language of personal resonance. Taylor provides the framework and, I suppose, the yardstick for such a language. By the same token, his philosophical exposition of contrast and decision making benefits from an encounter with some of the dialectical and some of the most incommensurable elements of language that are to be found in this book's most textually aware critics, Paul de Man and Fredric Jameson. Stanley Cavell's commentary on deconstruction and on Empson provides additional key components, namely, the specification of which elements in a literary text impose claims upon other speakers' use of language.

In the final analysis, the commentaries offered in this book come back full circle to the pragmatist issue of a literature without foundations and one that supports the plurality of modern society. At its most developed, a situated, textually determined, personal language of resonance should not preclude a multiplicity of voices. And it should leave space between different institutions and cultures that may inhabit the same democratic society. The space between is not a void of ethical neutrality or indifference, however, but rather the as-yet-underdetermined replacement of our old philosophical vocabulary by the discovery of the meeting points of our plural convictions. It is a space, finally, in which recent concepts of literature may be realized and fulfilled.

Acknowledgments

Research grants from the Social Sciences and Humanities Research Council of Canada provided time to write this book and support for the preparation of the manuscript.

The comments of several colleagues at McGill have improved this book. I thank David Hensley, Charles Taylor, James Tully, and Sarah Westphal. Martin Kreiswirth and Christie McDonald invited me to present portions of the manuscript as lectures and offered lots of encouragement at various stages of the book's development. Stephen Ahern and René Hulan, my research assistants, verified bibliographical information. It is a pleasure to thank Jonathan Brent and Paul Fry at Yale for their interest in and support of my work.

Philosophies of Language without Foundations **PART ONE**

1 Pragmatism, Expressivism, and Deconstruction

In the first part of this book I attempt to combine features from three contemporary philosophies of language in order to describe how personal and collective convictions may arise from the study of literature. The three philosophies of language are expressivism, as it is defined in the writings of Charles Taylor and Stanley Cavell; deconstructionism, as exemplified by the writings of Paul de Man after 1970; and pragmatism, as it is used in recent essays by Richard Rorty and Stanley Fish.

This introduction is largely devoted to an outline of the main concerns of each philosophy of language, starting with the pragmatists, and to a brief account of why I believe that, in spite of well-known differences which have kept apart the philosophers and critics who hold each position, they reinforce each other and work together in important ways for the present-day study of literature. I would go so far as to say that together these philosophies of language clarify what can and cannot be accomplished within the literary disciplines.

Pragmatism

What do I mean by the term *conviction*? It is not commonly found in studies of literature or literary theory, and I would not want an unfamiliar term to cause any confusion about this book's objectives. *Conviction* seems to me the best term for indicating that the philosophical scope of this book belongs within the bounds of modern pragmatism rather than within the tradition of inquiries about literature's truth value or its aesthetic status. Establishing a conviction about the rightness of a work of literature for oneself is, according to pragmatists, the philosophical task of literary studies. Though difficult to define or systematize, the development of personal and collective convictions is the function of works of literature. The critics and philosophers I shall discuss in this book are those who illuminate what is involved in that literary function whether or not they explicitly identify themselves with a pragmatist point of view.

By *conviction* I also acknowledge the fact of plurality and the kind of philosophical challenge that plurality poses. I intend to keep in play these questions: How does a reader acquire and then maintain a particular stance toward a relatively small corpus of literary works? Why should that particular reader's insights be of value to any other reader? Is it necessary to reconcile multiple readings of works of literature and, if so, to what degree of generality? How does reading, as a specific interpretive activity, connect with a person's other verbal activities or participation in other cultural events?

The plurality of topics and approaches that presently makes up the academic discipline of literary studies arises from the effort to match the value and significance of particular authors or works of literature to the convictions of an increasingly heterogeneous readership. Peter Railton describes heterogeneity and pluralism as a moral dilemma, but his words are equally relevant to the study of literature:

Our moral thought and practice have multiple origins in human history and anthropology, bearing traces of sacred as well as secular conceptual schemes, of changing folk and scientific theories of mind and society, of codes of honor and retribution as well as norms of beneficence and fairness, of expedient social and political compromises hammered out in specific historical circumstances by competing interests under shifting power relations, and even of previous philosophical attempts at unification and legitimation. It is only to be expected that any new effort to find—or develop—coherence and system in moral discourse will face some pretty recalcitrant phenomena. (720)[1]

Nevertheless, people who become deeply concerned about morality, and literature, do require philosophical guidance in order to give some stability and coherence to all these recalcitrant phenomena. The philosophical issue of how to reconcile multiple and often opposing interpretations and theories of literature parallels the issues associated with pluralism in ethics and politics. Susan Wolf writes, "The pluralist believes . . . that no principle or decision procedure exists that can guarantee a unique and determinate answer to every moral question involving a choice among different fundamental moral values or principles . . . pluralism has implications for the way we understand issues concerning moral objectivity and moral relativism" (785).[2] Traditionally, these implications have moved in the direction of subjectivism and relativism, which deny the possibility of resolving conflicts and commensurating different values and beliefs. For Wolf, however, "a plurality of values pulls one in different directions" (788), and this fundamental experience of contradiction encourages the pluralist to look for ever-more-complex and more finely determined limits and constraints to what is acceptable moral thought and action. The task of apprehending these limits and constraints becomes the actual practice of moral reason, and in a genuinely plural mode, it involves a mixture of "dialogue, logic, argument, perception, experience" and reflection. Pluralism, once its multiplicity and diversity is grasped, makes the traditional meanings of objectivism or relativism irrelevant. What matters to morality, and I would say to literature, is the quality of the determination that constrains agents in the full knowledge that perfect harmony is out of the question. As Railton says, "Values might be the sort of things that are indeterminate and incommensurable in various ways, and our intuitive sense that certain moral choices involve genuine dilemmas can be seen as expressing simultaneously this idea of indeterminacy or incommensurability, on the one hand, and the idea of genuineness, on the other" (740). The underlying argument of this entire book is based on the same point, but with regard to the language of literary texts. To what degree are the plural strands of language commensurable, and what does the effort to determine that degree, in the name of textuality, express about genuine, if not foundational, humanistic values?

Pragmatists, like pluralists, argue that the lack of an objectivist framework for discussing morality or art makes no claim on behalf of subjectivism or relativism or irrationalism.[3] Rorty and Fish have tried to show that separating a discourse about belief, value, and agreement from a discourse of legitimation and justification does not entail any of these dire consequences.[4] I shall rely on Rorty and Fish to further the position I am developing in this book, but only up to a point. They are useful in disengaging philosophical questions about convictions and beliefs from universal, or generic, questions either about literature as a whole or about the ideal reader without regard to local differences of gender or ethnic background or linguistic community. For pragmatists, there is no point in eliminating cultural differences for the sake of answering concerns about subjectivism and relativism, especially if these concerns are not as worrisome as they might first appear. So, while pragmatists recognize a deep connection between convictions and important cultural differences, they do not seek to scale or reduce those differences to universal principles. The pragmatic shift within our present culture reveals itself in the fact that philosophical answers do not generally appeal to what Richard Shusterman calls "transparent fact, absolute or univocal truth, and mind-independent objectivity." For, he continues, "such ideas underwrite the possibility of attaining some perfect God's-eye grasp of things as they really are, independent of how we differently perceive them, a seeing or understanding that is free from . . . corrigibility and perspectival pluralities."[5]

Persisting concerns about relativism and subjectivism seem to acknowledge the weakening of universals as well, but negatively rather than positively. For pragmatists, the end of universalist modes of inquiry eventually entails the end of the relativist and subjectivist dilemmas. Without a core of universal truths around which all epistemic inquiry spins, the need for terms like *relativism* and *subjectivism* disappears.[6] Lack of agreement, or what I am positively calling plurality, does not signal error or the complete absence of standards.

The pragmatist position requires deep convictions on the part of cultural players like poets and philosophers but does not require that *deep* mean the same thing to each speaker in order to make society coherent. What matters is discovering where one stands in the web of multiple vocabularies and beliefs, and what exactly is entailed in moving from one strand to the next. The pragmatist definition of social coherence is well expressed in the writings of Martha Minow on cultural differences and American law and by Martha Nussbaum in her essays on the English novel. Minow suggests that in matters of law, "[we] should strive for the standpoint of someone committed to the moral relevance of contingent particulars," and quotes Charles Sanders Peirce in support: reasoning about justice, to take a key example, "should not form a chain which is no stronger than its weakest link, but a cable whose fibers may be ever so slender, provided they are sufficiently numerous and infinitely connected."[7] Nussbaum provides a similar image when she writes, "We reflect on an incident not by subsuming it under a general rule, not by assimilating its features to the terms of an elegant scientific procedure, but burrowing down to the depths of the particular, finding images and connections that will permit us to see it more truly, describe it more richly" (quoted in Minow 381).

The emphasis on breaking down generic and universalist vocabularies in favor of local forms of understanding brings pragmatists into contact with very specific views about language. The pragmatist view of literature orients the discourse about conviction away from the demand that literature justify itself to its readers by its special ability to represent universal meanings and situations. Ultimately, the very term *literature* needs to be broken down into the different vocabularies that may coexist within single works or that may serve different interests within a community of readers.

But pragmatists like Rorty and Fish founder when they assume that the major stumbling block to a multiple discourse about convictions is the doctrine of linguistic representationalism. Rorty calls this the view of language as a medium.[8] Reducing the emphasis on linguistic representationalism is an important step for pragmatists because it allows them to map all the different purposes to which we put language and to show, further, that languages whose primary function is the description of phenomena are not necessarily master vocabularies for all others. But that insight alone does not seem sufficient for maintaining a strong connection between the use of language and the development of convictions. Fish's position on the coherence of an interpretive community takes pragmatism to a radical extreme because it reduces all uses of language to sheer persuasion and contextually dependent meanings. He offers a picture of a highly adaptive and flexible community of interpreters as an alternative to the pseudoidealized work of literature. But he identifies belief with utterance so completely that speech-acts, rhetorical devices, and poems become interchangeable units of meaning, practically devoid of any linguistic structure. Accordingly, different types of language cease to have any role in the actual shaping of belief and identity. Fish sees every utterance as an immediate expression of a belief, and he discusses language in general only when he is required to point out the fallacy of the medium-theory.

I would agree with the emphasis on the use of words as a transaction between speakers rather than upon words as primarily carrying previously formed messages between speakers. But even so, the use of words would remain a very impoverished way of understanding the role of language if it serves only to attack the primacy of things like literal meaning or referentiality or formalist poetic autonomy. If words have uses and if uses require beliefs, then some uses and some word-chains will still count more than others, some values will prevail, and speakers will on occasion not only change beliefs but also interpret and debate beliefs in order to strengthen them. In the absence of any ranking of beliefs and values, traditional accusations of subjectivism and relativism are bound to persist. Railton makes the point that in order to recognize plurality and to see that recognition as part of a nonfoundationalist philosophical project, analysis and reflection have to be based on high quality determinations of conflict or incommensurability. Do pragmatists offer sufficient determinations of plurality, incommensurability, and difference?

In positing a direct connection between utterance and belief, pragmatists call attention to what matters in debates about literary meaning and value: how works of literature promote and develop everyday convictions. Furthermore, pragmatists maintain that these convictions cannot be sustained independently of the actual task of commenting upon and circulating particular works of literature. Literature ceases to exist when it is looked upon as an inert repository of meanings or when it is compared to what Rorty calls the "real language" that represents the world of atoms, genes, neurons, and man-made circuitry. Rorty puts it succinctly when he says that what differentiates poems from these real languages is the fact that various definitions of persons may actually come about from the perspective of a particular poem, whereas personhood has never been strongly identified with one of these other real languages.[9] What do poems have that give rise to convictions about identity which cannot be replaced by controlled descriptions of sub-human things and their relevant properties?

If, within a plural culture, convictions are what knit together the different discourses rather than object properties or truth values, and if these convictions do offer a coherent if not a global perspective upon a person's attachment to different beliefs and values, and if acting upon convictions requires a strong identification with a way of speaking rather than a simple medium of communication, then we will want a much fuller account of how our languages and literatures enable persons to hold and modify convictions.

Rorty and Fish do recognize a high degree of plurality within language. Rorty writes about culture as being made up of a variety of vocabularies, ranging from the most publicly shared scientific and political ones to the most idiosyncratically personal and private ones. And, more important, he sees no reason for mixing them: "If we avoid [reducing all vocabularies to other vocabularies], we shall not be inclined to ask questions like, 'What is the place of consciousness in a world of molecules?' 'Are colors more mind-dependent than weights?' " (*Contingency* 11). Fish does not talk about vocabularies, but he does attempt to promote pluralism by his relentless attack on any theoretical discourse which assumes the slightest gap between a literary text and its readers' social context. The upshot of his position is the realization of multiple contexts for discussing literature rather than of consistency and regulation of interpretation based upon the intrinsic meaning of any given work of literature, including the most canonical writings by Shakespeare, Milton, and Spenser. Pragmatists emphasize creativity, diversity, and the susceptibility of changing our norms and beliefs; in short, they emphasize our utopian potential in a world free of philosophical worry and political tyranny.

But this picture of an emergent utopian culture is precisely where pragmatists differ from other pluralist philosophers. At the point where we are led to expect contact with other speakers' beliefs and values, Rorty offers us ever-shifting metaphors and ironies. The literary terminology emphasizes the supposedly creative side of our emerging utopian culture and the fact that social solidarity is a matter of discovering the difference between the familiar and the unfamiliar, a distinction captured very nicely by terms like *metaphor* and *irony*. But even in a culture without justifications and foundations, are metaphors and ironies capable of sustaining convictions and negotiating differences?

The term *conviction* suggests a kind of speaker rather than the product of a theory. Nevertheless, a great deal remains to be added to this term if I am to take it beyond the pragmatist's definition of literature as persuasion, irony, and metaphor. Before I turn to Taylor, Cavell, and de Man I would summarize the pragmatic role of conviction in three ways:

1. Convictions that spring from the concrete and plural lives of persons do not contribute to traditional philosophical searches for abstract, universal

truths and values. Nevertheless, the generic vocabulary of the great Western tradition of philosophy may form a large part of highly articulated pragmatic convictions.

2. Convictions do not appear as representable things in and of themselves, separate from their concrete embodiment. The language of convictions, therefore, does not function like a representational medium.[10]

3. Convictions are what philosophy and literature look for in order to give depth and shape to personhood, but the source of convictions does not lie in ontology or epistemology or in any justification external to embodied personal identity.

The primary task of this book is to develop and refine these points. The primary difficulty is to distinguish this task from radical pragmatism, on the one side, and from the hermeneutical philosophical project, on the other, which also attempts to picture an embodied speaker who challenges the primacy of epistemology and instrumentalism. There is an added complication in the fact that pragmatism is often looked upon as one outcome of an empirical, goal-directed, instrumentalist culture, and so becomes a target of modern hermeneuts like Taylor. To date, Taylor and Rorty appear as opposites, and I shall not attempt to smooth over all of their fundamental disagreements (see note 8). Nevertheless, I shall argue that each makes an indispensable contribution to our understanding of pluralism, of the types of convictions that arise from it, and of the type of linguistic embodiment that may arise within a society of pluralized discourses.

Jeffrey Stout has written on Rorty with a similar idea in mind: he would like to find a moderate view of pragmatism in Rorty's works.[11] I share with Stout a deep respect for Rorty's awareness and acceptance of just how plural our morality and culture have become. What sort of agreements and values emerge from that pluralism? How does Rorty's work contribute to the task of personal individuation and to a moral awareness that would replace the traditional philosopher's search for grounds and reality principles upon which to anchor truthful, objective utterances? Like Stout, I think that pragmatism is better equipped to recognize and deal with the multiplicity of group identities and moral values than any other school of philosophy. But as he says of the term *pragmatism*, "Using the label too freely or too early in the game" risks a "premature dismissal" of a critical approach that relies upon it (243). A radical version of pragmatism which levels all discourses as equals and which refuses all critical adjudication should be dis-

carded. Stout's moderate pragmatism, however, provides just the sort of guidance
that the philosophy of justification fails to offer:

> It is doubtful . . . that very many people use such a picture [of "a special
> something . . . within the human breast, or . . . a transcendent Moral Law
> replete with propositions about human rights . . . 'out there' "] to hold up
> their first-order moral beliefs and dispositions. To suppose otherwise is to
> make the entire populace out to be philosophers. Our fellow citizens are
> not nervously awaiting vindications of philosophical pictures before pro-
> ceeding to hold each other valuable. A modest pragmatism, fully
> understood, would encourage us to view most of our first-order moral be-
> liefs as more certain, and most of our dispositions as more worthy of
> confidence, than any of the pictures philosophers have introduced in hope
> of explaining and grounding them. (253)

Stout carefully reviews passages from Rorty's writings in order to focus attention
on the moderate steps that lead up to the pragmatist's sense of confidence, certainty, and value. While it is true that pragmatists put "moral propositions on a
par with propositions of other kinds" (249), the outcome is not the radical assertion that all propositions are social artifacts, whether the topic be the poetry of
Philip Larkin or the neurobiology of Daniel Dennett. Moderate pragmatism
heightens the definition of conviction not by radical reduction, but by the rather
subtler insight that the difference between Larkin and Dennett will not be furthered by invoking correspondence theories of meaning or representational theories of language. The difference in language and personal interest between Larkin
and Dennett is not grounded in their attachment to different object domains of
reality. Larkin's discussion of the fear of death is not valuable to readers because it
corresponds to something such as "the fear of inexistence as such" (Rorty). Stout
writes,

> In the eyes of a modest pragmatism, true moral propositions correspond to
> the moral facts in the same (epistemologically trivial) sense that true scien-
> tific propositions correspond to the scientific facts. . . . Since modest
> pragmatism finds the idea of correspondence to undescribed reality inco-
> herent when pressed into epistemological service, it allows us to upgrade
> moral truth to philosophical respectability without inventing what J. L.
> Mackie called "queer" entities (like "values") with which moral proposi-
> tions might correspond. (250)

In the conclusion to his analysis, Stout finds a purpose for Rorty that I would adopt as an important feature of the design of this entire book. The implication of putting aside the demand for correspondence to reality is neither radical utopianism nor the lack of commensuration between types of language games. For Stout, it is in fact almost the exact opposite: a renewed effort to break down the idea that cognition belongs to the scientist, social practices to the moralist, and aesthetics to the strong poet. All these are "diffused throughout the culture, inseparably interrelated" (263). Pragmatism's chief opponent is not epistemology or rationalist social critique but rather existential freedom. Upon that point I would form a bridge between Rorty's pragmatism and Taylor's expressivism.

If modest pragmatism returns us to a deeper sense of our participation in multiple uses of language, then the task of criticism becomes that of truly taking on those uses, of giving them the weight they deserve in the absence of any freestanding entities upon which their truth is vouchsafed. Existentialists seem to have made the same point in terms of human freedom; Rorty calls it the rise of utopian culture. In answer to both, Stout's modest pragmatism shifts philosophical inquiry toward linking particular uses of language to the central defining role in culture and law that metaphysical discourse previously occupied. Through which uses do we confront choices about what to call right? The use of language, once grasped and taken seriously, begins to show us that the absence of special true entities that justify language does not make language an arbitrary exercise. The point of philosophical departure lies in becoming aware of the vocabulary that already exists as a practice. Through moderate pragmatism, uses of language become choices among and between plural values within our contemporary society rather than ironies and metaphors.[12]

These choices, which Stout brings into view for the first time in the context of pragmatism, have very far-reaching implications. Through a more finely textured inquiry into choices, the idea of an embodied speaker, which I introduced earlier, undergoes substantial development. Instead of arguing about whether pragmatists are social reductionists, a sophisticated, moderately pragmatic picture of how we use language brings into view the idea of a speaker situated between different discourses. Instead of the radical incommensurability of talk about Freudian narcissism and moral heroism, Emerson and Gnosticism, anthropological ritual and literary criticism, choices bring plural discourses into focus as contrasts.[13] Not all uses need be contrasted, but it is likely that those that are at least partially commensurable will be of the greatest concern, especially in a society in which persons hold multiple and often discontinuous identities in their work, their family romance, their cultural pleasures, and their legal awareness, and in which transitions between identities occur, as Stanley Fish has quipped, by doing what comes naturally.

Taylor defines *expressivism* as a "language of qualitative contrast," built upon crucial moments of moral choice in the personal history of human agents. As a philosopher addressing political and moral theory, Taylor aims his expressivist language at certain forms of epistemology and objectivism which render human agents inarticulate about their relations with each other. The interrelatedness of agents is a central concept within Taylor's much larger humanist, indeed Hegelian, project. That project offers a merging of individual and collective being in opposition to any type of social theory based in a simple distinction between atomism and communitarianism, the good or rights of the individual or those of the community. Taylor's immediate relevance belongs to the issue raised by Stout, however, which is the articulation of choice. Taylor pictures critical moments of choice as intrinsically based in language, as the necessary entry of the moral agent into a public sphere of discourse and reflection. But to answer other, contending theories of language and the public sphere, Taylor places great emphasis on the quality of the determination within the agent's language of contrast. Language, therefore, is not only the point of fusion between personal and collective existence but also an intrinsic expression of that fusion. That expression is capable of meeting Railton's criterion of the right degree of determination of incommensurablity, difference, and plurality. In linking the human action of deliberation, specific features of language, and the problem of highly determined expressions of incommensurablity, Taylor advances the pragmatist mode of inquiry. Plurality and social context do not disappear but rather are rendered in sufficiently complex terms to determine exactly the sorts of choices that are required in a genuinely plural society and culture. The question which this book poses is, What specific role does literature have and how are these links furthered by literary theories about textuality?

Expressivism and Deconstruction

If pragmatists are commonly mistaken for relativists, then expressivists are commonly mistaken for interpretive holists. Richard Shusterman makes this point in writing on the relation between pragmatism and hermeneutics, and so does James

Tully writing on Charles Taylor as an exemplary hermeneutical thinker.[14] Both essays help me bring into focus the specific contribution of Taylor's expressivism to the general outline of the first part of this book.

Shusterman and Tully take up similar topics from different but complementary points of departure. Shusterman calls himself a pragmatist very much in the spirit of John Dewey; Tully limits his own approach to a correction of universalist critical theory by way of a modest application of Wittgenstein on custom. Both writers face the same problem: Does the turn away from a set of foundational principles (in critical theory), in favor of a nonfoundational plurality of criticisms in politics and art, commit us to the idea that everything is interpretation, based in perspective or (in the positive, Gadamerian sense) prejudice? Shusterman provides a clear summary of how hermeneutical holism has intruded upon the pragmatist dismantling of the foundational discourse of objectivity and univocal, mind-independent truths and realities:

> It is easy to confuse the view that no understanding is foundational with the view that all understanding is interpretive. Yet this confusion of hermeneutic universalism betrays an unseemly residual bond to the foundationalist framework, in the assumption that what is not foundational must be interpretive. It thus prevents the holists from adopting a more liberating pragmatist perspective which . . . can profitably distinguish between understanding and interpretation without thereby endorsing foundationalism. (120)

Nonfoundationalists wish to avoid the notion that everything that differs from objective reality is a product of interpretation, or that interpretation replaces objectivity completely. Like relativism, hermeneutical holism appears to be a pseudoproblem that has been carried over from traditional philosophy's excessive concern with justifications and sovereign principles. In response to the exaggerated significance of interpretation, Tully and Shusterman quote the identical passage from Wittgenstein's *Philosophical Investigations,* section 87: "As though an explanation as it were hung in the air unless supported by another one. Whereas an explanation may indeed rest on another one that has been given, but none stands in need of another—unless *we* require it to prevent a misunderstanding" (quoted in Tully, "Wittgenstein" 180, and in Shusterman 130–31). Shusterman elaborates: "Understanding grounds and guides interpretation, while interpretation enlarges, validates, or corrects misunderstanding. We must remember that the distinction is functional or relational, not ontological. The prior and grounding understanding 'which is not an interpretation' may have been the product of prior interpretations, though now it is immediately grasped" (131).

I cannot do justice to the full complexity of Shusterman's and Tully's essays because it would take me too far afield from the main concerns of this book; most of their two essays is devoted to filling in the meaning of *understanding* in terms of what is familiar and stable in normal social interaction. In the final analysis the approach I put forward in this book probably would not mesh well with the primary philosophical goals of these two theorists, for I am less concerned with the general background or context against which interpretations occur, and rather more with what goes into the specific moments of interpretation once these can be identified. Just as there is no radical separation between understanding and interpretation, so there is no radical separation between literal and metaphorical language. But the burden of accounting for these differences remains. I have let pragmatists like Rorty and Fish already carry the burden of providing notions of embodiment, contextualization, and practice as the point of philosophical departure rather than any sort of foundationalist discourse about ontology or epistemology. The crucial significance of Shusterman's and Tully's essays at this stage in my exposition lies in their efforts to specify a moment of reflection that truly deserves to be called interpretive.

The pragmatist's effort to recognize and adjust to the plurality of discourses about things like rightness, beauty, morality, and solidarity seeks to replace abstract justifications with particularized, but connected, convictions. These convictions have implications for the kinds of selves we picture at work in our society and for the kinds of relevance we attach to large terms like *literature, tradition, natural law*, and more recently *gender identity*. But an emphasis on convictions does not seek to replace objective reality with subjective interpretations—which would indeed hold us to the kind of upside-down foundationalism mentioned by Shusterman. The best outcome of a pragmatist point of departure would be the narrowing down of interpretation to precisely those moments of conflict, change, or transition between discourses that impose unusual demands upon us.

In order to overcome the spectre of hermeneutical holism, Shusterman and Tully turn toward a consideration of the customary, the practical, and the everyday. We inhabit these forms of life without special study. We feel "at home" in them, as Wittgenstein put it (quoted in Shusterman 131). Only on those occasions when there is a special cause to feel puzzlement, doubt, or incongruity is interpretation demanded, according to Shusterman—a point I would endorse in principle but without much enthusiasm. For all the difficulties begin as soon as we try to specify and define those occasions, and that is where Shusterman's own thinking becomes hard to follow.

Shusterman puts most of his effort into reassuring his philosophical peers that custom and practical experience will do the work that had been previously assigned to objectivity and proof, but strangely he concludes that the last traces of hermeneutical holism remain in the writings of Derrida and Rorty (see 128). In positing a strong connection between language and understanding, Derrida and Rorty seem to make the interpretation of language essential to understanding in general. Subjective perspectivism is replaced by total linguistic mediation of reality. In response to his own characterization of their work, Shusterman returns to direct understanding and experience once again: "But neither we nor the language which admittedly helps shape us could survive without the unarticulated background of prereflective, non-linguistic experience and understanding. Hermeneutic universalism thus fails in its argument that interpretation is the only game in town because language is the only game in town. For there is both uninterpreted linguistic understanding and meaningful experience that is non-linguistic" (128).

The gratuitous attack on linguistic holism, and specifically on Rorty and Derrida, impoverishes the overall effort to specify what counts as interpretation. It confuses the pragmatist-deconstructionist questioning of the primacy of representationalism with the reductive hypothesis that everything is language. If anything, the advantages of pragmatism and deconstruction lie precisely in the fact that language is never conceived holistically from the outset. There is no language as such in the writings of Rorty, Derrida, de Man, or Fish. The breaking down of monolithic and generic definitions of language in favor of multiple, even contradictory uses or of internal differences between logical and rhetorical aspects points us in the required direction of specifying moments of particular incongruity, doubt, and puzzlement. The goal of pragmatism and deconstruction is not to turn everything into language for the sake of either hermeneutical holism or linguistic nihilism, but rather to acknowledge the inescapable plurality of language games at work in literary and philosophical discourse and thereby to seek out the crucial juncture points and degrees of commensurability between them. I shall argue later in this book that lack of perfect commensuration within and between texts, which is recognizable only after we stop using *language* as a transparent term, in fact strengthens and supports the very situatedness in culture that Shusterman seeks.

A good part of this book will be devoted to expanding this line of inquiry, but it cannot be furthered until I have introduced the role of Charles Taylor's philosophy of language. Tully, if not Shusterman, provides the last section of the bridge I am building between pragmatists and Taylor in his specific comments on Taylor's work. When Tully questions Taylor's interpretive holism, he has in mind two different arguments. The first has to do with a rejection of any holism, including Taylor's or for that matter Habermas's, in the name of pluralism and in the name of the conventional, or what is called understanding rather than interpretation. In this respect he and Shusterman are in agreement. Even on a subject as vital as human rights and democracy, Tully points out the multifaceted uses of the term, which nonetheless achieve a certain coherence on the level of everyday practice:

> Rightness, for example, is a ground in virtue of our confident abilities in using it as the hinge around which our reflective questioning provisionally turns; not in virtue of a transcendental property of the concept nor of an explicit process of reaching agreement and consensus on it (for in the circumstances we already have this). To say, for example, that the only valid form of political justification is an appeal to rightness is to say no more or less than in our current liberal language-games of politics we justify our proposals by appealing to standards of rightness in one form or another. . . . "Rightness" belongs to and is a constituent part of a wide range of uses of justification in our political language-games, but is not an independent determinant of the political. ("Wittgenstein" 190–91)

Tully's emphasis on use rather than transcendental justification is what links him to the pragmatists and what gives rise to his criticism of Taylor. Can Taylor's views on situatedness, the philosophy of language, and human agency, which play a central role in this book, be detached from the transcendental program that seems to have given rise to them? Tully calls attention to this issue when he writes that for Taylor, "interpretation is not simply a method, procedure, or one activity among many, but that being engaged in the activity of interpretation is our basic way of being in the world. In granting ontological status to the activity of interpretation Taylor acknowledges his debt to the famous argument of Hans-Georg Gadamer in *Truth and Method*" ("Wittgenstein" 192).[15] In privileging interpretation as a foundational concept for things like human dignity and a political, civic order,

Taylor seems to overplay its significance. His effort to wrest an ontological picture of humanity out of our interpretive activity has a strong tendency to seek universality and transcendental first principles. Rather than let a picture of rights, for example, emerge out of the interplay of a variety of traditions, Taylor, like Habermas, would look for an essential within that play that would ground rights in a much deeper way. The name for that deep grounding, according to Tully, is interpretation. Through interpretive activity, the gap between the individual and tradition, between language and consciousness, is not only closed but raised to a higher level of human being.

Much more needs to be said on the topic of Taylorean ontology, and I shall return to it in chapter 3. But for the moment, I shall follow the pragmatists and avoid ontological arguments. Once ontological issues are bracketed, Tully's other argument is to separate *interpretation,* in the strong sense given to it by Taylor, from *use,* the term the pragmatists deploy against the notion of language as a medium or a representation of something outside it. *Use,* for example, is the key operative word in Tully's earlier comments on how rights exist within a democratic society: rights are not represented by a discourse about them but constituted by the very circulation and contestation of talk about rights within different political sectors and interested parties. *Use* not only forms the stable background of everyday practice and understanding which does not require interpretive activity; it also prevents an "unnecessary shuffle" on the level of linguistic theory:

> Wittgenstein wrote the following, synoptic remark: "It is not interpretation which builds the bridge between the sign and what is signified //meant//. Only practice does that." Interpretation, like intuition, is an "unnecessary shuffle" (section 213). . . . Interpretation is a reflective activity that we engage in when we are in doubt about how to grasp or understand a sign that is in question. . . . To interpret a sign is to take it *as* one expression rather than another. In contrast, to understand a sign is not to possess a sedimented opinion about it or to take it *as* something, but to be able to grasp it; that is, to act with it, using it in agreement with customary ways (section 241). . . . Conventional understanding does not involve implicit interpretations (or representations) to bridge the gap between thought and action, language and reality, because no such gap exists. (195–97)

When Tully links the definition of use to a particular theory of language, he provides Taylor with an opportunity to reply. This opportunity was lacking in Shusterman's unexpected swerve into "unarticulated experience" as a form of life that exists beyond the concerns of linguistic theory.

It is one thing to assert with Rorty or Wittgenstein or even Taylor himself that we do not gain any philosophical purchase on reality by positing a special representation of it through the medium of language. For these philosophers, a sense of social belongingness, or personal and community identity, is of primary importance. They place the emphasis on forms of discourse that bring the concerns of speakers into contact with each other rather than turn speakers into vehicles of a depersonalized reality principle. But it is another thing to attempt to fit central forms of discourse—about rights, for example—and all sorts of customary behavior into one undifferentiated concept of use in order to attack representationalist sign-theory. True, we do not want the moment of interpretation to become either all-encompassing and universalist or an "unnecessary shuffle" in the name of endless reflection. But how far can use be extended? how capable is it of handling shifts between the customary and the critical, those key points of conflict between, for example, subjective rightists and natural law rightists? Use, as attached to the meaning of a linguistic sign, would have to undergo complex definition in order to handle that sort of conflict.

Tully contextualizes Taylor in an important way for this book when he limits interpretation to taking a sign as one expression rather than another, as a contrast in short. Taylor's essays on human agency and language and theories of meaning are built upon this crucial moment of contrast. Out of the agent's construction of contrasting expressions of how to act, Taylor elaborates a complex picture of (a kind of Hegelian) situatedness replacing absolute freedom, of commensurability and cultural difference, and of symbolic versus designative language. In the long run, his goal is to fill in the moment of contrast in ever-finer detail by attacking all sorts of generic terminologies and instrumental forms of reasoning.

That his picture of contrasted, situated decision making rests on ontological premises about what makes humans essentially what they are remains a debatable point. More pressing for my purposes is that Taylor's picture of contrasting choices connects with the pragmatist position of Jeffrey Stout. Stout concluded that the only way pragmatism could take hold as a social philosophy was through a strong definition of choice, which would obviate notions of existential absolute freedom. But that is where pragmatism seemed to reach a dead end. How are nonfoundational contingency and utopianism to be distinguished from absolute freedom? How can plurality be made consistent with notions of personal coherence and a deep situatedness in society? Thus far the pragmatists have shown that we cannot expect to answer these questions all at once as was attempted in the old philosophy of epistemology and linguistic representationalism. Their hunch seems to be that there is some sort of a connection between personal choice, a complex social matrix of values and multiple strands of identity, a rejection of holism, and a philosophy of language that avoids representationalism.

For Taylor, these connections are drawn closer together and given a finer articulation through what he calls a "language of qualitative contrast."[16] The language of qualitative contrast is not a global formula for all interpretive activity; as I read Taylor, it is not at all holistic. Rather, Taylor pictures human agents involved in critical choices in exceptional circumstances. The very definition of choice must be made coherent by presenting different options as in some degree incommensurable. Without difference, there is no real choice. Out of this moment of choice, Taylor explores how the articulation of contrast places speakers between different elements of language at the same time as it places them between different values and beliefs. There is no one-to-one correspondence between the sign elements of language and scientific rationalism or between rhetorical moments and human emotions and feelings. Categories of language do not represent different sorts of reality. Nevertheless, tensions exist between the articulate capacities of different forms of language, and these in turn may influence and on occasion determine the personal awareness and values of a particular speaker.

To some extent, these sorts of tensions are much more familiar to literary theorists than to philosophers. If the articulation of contrasted meanings is (nonontologically) central to the agent's efforts to become coherent and situated, then contrasts in meaning are likely to involve much more than one sign's meaning versus another's or a detached sign versus a sign in use. Taylor's complex view of language seeks to return the speaker to the ordinary and the familiar but avoids reducing this return to mere sign use. Contrasts may involve the expressive possibilities of sign versus symbol, poetic versus designative language, Freudian symbolic formations versus the vocabulary of higher and lower moral values. The language of qualitative contrast is a vehicle of social becoming and personhood, and it is adaptable to the multiplicity of articulations captured in the writings of the pragmatists. But Taylor works the concept to the point where it is capable of making interpretation into a moment of choice and affirmation, thereby shaping the speaker's identity. Expressivism is the shorthand term for the personal identity that emerges out of the human agent's constructed language of contrasts.[17]

I am focusing upon Taylor's language of contrast in order to strengthen the links between plural vocabularies and critical moments of interpretation. These links must be seen at the outset as an essential feature of this book. Taylor offers a way beyond interpretive holism and any facile opposition between hermeneutics and science, but he also sharpens the recognition of plural values and vocabularies by seeking those forms of expression and belief that demand choices and partial commensuration. (Full commensuration, as I shall discuss later, would not only deny plurality, but would also render the act of decision incoherent by canceling one of the terms that first gave rise to the need to make a decision.)

The last point which must be made in this chapter concerns the connection of pragmatism and Taylorean expressivism to deconstruction and to other writers discussed in this book, Stanley Cavell, William Empson, and Fredric Jameson. Rorty and Fish have already embraced deconstruction as an ally of pragmatism because it seems to agree with pragmatism on issues like antirepresentationalism in language, on the nonexistence of transcendental foundations, and on the contingency of changes in belief and value, what is sometimes seen by critics of both approaches as their nihilist and relativist strains. I deliberately place Taylorean expressivism between Rorty and de Man in order to obstruct just these sorts of general comparisons. Taylor introduces the necessity of specific contrasts of meaning and value to the construction of personal identity. In the literary disciplines, the closest analogy to this degree of specificity might be found in the theories that attempt to determine the rhetorical structures of literary texts. Contrasting forms of language within a text need to be drawn very finely. Terms like *irony* and *metaphor* are not fine enough, but they do remind us that determinations of textual structures have no special philosophical foundations. I take from the pragmatists the idea that the product of such moments of interpretation is a nonontological embodiment within a social matrix. But I take from deconstruction the most precise and finest analysis of the multiple forms of language that are likely to be involved in moments of contrast that specifically demand interpretation.

In using the word *text,* I anticipate suspicions of reductionism in the minds of some readers. There is a familiar assumption, found in Shusterman's essay, for example, that deconstruction says, "Il n'y a pas de hors-texte." But *text* is a better term than *language* or *irony* or *vocabulary* because it calls attention to what specific forms of language are at work in a complex linguistic claim, one that fits the criteria of a Taylorean expression. Taylor's language of contrast succeeds the use doctrine of pragmatism because it allows central values like rights and virtues and freedom to situate themselves in the identity of speakers through a decision-making process which builds in a lack of perfect commensuration between meanings and values and personal identities. It does not deploy central terms like *rights, freedoms,* and *the good life* from the outset as self-evident truths which need only be presented to the speaker. Taylor's philosophy of language demands the actual apprehension and acquisition of the meaning of central features of personhood through the determination of degrees of commensuration, conflict, and comparison among inescapably plural values and forms of life in modernist society.[18] *Deconstruction,* as I intend to use the term in this book, adds a further degree of refinement by allowing Taylor's language of qualitative contrast, his primary vehicle for measuring commensuration, to take on more highly determined textual forms. At no point would I attempt to reduce historical reflection or personal identity to generic textuality or to make the reading of a text into another version of hermeneutical holism. More important, I do not believe deconstruction does this either. Its significance has been missed, I think, because of a prevailing under- or overestimation of the functions of language. The whole middle ground between a developed Saussurean sign theory of language and hermeneutical holism is precisely where literary theories like deconstruction may refine the terms of the debates within the philosophy of language.

Not all the features of Taylor's philosophy of language are capable of being harmonized with pragmatism and deconstruction. But the connection between embodied moments of interpretation, plural, partially commensurable meanings, and a process of decision making and identification is what I am attempting to refine and picture in juxtaposing Rorty, Taylor, and de Man. De Man, in particular, demonstrates what sort of critical economy is possible once this connection is grasped. His influence is apparent in the design of this book, as I develop the language of contrast, in all of its social and ethical implications, through a highly determined set of textual claims that arise from the work of literary critics like Empson, Fish, and Jameson. Nothing in deconstruction suggests that a textual claim and a person are identical with each other. It simply avoids any generic view of language and thus heightens the definition of commensurability and contrast.

What role belongs to Cavell in this project? Cavell writes primarily on the

S. Cavell

problems of modern skepticism and solipsism. His use of these terms is somewhat fanciful, but generally he uses them to point to a failure of linguistic attunement between speakers which is beyond the remedy of ordinary language philosophy, what Shusterman and Tully identify in Wittgenstein's term "understanding." For Cavell, the skeptic's removal from ordinary communication is provoked by an impossible-to-satisfy need for certainty, proof, and demonstration. While these needs may go under the guise of epistemology, they really dig the skeptic deeper into a pattern of withdrawal, which may end tragically. Shakespeare's Othello is a literary example of Cavell's skeptic.

I defer until chapter 4 a detailed explanation of Cavell's position and of his rather oblique terminology. Cavell's concern with skepticism raises some final issues about expressivism and deconstruction, however. Complexly built linguistic claims come more clearly into focus through Cavell's investigation into the skepticism that lies beyond ordinary language philosophy. In positing an extreme of withdrawal and failed linguistic understanding, under the rubric of skepticism, Cavell develops a highly sophisticated picture of what forms of language are strong enough to return the speaker to social life. He expands notions of expressivism in his discussion of how speakers enact themselves, answer or acknowledge each other, and respond to very specific, nonholistic forms of language, or claims. The determination of a claim against a background of ordinary linguistic understanding is a special feature of Cavell's writings. Cavellean claims further the identification of the critical, truly interpretive moment. The linguistic account of a claim is missing from the pragmatist's use doctrine and from Taylor's largely hermeneutical theory of contrasted meanings.

One of the key elements of Cavellean claims is the decision to enact oneself in a community of speakers, and this decision is framed very closely by elements of poetry and the sublime. Pragmatists lack a definition of a claim and assimilate all vocabularies either to ironies (Rorty) or to forces (Fish). One of the pragmatist's goals is the dissolution of the literature/language distinction, thereby making all uses of language comparable and all interpretive activity a matter of collective agreement. Fish does try to extend terms like *force* and *persuasion* in order to uphold some sort of coherence within the interpretive community but falls far short of Cavell in demonstrating how literary texts serve any particular communal function. Taylor leaves the moment of contact between speakers as a mystery or a revelation. Only Cavell, to my knowledge, bridges this theoretical gap by aligning contrast, decision, individual, and community in the form of a language that imposes strong claims. Although these claims are designed to answer skeptics, they prove to be valuable insights into the role that literary texts may play in pragmatist and expressivist philosophy. Literary texts are those that produce strong linguistic claims and thereby bring speakers into a high degree of attunement. This attunement is beyond customary forms of understanding but does not substitute for it. The claim of a literary text is special, as is the act of interpretation. If Taylor's expressivism can be detached from his ontology, then I hope that Cavell's literary version of expressivism can be detached from assumptions about the prevalence of skepticism.

Deconstruction is commonly equated with skepticism, and it is not surprising to discover that Cavell has tested this connection. It is also not surprising that he focuses his criticism of deconstruction on the meaning of the word *decision*. Paul de Man's emphasis on the undecidability of meaning seems to Cavell a challenge to the decisions and claims through which speakers enter a public realm of common understanding. If deconstruction is comparable to skepticism, it can be so only in a weak sense, which can be left to the control of ordinary language philosophy. For Cavell, de Man's assumptions about universal undecidability of meaning deny ordinary usage and ordinary transactions between speakers.

Examined more carefully, however, Cavell's criticism of deconstruction raises further questions about literary texts and decisions. I shall argue that deconstruction is not a weak version of skepticism, rooted in perpetual doubt and uncertainty, but rather a final correction to expressivist philosophy, complementary to it if anything. De Manian undecidability does not apply to most uses of language; it makes no sense to deconstruct ordinary usage at all, as if it were another skepticism. *Undecidability* is deconstruction's term for signaling the lack of perfect closure of linguistic elements, even in the final analysis. That does not imply an indifference of meaning or outcome; it rather implies a strenuous effort to specify and locate the exact degree of closure possible, and this effort I believe is consistent with the strands that link Rorty's pluralism, Taylor's situatedness, and Cavell's ideas about linguistic claims.

In outlining this book's concerns, I have portrayed deconstruction as a refinement upon expressivism and expressivism as a refinement upon pragmatism. But in the practical task of expounding a synthesis between these philosophies of language, I must follow a different order. Taylor must be considered first because he provides the basic conceptual framework of the language of contrasts, of how the articulation of contrasts defines situatedness within a modernist, plural society, and of how the determination of the proper degree of commensurability between different values and identities offers a better form of coherence than may be found in universalist critical theory. As added background to Taylor's concerns, I begin with a discussion of two philosophers, Harry Frankfurt and Bernard Williams, who play an important role in Taylor's own conceptual formation.

With these important issues on the table, I proceed to develop a specifically literary version of the expressivist philosophical position. Taylor cannot be adapted directly into discussions about literary theory. His philosophy of language must be modified through the concept of text, which is the important contribution of the literary theorists discussed in this book. Although Taylor recognizes a multiplicity of functions within the field of language, they do not come together for him in ways that specifically illuminate literature's ability to situate readers and speakers.

Cavell's essays on literary theory and deconstruction begin to introduce some of the issues about language that move the discussion beyond very large contrasts between, for example, literary symbolism and instrumental nominalism. Cavell starts the task of pinpointing expressive forms of language, the ones that do indeed situate speakers, within a recognition of discontinuity between certain types of literary utterances and ordinary speech. This recognition begins to approach the definition of forms of language that could be called textual.

Empson complicates the pragmatist/expressivist position with an alternate type of use doctrine. He offers a complex definition of use that gives literary texts an important role in shaping social norms. In that respect his approach to works of literature is comparable to that of the pragmatists. Cavell expresses a debt to Empson for the definition of key elements of language that contribute directly to this shaping. What remains to be explained, however, is why Empson's Othello is antithetical to Cavell's. Why does Empson's Othello lack tragic qualities? Empson, virtually in opposition to the approach that Cavell takes to Shakespearean tragedy, raises questions about the link between the determination of a piece of writing as a text in an ordinary sense and the particular degree of situatedness such a determination may provide. For Empson, Iago's popularity as a vice figure is really part of the emergence of the language of individuality which, historically, becomes necessary for all speakers to adopt. The kind of language Iago speaks is in the long run more important to the pragmatic work done by the Shakespearean text than the tragic skepticism and doubt portrayed in the language of Othello. Which is more important to a language of personal identity? Empson provides the occasion to pinpoint the difference between a use and a claim in finer terms than can be captured in the generalized opposition between pragmatism and skepticism or between ordinary understanding and isolated tragic misattunement. This issue becomes crucial for assessing the limits of a pragmatic situatedness not only in Empson, but also in Stanley Fish's equally strong effort to normalize the communal function of tragedy in a play like *Coriolanus*.

I have included a chapter on Jameson as the true foil to de Man and deconstruction, for his dialectics of language does seek total symbols in art and culture that would offer as complete a picture of one's historical moment as possible. It is the dialectical approach that would reconcile text, culture, reader, and history following an initial determination of what seems to be textually absent or missing (the structuralist-Marxist jargon for contradiction and incommensurabililty). Jameson, as perhaps the most dialectically minded critic writing in English today, poses important questions about the modified deconstructionist approach that I take, because he, too, would establish a link between the sociohistorical situatedness of the reader and a very highly determined form of textual structure. The question that his work poses, in opposition to deconstruction, is whether the link between textual determination and situatedness should take on dialectical form. Just as Cavell's questions about linguistic claims exceed his concerns with skepticism and Taylor's expressivism exceeds his indebtedness to logocentric philosophy, so a dialectical theory of textuality exceeds Jameson's particular defense of structuralist-Marxism. As a writer who combines a sophisticated theory of textual structure with a philosophical position on the conflicts faced by human agents in a postmodern society, Jameson must be addressed within the terms of this book's project. Finally, de Man's deconstruction of the Hegelian dialectic provides the sharpest definition of textuality that may be found in contemporary literary theory. I conclude this book with an attempt to flesh out the significance of de Man's work on the theory of a text by questioning what form of situatedness it provides in conjunction with the issues raised by Rorty and Taylor.

Each of the theorists studied in the second part of this book provides a powerful insight into a form of language that is realized first and foremost in the linguistic tensions that define a literary text. The definition of a text is not generic or easily generalizable, but it does perform, in varying degrees and in varying combinations, the work of situating a reader in an expressive linguistic mode. Explaining that form of situatedness nonfoundationally, to the highest degree of nonrelativistic personal coherence, and in recognition of the ongoing plural nature of the language against which it emerges is the task of the second part of this book. The determination of a textual crux gradually becomes the equivalent of a definition of situatedness in language, an equivalence that may be deepened, rendered in increasingly complex terms, and given personal resonance.

The product of these determinations of textuality will be neither a theory of literature nor a comparative methodology. The critics who are making the greatest contributions to a determination of textual instances of language do not necessarily affirm pluralism by openly engaging conflicting histories, cultures, and laws among their readers. But if the link between higher degrees of textual determination and a nonfoundationalist means of situating a reader does work, then that link can be made consistent with the expression of those interests within a heterogeneous readership. Although it would be difficult to classify this philosophico-textual project as a direct contribution to literary theory, practical criticism, or the politics of interpretation, it does attempt to add personal resonance to these practices of self-articulation through a local sense of what is important, enabling, and influential about that narrow segment of world literature we identify as our own.

2 Beyond Relativism and Holism

In chapter 1 I rejected an approach to language and literature based upon universal justifications and objective foundations in favor of one based in personhood as inescapably plural and made up of critically acquired convictions. I also suggested that contemporary pragmatists like Rorty provide a general outline of what a postfoundationalist person looks like, and I agreed with Rorty's assertion that such persons are already familiar within our culture. But the Rortyan picture meets a great deal of philosophical resistance because the convictions that are now supposed to hold us in place and take on the job of foundations are not easily disentangled from the traditional philosophical issues of relativism and subjectivism. Why does one conviction count more than another? How can they be compared and assessed? In what sense are psychological events, human rights, and poems the products of convictions in more than narrowly personal terms?

The key questions about convictions concern the stability and integrity of personal identity in a world that is no longer *foundationally* whole as well as the types of conflict and choice that occur when plural convictions overlap. Moderate pragmatists and some sophisticated Wittgensteinians want to develop a nonfoundationalist and a nonreductionist account of social context, normative behavior, and ordinary experience in order to answer these questions. They attempt to disarm the problem of relativism and subjectivism by showing that these problems can be made to disappear along with foundationalism. Relativism and subjectivism are attached to very specific definitions of truth and knowledge. And these definitions, in turn, depend upon foundationalist concepts like the cognitive or epistemic states of the subject's mind, the theory of true and false correspondences, and an objectivist definition of reality. Moderate pragmatists argue that other sorts of definitions—of personal consistency, of important social and ethical values, and of human labor upon nonhuman objects—can continue without putting them in a supporting epistemological framework. The work of these definitions occurs in the customary contexts and so-called ordinary experiences to which they are closely connected.

But the shift from epistemology to situation and social context is not specific to the new pragmatism. The same shift occurs in feminist theory and the social sciences, in Gadamerian hermeneutics, and in many versions of the Marxist critique of Enlightenment ideology. The philosophical and political assault on the primacy of epistemology has put into circulation a common vocabulary of context-specific behavior, the social position of the knower, interpretive bias, antitheory and praxis, and interpretive holism. This vocabulary, however, has not freed itself from concerns with relativism and subjectivism. The meaning of *context* and *ordinary experience* needs a great deal of weight if it is to do the work that foundational discourse did previously, namely, provide central terms of reference for political justice, morality, pleasure, labor, and so on. Most of these central terms in our culture are the product of foundationalist discourse even though we may no longer view them as being justified by a special language spoken by the real world.

Debates about the relativity of interpretation and meaning are now just as likely to occur within pragmatism as they did previously in the philosophy of the social sciences and hermeneutics.[1] In chapter 1 I offered an approach to literature that would put together three issues: a strong definition of the choices faced by agents in a plural society; a focus on the interpretive moment rather than the ordinary or customary background; and a finely grained textual view of language.

I suggested that an analysis of these three issues would give notions of context and situation the weightiness that used to belong to foundations, with the additional caution that the key interpretive moments faced by a human agent cannot be completely assimilated to all customary and ordinary contexts of behavior. My overall argument is that a pragmatist equivalent to hermeneutical situatedness can be found and developed in a particular, Taylorean concept of choice in language and that this language can be found and further developed in a particular, deconstructionist view of a text. Relativism and subjectivism are overcome through situatedness. Situatedness, as originally developed by Hegel and adapted by Taylor, is the passing beyond an atomized subjectivity by becoming deeply embedded in the ethical values of the historical and cultural moment. It overcomes relativism because it prevents the arbitrary profusion of and undecidable juxtaposition of alternate points of view, which seems to leave each to its own local community. The pragmatist twist is to allow this embeddedness to occur through deliberation and choice without denying the presence of ongoing, plural, and perhaps contradictory values in the society at large. In other words, it is a situatedness without a teleology or an ontology and without holism.

This chapter draws two of these strands of argument closer together: (1) the specification of values and terms that have the density and weight to situate the agent, without denying pluralism; (2) a concept of choice that provides an agent with a coherent outlook without attempting to commensurate conflicting values. It then remains to be seen how Taylor's philosophy of language further develops these connected arguments.

Bernard Williams's essay "Relativism and Reflection"[2] refuses to equate the philosophical significance of the word *reflection* with an insight into culture as a whole. He therefore supports the effort of other philosophers who attempt to overcome interpretive holism. But he is equally concerned with the risk of mistaking discontinuity between values within a society for an endorsement of relativism. For relativism would seem to sanction as many values and forms of behavior as there are different social contexts. In effect, relativism stands as a dangerous temptation once genuine pluralism is recognized within society. It levels all values as equal and as beyond critical assessment, and it therefore steers the discussion away from the effort to locate terms of central, if not foundationalist, value.

Williams attacks relativism, like some pragmatists, by questioning whether indeed it is a real problem for philosophy and ethics. It seems to arise as a problem primarily for philosophers who begin with a falsely homogeneous view of culture in the first place. "A fully individuable culture," Williams writes, "is at best a rare thing. Cultures, subcultures, fragments of cultures, constantly meet one another and exchange and modify practices and attitudes. Social practices could never come forward with a certificate saying that they belonged to a genuinely different culture, so that they were guaranteed immunity to alien judgments and reactions" (158). And yet the bestowing of such an imaginary certificate is what pro- and antirelativists appear to debate, all the while slipping into a monolithic picture of an individuable culture. Rather than reflect upon the conflict of various cultural components, a task by no means easy to engage, relativism's aim is "to *explain away* a conflict" (156), either by reducing apparently incompatible statements to a "logical form that makes them straightforwardly compatible" or by accepting the genuineness of a conflict and finding a sense "in which each may still be acceptable in its place," and "relative" (in relation) to one foreign or ancient or primitive culture (157). Both forms of relativist thinking bypass a moment of reflection in which the agent is genuinely caught *between* cultures and practices.

Williams suggests that relativism as an approach to cultural difference sustains itself by continuing to falsify cultures as totalities, distinct in time and space, though the effort required to describe the totality of a culture becomes greater and greater. In time, he believes, relativism causes a profound sense of dissatisfaction because the mere admission of cultural difference is such a "blank and unresponsive" stopping point for consciousness that it is "incredible that this consciousness should just leave everything where it was" (159).

Williams is careful to take into account both the present-day liberal and conservative uses of relativism that weaken the task of reflecting upon our positions between cultures or between elements of our own culture. For the liberal, the dislocations and uncertainties brought on by reflecting upon cultural difference can be made into a virtue, a form of universal tolerance. For political conservatives, by contrast, immersion as deeply as possible within one's own traditions can be turned into a special virtue, leaving no place for the traditionally minded to reflect at all upon their difference from other members of the society.

For Williams, the true starting point for overcoming relativism and entering reflection is seeing "whether the contrast of our outlook with another is one that makes a difference, whether a question has to be resolved about what life is going to be lived by one group or the other" (160). The contrast must be incapable of being assimilated to the observer's practices and norms; rather, it forces into consciousness a rejection of these practices as unacceptable without positing a mutual understanding, without assuming that the observer and the societal other are capable of inhabiting the same conceptual framework. Williams gives the example of witnessing members of an alien society practicing ritual killings or launching murderous injunctions. The point of the rejection is to feel the depth of our belonging to a culture that is in conflict with another culture. The conflict is brought to the surface of our attention without resort to a special critical effort at conceptualization. The observer standing outside the practice of ritual killings is being made to feel *her* place inside her culture's rejection and knows full well how trivial a relative response would be to such a witnessing.

Ritual killing is of course a loaded example for Williams to choose for a Western readership. But I think the harsh example is intended exactly to make us feel the point of a relativist response. It would be difficult to tolerate ritual killing simply because it is part of the worldview of group A and makes no claim upon the basic constructions of the world I inhabit. Were it possible to adopt a relativist stance toward exposure to ritual killings, the sense of rejection, conflict, and difference would lose force by being distanced outside the observer's societal perspective.

Furthermore, there is a subtle element of holism in the disengaged viewer's response, since it assumes the unity of cultural beliefs and practices within the foreign practice and experience. As Hubert L. Dreyfus has pointed out, once culture is conceived as a whole, the only change possible is a nihilistic dismantling of fundamental structures or, in practical terms, a colonization, since the one culture has to shift all at once.[3]

Does that mean there is some justice in a ritual killing? or that justice is relative to a particular culture? Not at all. These questions are tempting to answer but misleadingly posed. Williams is after a principle of justice and critical reflection that avoids conceptual totalization. The same would be true of what he terms the notional or fantastic reconstructions of past eras, like utopianism, neo-medievalism, or the image of life in the Bronze Age constructed by an archeologist. As conceptual constructs, the images of such societies can be refined to increasing coherence, but they never become real options, real spaces inhabitable by agents. At best, they could become optimistic personal fantasies.

How, then, can we reflect nonrelatively so as to recognize conflict and bring about change? As an ethical philosopher, Williams is interested in only one answer to the question: " 'Just' and 'unjust' are central terms that . . . can be applied to societies concretely and realistically conceived" (165). But the extension of these terms over a plurality of modern societies and over the history of the Western European state does not lead to any conceptual smoothing over of differences. Some states identify justice with global egalitarianism, some with natural rights, some with a clear hierarchy, legitimated by god or by myth. In calling all these states just or unjust one is not making a "pun or linguistic error," as if the terms were abusing the single concept. As I understand Williams, his point is that the terms *are central,* an expression of our most pressing, demanding sense of our place in a social structure, but the terms cannot be said to represent that structure holistically. Instead, they measure the weight and strength of our need to respond to a variety of claims made upon us.

Conflict is not one of Williams's goods, however. If reflection is in the first instance an acceptance of the limits of any cultural stance in the face of real alterity, it is next a process of growing more deeply and passively into that stance. In describing how a stance enters a cultural network without abstract justification, Williams critically downplays the usefulness of *knowledge* (his synonym for *certainty* that arises Socratically through reflection) and *decisions* and replaces them with terms like *conviction* and *confidence*: "No amount of faith in cognitive certainty will actually bring about ethical conviction if we cannot agree on what we are supposed to be certain about" or what we are to decide. *Confidence* refers to the way an individual holds on to belief even when consciously challenged, and it in no way implies mere individualism. It is a shared experience: "It is a social and psychological question regarding what kinds of institutions, upbringing, and public discourse help to foster it. . . . Confidence is both a social state and related to discussion, theorizing, and reflection" (170).

As a nonessentialized picture of faith in socialization, Williams's analysis is admirable, but it is all resolved a little abruptly. The reflective struggle of the agent is given over to a wise passivity. It may be true to say that we can manage remarkably well, behave ethically, and overcome relativism without transcendence, epistemic certainty, or any other absolute intellectual moves. But is that sufficient argument against some form of reflection and decision making? If reflection can be modified as a situated and coherent stance, why not explore equally real options?

Williams's essay seems to me an excellent point of departure for many concerns I want to raise in this book. He helps to orient my discussion at a broad level by disarming premature charges about relativism in a book that does not propose a holistic system or theory. But we need to add a few more layers of color to the outline we have so far.

How much change or conflict does reflection allow in its progress toward confidence? and how many of these changes count for other agents? or require communicative exchange between agents? Most of all, how does the task of reflection lead to the acquisition of central terms of reference like *justice* or *rights* or *cruelty?* I agree with Williams that central terms like these form a basic orientation within one's society. And I agree that the specification of these terms may come about in moments of special conflict, perhaps even shock. Once felt, there is no return to the safe option of relativizing cultural and political difference. I differ from Williams, however, in wanting an active, if not global or holistic, process for maintaining and developing the central terms of an agent's political and cultural outlook.

I can begin to address these questions with a few remarks on reflexivity and wholeheartedness made by Harry Frankfurt.[4] Like Williams, Frankfurt challenges the concept of a self modeled on a hierarchy of faculties or on complete psychological integration of all impulses, desires, and purposeful actions. The principal obstacles he seeks to overcome, however, are not relativism and essentialism but the "wanton" and the agent who thinks he is capable of "doing what comes naturally." It is as if he were writing in anticipation of Stanley Fish's most recent portrayal of professionalism and interpretive practices. Frankfurt returns us briefly to the states of reflection and decision which Williams does not develop and adds the important issue of how to *express* personal identity. Frankfurt does not use that term, but he is working on this assumption:

> It is a salient characteristic of human beings, one which affects our lives in deep and innumerable ways, that we care about what we are. This is closely connected both as cause and as effect to our enormous preoccupation with what other people think of us. We are ceaselessly alert to the danger that there may be discrepancies between what we wish to be (or what we wish to seem to be) and how we actually appear to others and to ourselves. (163)

I would like to reformulate these concerns along linguistic lines, which will allow me to bring into play Charles Taylor's work on agency and expression. But for the moment, I shall focus on Frankfurt's elaboration of *immanent reflexivity* as a bridge between Williams and Taylor.

Frankfurt begins his discussion of reflexivity with consciousness, which may be crudely defined as an awareness of features in one's environment that cause one to discriminate between these features, say colors, sounds, degrees of temperature. But such neurobiological consciousness is far from equivalent to a state of reflection, and in fact has led neurobiologists to ask, jokingly, what good is consciousness if we can perform most logical and creative activities without it? Perhaps consciousness is the source of our silliest illusions about inwardness as a special philosophical state, which in fact has no important role to play in human reasoning.

In the crude reflector model of consciousness, one shivers with cold, then becomes conscious of shivering with cold; or one becomes conscious of being conscious, and so becomes self-conscious; etc. One way to give a purpose to this regressive awareness is to turn it into a hierarchy. Within a hierarchy, second-level consciousness would control or judge first-level consciousness, leading to such mental constructs as strong and weak will power and ego ideals. But Frankfurt's point about such straightforward hierarchies is the same as Williams's: a higher-order volition is not sufficient ground for determining action "unless the higher-order volition were *itself* one by which the person *really wanted* to be determined" (166). Terminating the hierarchy at any particular point would be arbitrary without this element of choice and investment in the choice. Consciousness primarily as a distant reflection or a higher level is as wanton and disintegrated as unconscious behavior, perhaps even more so, since all it seems to do is increase the number of critical components without strengthening the identity of the agent.

Frankfurt gives a subtle twist to this reductive hypothesis when he refuses the "infinite regress" of making consciousness equal "consciousness-of," as if it were a mere reflector of a first or primary state of awareness. Consciousness can be seen to contribute to the formation of identity once its reflective structure is not made secondary, peripheral, or genitive, but *immanent* "by virtue of which every instance of being conscious grasps not only that of which it is an awareness but also the awareness of it. It is like a source of light which, in addition to illuminating whatever other things fall within its scope, *renders itself visible as well*" (162; my emphasis). In rendering itself visible (a difficult phrase to decipher), Frankfurt's consciousness does not seek to represent or image itself; it is not a question of a mimesis of an internal mental image, the so-called mirror of the mind debunked by pragmatists like Rorty.

The discriminating or noticing activities of a conscious state express themselves as *decisions* and identities on the part of the agent. The agent discriminates, chooses, identifies with the choice and renders the choice public, subject to approval by others. The point of consciousness is not mentality or interiority, in Frankfurt's view truly useless states as such, but the process of individuating oneself. It is reflexive because the object of consciousness is the constitution of one's identity through a variety of decisions (a stronger version of initial discriminations), and it remains an open question to what extent this identity can be said to govern actions in the name of some unified will: "A person may fail to integrate himself when he makes up his mind, of course, since the conflict or hesitancy with which he is contending may continue despite his decision. All a decision does is to create an intention; it does not guarantee that the intention will be carried out" (174).

The decision is immanent because it is not representable as a hierarchy or a totality. Like Williams, Frankfurt preserves the possibility of conflict in this subtle complex of reflection, decision, and identification:

> When someone identifies himself with one rather than with another of his own desires, the result is not necessarily to eliminate the conflict between those desires, or even to reduce its severity, but to alter its nature. . . .
> Quite possibly, the conflict between the two desires will remain as virulent as before. What the person's commitment to the one eliminates is not the conflict between it and the other. It eliminates the conflict *within the person* as to which of these desires he prefers to be his motive. The conflict between the *desires* is in this way transformed into a conflict between *one* of them and the *person* who has identified himself with its rival. (172)

That is about as far as the notion of wholeheartedness can take us. It is a process of identification without the implication of a completely fulfilled or realized personality.

Although Frankfurt begins his essay on wholeheartedness in terms of consciousness, it seems to me that the sort of reflection he develops takes the discussion of consciousness as a pretext for a theory of nonholistic decision making. As reflection is developed into partial identity and decision, filling in many gaps left in Williams's essay, Frankfurt makes no final effort to tie up all the references in his essay to neurobiology, physiology, and moral psychology. Instead, the figurative expression of illumination is unpacked and seems to summarize an ongoing process that begins as apperception but is finally directed at a self-critical exercise, something like an introspection. Frankfurt calls it *de-liberation*: "A person who is deliberating about what to do is seeking an alternative to 'doing what comes naturally.' His aim is to replace the liberty of anarchic impulsive behavior with the autonomy of being under his own control" (175). Through a nongoverning reflection, a reflection which will neither determine or control all actions nor result in a feeling of certainty, agents make specific identifications authoritative for themselves, all the while allowing for multiple and persistent conflicts in the social environment. Unlike mere consciousness, this reflexive exercise of autonomy, which is by no means perfect freedom to choose one way or the other, is indispensable.

Pragmatists like Rorty or Fish maintain the uselessness of self-consciousness because they equate it with mere distance from an immediate practice; without the principle of governance, the act of looking at oneself seems pointless. In contrast to Frankfurt's position, however, the pragmatists' attack is misplaced, a heavy salvo of artillery aimed at the wrong target. We can indeed drop the notion of consciousness as an elevated mirror of activity, and drop with it the futile effort of investing this mirror fantasm with special powers to govern our actions. But it does not follow that reflection is demolished and that we return to unmediated social practices of all sorts. Reflection, in Frankfurt's vocabulary, is the *limited freedom*, not pure, detached freedom or pure disengagement, to move between conflicting interests and goals. Immanent reflection is never completely freed of competing pressures upon the formation of human identity. Instead, it builds an image of its direct participation in the decision to go one way or another; it is personal wholeheartedness without theoretical or practical holism. And as Frankfurt intimates, once grasped, it begins to illuminate how we come to be concerned with each other and with others' opinions of us.

We are now touching on an expressive sphere of behavior in which language, conceived as a multiplicity of strongly identified expressions rather than a holistic sphere of expression, begins to play a stronger role. With partial but coherent decision making as a premise of a strong identity now in view, and with relativism replaced by central terms of reference, we can turn to a discussion of the role that language plays in all this. Charles Taylor is the contemporary philosopher who has gone farthest in linking language to the construction of human identity. Specifically, his language of qualitative contrast builds upon Frankfurt's distinction between first- and second-order decisions and identity. Further developed, Taylor's philosophy of language attempts to define the central terms of reference within a culture, which he calls hypergoods.

Taylor and the pragmatists directly engage contemporary political and moral issues. Situatedness, for example, in Taylor's writings is offered as a critique of liberal individualism, natural rights theories of justice, and all utilitarian ethics. It is difficult to isolate his writings on language from some of these issues in political philosophy and in the history of political theory. And it is equally difficult to avoid applying Taylor's account of expressivism as a direct critique of mimetic theory or sign theory in the literary disciplines. But to pursue these lines of argumentation would lead to a very different sort of project from the one I am attempting. As someone who is already writing within the literary disciplines and who wishes to place the study of literature in a socially relevant context, I shall follow Taylor's analysis of decision, expression, and situatedness in order to find within the textuality of literary works the sorts of convictions and central meanings which Williams and Frankfurt seek.

Charles Taylor on Situatedness, Incommensurability, and Symbolic Language

The philosophical writings of Charles Taylor have been overlooked within the literary disciplines, though he is of equal stature to Foucault and Habermas in the field of political philosophy and comparable in influence to Rorty, Derrida, and Lévi-Strauss in the philosophy of the social sciences. Aside from a brief commentary by Charles Altieri, I have been unable to trace any sustained reference to Taylor in the vast bibliography of literary theory, where Foucault, Derrida, and Rorty are cited widely.[1] This situation is likely to change with the recent publication of his *Sources of the Self: The Making of the Modern Identity,* a historical analysis of the implications of modernity in ethics, political theory, and literature.[2] This major work contains the first extensive use of literary sources in Taylor's exposition of a particular view of selfhood and language.

Rather than focusing directly on *Sources,* this chapter traces Taylor's concept of choice, the necessity of its articulation, and its consequences for positioning the human agent in a social and ethical context. I want to show the central relevance of Taylor's work to the development of issues in contemporary literary theory that involve the determination of a piece of language as a *text*. Specifically, I am concerned to show a connection between definitions of textuality that arise from the work of literary theorists and Taylor's language of qualitative contrast, its grasp of a principle of incommensurability, and its resolution in Taylor's concept of situatedness. These Taylorean concepts lead directly to a better understanding of the role of literary studies in a pluralist and nonfoundationalist society. At the same time Taylor's own views need to be modified in response to complex, progressive concepts of textuality within literary theory.

Taylor's work enables me to advance my discussion of reflective choice but also to take the discussion into questions about different, perhaps even antithetical, forms of language. The specific differences and syntheses of forms of language, tested and affirmed in acts of choice, bear upon the value of contemporary literary theory in a pluralist society. Specific articulations of choice allow a coherent critical position to develop out of a plurality of language games at work in our society. Articulations of choice avoid what I would consider to be unattractive versions of pluralism that present a multiplicity of little self-contained interpretive communities or a postmodernist expansion of vocabularies which do not enter into dialogue with each other. Taylor's analysis of choice, and the situatedness it gives rise to, may give back to the literary disciplines a sense of what moves agents to adopt or reject various features of language across a plurality of linguistic contexts, and it may enable the agent to discriminate important values within this movement. The aim of my discussion of Taylor is not to turn society and human agency into the product of language or to turn history and politics into literature. It is rather a matter of discriminating how a particular stance toward language may develop certain aspects of personhood, and then of seeing if some very highly determined forms of language, characteristically found in the discourse about the construction of a text, can take those discriminations a step further. Taylorean articulations of choice help to locate important moments of personal awareness and help to trace the stance of a linguistic agent in that web of vocabularies which Rorty, Minow, and Nussbaum speak of as an inescapable feature of plural societies.

Harry Frankfurt enables us to hold onto the concept of a reflective stance without assuming a governing distance from our immediate actions and impulses. Instead, he asks us to see reflection as immanent, as illuminating itself directly in the action of partially identifying ourselves with one action as against another. Immanent reflection is not totalizable, yet it seems to give a greater edge to our deliberate effort to assume a particular identity or stance than does Williams's notion of wise passivity. Taylor's analysis of the embodiment of the beliefs and values of a human agent, his effort to pinpoint what these philosophers call immanence, adds a new dimension: in the reflective awareness of plural values, difference of perspective, incommensurability of options for action—an awareness that is much more pressing and conflicted than Williams's reflective relativism—the immanence of the reflection can be achieved only *through the expression* of a strong decision. As Taylor develops the connection between taking a decision and expressing a decision in language, he acknowledges the influence of Frankfurt's description of partial resolution of conflict within a person, the sort of personal coherence that does not do away with the persistence of the source of conflict at large even if one side of the conflict is no longer an option for the person. How does a partial, deeply personal, reflective decision express itself? What is its language? and why is its language of special interest to a concept of human agency?

Taylor fights the tendency to lose a grasp on reflective activity which occurs when philosophers look for objectivist grounds or criteria. Reflection and expression are interdependent, so that the agent's decision *is* the capacity for expression. Once the connection is established, Taylor elaborates a larger view of the meaning of *situatedness,* which occurs in and around the terms of these expressions and decisions. Taylor does not say that language is the foundation of social identity. But he does argue that language is vitally important to philosophy's conception of human agency. Language is what enables the agent to perform the tasks of reflection and illumination, as they are defined by Frankfurt. Taylor's debates with social scientists and political theorists have addressed the way in which they hollow out human agency by universalizing it or by rendering it in generic terms which ignore the plurality of human agents. By extending the range and depth of these articulations, Taylor hopes to render the situatedness, or coherence of self and society, in more complex and edifying terms. Becoming a deliberate person, as in Harry Frankfurt's picture of an agent, involves a redescription of certain tensions that already inform the values of the agent.

Taylor's essay "What Is Human Agency?" contains a central counterinterpretation of the classic Sartrean case of the man torn between his patriotic duty to join the Resistance in wartime and his devotion to his invalid mother, who

cannot be left alone (from *L'Existentialisme est un humanisme*).[3] Taylor's interpretation of the Sartrean example of choice and conflict brings into focus his own
philosophy of agency and the language of qualitative contrast which is needed to
illuminate it. But before I can turn to this example and outline its relevance to the
arguments of this book, I need to take a small detour through some important
preliminary features of agency that Taylor puts forward.

The first feature has to do with the elimination of contingent, circumstantial
expressions of human agency. It is always possible to trivialize or magnify discussions of agency by trivializing or magnifying the circumstances under which it is
determined. Taylor leads up to the Sartrean case with a few ordinary examples,
such as the decision whether to take one's summer vacation by the sea or in a rich
cultural locale of obvious educational value, or to charge into battle on the front
line as a matter of courage or reckless indifference. Faced with numerous choices
in life, the human agent may come to think of volition and reflection as an ongoing
quest for a certain ideal of the good life or as a finite set of given options which can
be independently weighed on a case-by-case basis. But that picture of agency is
precisely what Taylor is seeking to overcome. The picture neglects the extent to
which the agent is involved in the *construction* of alternatives as the basis of
choice. Agency is not determined whenever there is a simple choice between
alternatives. Agency involves the construction of an essentially contrastive view of
a situation, whereas the act of examining desires or motivational urges may be
given to an agent as a contingent sequence of actions. Agency in a contrastive
perspective does not seek to eliminate one alternative in the face of the other but
rather seeks to extend the discrimination and awareness of alternatives for ethical
action over an entire pattern of behavior. The extension of a contrastive evaluation demands the self-definition of a stance, or what Taylor immediately calls the
"language of strong evaluation": "The alternatives in strong evaluation must be
contrastively described. For in strong evaluation, where we deploy a language of
evaluative distinctions, the rejected desire is not so rejected because of some mere
contingent or circumstantial conflict with another goal. . . . The conflict is
deeper; it is not contingent" (21).

In this passage, Taylor introduces *language* as if all speakers shared in it
nonproblematically. But for the moment Taylor is attempting to give the concept
of agency a certain continuity, beyond the numerous contingencies we all must
negotiate in everyday experience. He reaches for language in order to begin to
strengthen the definition of a core moment of contrastive decision making which

will have long-term implications once it has been taken. His point about evaluation is that poor accounts of agency will seek to disarm the stakes in a conflict by treating them reductively as erroneous linguistic descriptions, subject to objectivist correction (but then why should a more correct description automatically move us to change?)[4] or as circumstantial contingencies. The key element of contrast, captured in our language, is lost; or in Williams's terms, we become relativists by seeing our task as the complete dissolution of conflict.

Contrastive language concerns a "conflict of self-interpretations":"Which one we adopt will partly shape the meanings things have for us. But the question can arise which is more valid, more faithful to reality. To be in error here is thus not just to make a misdescription, as when I describe a motor-vehicle as a car when it is really a truck. We think of misidentification here as in some sense distorting the reality concerned" ("Agency" 22).

The term *reality* invokes an ontological vision of what makes a person good or dignified. Taylor suggests that a descriptive approach to ethical conflict would not only yield poor insights, but, further, would somehow distort a deeper reality about human being. The reality behind the act of choice signifies the transcendental strain in Taylor's writings. But language as a system of contrastive expressions, even as Taylor expounds it, does not necessarily refer to some special inner psychological state or some fundamental ontological division in the makeup of humanity. An attempt to hypothesize contrast as a better description of human being would be a misreading of Taylor (though one I concede he seems to invite).[5] Taylor is trying to give full recognition to the elements of reflection and self-constitution as partial identification, by deepening (in his vocabulary) the complexity of the decisions the agent must face.

Taylor argues that our reflective capacity to shape our identity out of personal choice needs to be closely bound up with the terms that confront us as incommensurable. The vocabulary we inherit from philosophy or literature may assist the process of reflection insofar as it enriches our capacity to articulate the choices out of which we constitute personal identity. Taylor would not view these vocabularies as verifiable descriptions of humanity, however, as if they were seen outside of their immediate relevance to the agent's task of articulation. Neither would he appreciate, at the opposite extreme, the sheer particularity of experience a philosopher like Nussbaum would associate with the narrative of a novel by Henry James or George Eliot.

For Taylor, articulation and the expressive merging of our identity and our language occur only after we have engaged in the effort to decide the importance of one value as against another, in full recognition of the fact that the two cannot be held together. In Taylor's view, we have thereby increased our general expressive capacity, become in a sense richer users of our linguistic resources, and that in turn has immediate implications for the depth at which values become situated within us. Taylor calls the "reflective choice between incommensurables" a "condition of articulacy" (24). In positing the inevitability of differences and incommensurables amidst the plurality of modern society, Taylor attempts to locate those special moments when a human agent is caught between those differences that are irreconcilable. Rather than split the difference into finer and finer gradations of vocabularies, as Rorty seems to do, Taylor sees agents acquiring their stance, or situatedness, within plural society in the articulation of the meaning of *between*. Betweenness becomes a very large part of Taylor's definition of the structure of the literature of modernity.

The Sartrean dilemma clearly involves contrast and choice: whether sympathy and duty to stay by one's ailing mother outweigh ethical duties to one's country in wartime. But Sartre's development of the choice is misleading, according to Taylor, because it is made to seem radical, a choice of one or the other obligation instead of a choice between them (the prepositions used by Taylor). At first glance, the idea of a total investment of self in one direction seems to attach great deliberation and responsibility to human agency, making it appear to be the very basis of value's enactment in the social world. But Sartre's characterization of choice as a radical expression of freedom leaves unexplained how the choices could come to be incommensurable in the first place. If values exist because we create them by our agential capacity to act one way *or* another, then all comparisons of values would have to be on an equally radical footing. We would not be able to reflect upon the responsibilities and decisions we uphold as agents, by which we identify ourselves, if the reflections were radical, a direct expression of agency. By a radical definition of agency, all choices would seem to be incommensurable. The existentialist radical definition of choice may be one way of committing ourselves to contingencies, and Rorty suggests that all choices are radically contingent once we give up foundationalist thinking. But situating our identity in an ethical context and measuring the individuality of our identity, Taylor argues, emerge only in acts of choice in which we experience incommensurability throughout the task of decision making. That experience is what radical contingency and choice seem to omit. Or in Hegelian terms, one could say that Taylorean choice not only cancels but also preserves contraries. Radical free choice is incoherent choice because the depth of investment it asks for makes it nearly impossible to articulate that depth:

> Now in this hypothetical case the young man has to resolve the matter by radical choice. He simply has to plump for the Resistance or for staying at home with his mother. He has no language in which the superiority of one alternative over the other can be articulated; indeed, he has not even an inchoate sense of the superiority of one over the other; they seem quite incommensurable to him. He just throws himself one way. (30)

An expressive stance for a human agent must emerge from a different analysis of incommensurability which involves a pull between alternatives. Only then can we speak properly of having made a choice; only then does the verb have any sense as an act of entering into a pattern of decision, rather than declaring oneself by fiat one way or the other.

For Taylor, acts of reflection can be realized only as they develop a language of contrast. I think Taylor is right to point out that radical agency practices an incoherent form of expression, "for it wants to maintain both strong evaluation and radical choice. It wants to have strong evaluations and yet deny their status as judgements" (32). The reductive connection between strength, or effort, and choice has to be broken, although on the surface they seem to fit together. Choices cannot be unidirectional; the effort of enacting values is always carried out in the midst of contradictions which need to be partially maintained to affirm the fact that we are involved in an ongoing process of decision making.

The Sartrean example is a striking one, like Williams's use of ritual killings to define the distance between different cultures. If we can leave aside the distracting extraordinariness of this particular decision for the moment, then the point that needs to be made has primarily to do with seeing the importance of incommensurability as the instigator of a proper definition of a decision. Within the larger context of a theory of decision making, incommensurability itself would have to be less radically defined. For now, it holds an important place as an indication of a kind of general lack of commensuration within a pluralist society, consisting of persons who may hold plural convictions, and as means of specifying the right degree of contrast that would invoke the necessity of a decision. Out of this decision and confrontation with incommensurable values and beliefs, Taylor goes on to build an extremely complex picture of human agents finding their right degree of coherence with each other. Determining that right degree, by sharpening and refining the terms that define a self in the midst of plurality, is the larger purpose of a discourse based in the recognition of incommensurability. The decision that does the work of refinement, by constructing the experience of incommensurability, is also the source of what most deeply situates a self in a modern society. The language of qualitative contrast maintains a very complex degree of specificity and refinement. But by virtue of its function as a bridge between different values, that same language shares in a wide vision of what is important, central, of paramount importance to an individual ethical stance. To be situated, therefore, is to bridge the gap between the highest values in a complex, internally differentiated society and to possess a high degree of immanent reflection upon who one is individually.

This concept of situatedness demands a combination of generalization and precision that is characteristic of the discourse within and about works of literature. The large question that remains is, Can the language of contrast that determines a speaker's situatedness, immanence in language, and personal coherence incorporate the language that is presently being determined in the name of textuality? The implications of this question are far-reaching and far exceed the terms of many debates about the status of literary theory in relation to a fixed textual object. For to investigate this question is to pursue a language of personal expression right at the core of the determination of the language of textuality as it is provoked (if not produced) by works of literature.

These types of questions point to what really counts about the relevance of Taylor to issues in literary theory and criticism. But the task of answering them leads us to look more carefully at Taylor's philosophy of language. Granting that we want Taylor to guide the discussion about situatedness and plurality, incommensurability and decision making, does his account of language provide us with the means to rethink certain issues in the field of literary studies?

In the account we have so far, the assumption seems to be that a better view of agency will lead, inevitably, to a better kind of social theory, one that avoids the pitfalls of abstract universalization and homogeneous measurements. But that outcome is not at all guaranteed, especially when the social nature of language is always seen to assist the realization of agency in a nonproblematic way. But what sort of societal coherence of expression and behavior does this imply? Qualitative distinctions and contrastive values as they contribute to the articulate practice of individual agents leave unanswered a further question: How do individual agents, as partial norms and identities, cohere with each other? Do individual agents drawing upon a generally available linguistic realm of contrastive expressions reshape that field in a decisive way for other agents? Taylor's essay on human agency turns in fact toward an introspective rather than a public characterization of choice and critical reflection. One of its conclusions about radicalism as depth rather than strength reads as follows:

> This radical evaluation is a deep reflection, and a self-reflection in a special sense: it is a reflection about the self, its most fundamental issues, and a reflection which engages the self most wholly and deeply. Because it engages the whole self without a fixed yardstick it can be called a personal reflection . . . and what emerges from it is a self-resolution in a strong sense, for in this reflection the self is in question. . . .
>
> Because this self-resolution is something we do, when we do it, we can be called responsible for ourselves; and because it is within limits always up to us to do it, even when we do not . . . we can be called responsible in another sense for ourselves, whether we undertake this radical evaluation or not. (42)

The first-person plural pronoun barely carries a sense of the collective; it merely offers an invitation, in politely passive form, for everyone to achieve this very individualistic state of ethical awareness.

Richard E. Flathman's discussion of Taylor as a political philosopher helps to define this problematic gap between private and public terms of ethical reference for human agency. Flathman points us immediately to a potential short circuit in Taylor's use of "contrastive language":

> Evaluating in the [Taylorean] contrastive mode, then, requires command of a conceptual system of some complexity. The items to be assessed *cannot* be experienced or understood particularistically, and the relations among them *must* be understood in a more or less closely specified and established manner. These modal cannots and musts, moreover, are normative, indeed typically moral, in character. To understand them is to know what, morally speaking, one cannot do and must do and it is to know that failure entails self-criticism (self-reproach, guilt or shame, remorse) and justified criticism by others (rebuke, blame, punishment). The agent must succeed in integrating and harmonizing her thoughts, her ac-

tions, and indeed her feelings. And as we will have occasion to emphasize below, this means that she must harmonize herself with the other agents who, together with herself, make up the community of which she is part.[6]

There seems to be a too-rapid shift somewhere in Taylor's concept of situatedness. The careful maintenance of critical decision making in a state of partial self-integration gives way to a pressure to become deeply situated in some strongly normative community. The language of contrast so essential to the development of the reflective capacities of the agent is reduced, on the next level of social behavior, to the community as normative, moral judge. As the reflective agent acquires more and more capacity for contrastive evaluation, a paradox develops: contrasts on the communal level of interpretation seem fixed and determinate. Collective agency as communal participation seems to carry over the whole idea of situatedness but now renders it devoid of the contradictory, incommensurable content that gave rise to it in the first place. There is a loss of mediation somewhere between these levels of analysis.

Flathman begins to note this loss in the way Taylor's concept of situatedness turns into a requirement that the agent accept the community's ultimate governance of the meanings of the contrastive language of moral evaluation:

> Despite the prominence of the concept "self" in [Taylor's] discussions, talk of the agent exercising control over her dispositions and character should not be taken as an endorsement of the theory of freedom as self-dependence. Oppositions such as "courageous-craven" are established in any number of communities, any number of languages. But to know that *these* particular acts are craven is to command criteria that are established in the community in which one is thinking and acting. . . . It does not follow that the genuinely free person invariably accepts the norms of her community; indeed Taylor argues eloquently that the genuinely "responsible" person is critical of the deepest norms of her community. But there is a powerful tendency in Taylor's argument to understand "free activity as grounded in the *acceptance* of our defining situation." (73)

The tension in the concept of the norm differs from the contrastive criteria used in becoming a member of the community. Situated contrasts, as we saw, demand a kind of mutually modifying attitude toward alternatives. There are no absolute criteria for judging between national and familial duties, and no absolute legitimation of the concept of justice under the terms of one nation's constitution or sociopolitical history. The primary task of situated agency in this context is articulation, summed up nicely by Flathman:

> Assessing communal norms is first and foremost, though not exclusively
> . . . a process of grasping, clarifying, and perhaps adjusting relationships
> among the multiplicity of beliefs and values, conventions and rules, practices and institutional arrangements, of which the community in question
> has come to consist. . . . It is continuous with those processes through
> which individuals seek to understand the array of their own desires and interests, beliefs and expectations, and attempt to discern and to contribute
> to consistency and continuity, coherence and integration, among them. It
> involves an attempt to articulate what is already present, perhaps in inchoate form, in day-to-day thinking and experience. (77)

As articulation becomes more coherent it implies a strong effort to establish a coherence of identity between individual and community, the continuity that Flathman mentions. But one does not entail the other. In order to maintain a kind of coherence proper to expressive agency, namely, the link between identificatory investment of self and the pull of contraries within a genuine decision, Taylor proposes an important role for linguistic articulation. He sees the development of articulation as a constitutive event. But Flathman correctly points to the return to a quasi-representational function for language, as a reflector of other kinds of normative activity that need to be aligned with each other within the community, as a clarification of what is already present. Agency, linguistic expression, and incommensurable stresses are eventually transformed into variables or equation marks, which allow agents to cohere with each other by rejecting, as Flathman notes further, norms that are "inconsistent, disjunctive, and make mutually incompatible demands." So the agent comes to affirm and strengthen a gradual process of rational change and improvement in civil society.

The commitment to community is an admirable feature of Taylor's social philosophy that should never be given up too lightly, if at all. My concern remains, however, that this process of social development, initially a great improvement over abstract social scientific generalizations, fails to build upon its own strong account of human agency and its links to an expressive realm of language. Taylor goes further than Frankfurt in his focus upon the exact terms of entry into the public sphere. He allows claims to be imposed, criticized, and reformulated without robbing them of their immanence. But it now looks as if immanence is practically synonymous with normative behavior. My point is not that we should be against norms, agreed-upon values, and rational inquiry. It is that the content of these norms and values is devoid of conflict, and eventually of plurality, when they reach the level of collective decision making. The need for agents to recognize the way in which competing claims are imposed and critically revised has been elided, so that eventually all the agents in a particular community appear to speak mono-logically rather than dialogically. Although the whole topic of language is central to Taylor's social philosophy, there seems to be an unexamined limit to the con-ceptual strains it can bear as the medium par excellence of human agency.

Taylor's most recent work, *Sources of the Self,* differs from the earlier essays on language and agency in its incorporation of literary works and different levels of vocabulary within the definition of a situated agent. But for that reason it also makes even more clear the impasse that Flathman is addressing. The added refine-ment of the linguistic analysis keeps to the view of language as special sort of public space, reducible neither to atomistic nor communitarian spheres of expres-sion, but the manner by which the agent's situatedness is upheld in language remains ambiguous. The introspective moment grasps the central but nontotaliz-able words that define moral awareness. These words make up a vocabulary of "hypergoods," which displaces the weaker functional and aesthetical vocabu-laries Taylor associates with a constricting "ethics of inarticulacy" (see *Sources* 53–90). Terms of politeness or prohibition are functional because they are rulelike; they set certain minimal conditions for social cooperation. Aesthetic terms for sensibility and enjoyment support a notion of individualism. But hyper-goods are like Williams's central terms. They are necessary to the entire sense of who one is, the society one belongs to, the standpoint of one's entire moral orientation.

Taylor is right to pick out of human discourse those special hypergood words like *freedom* and *dignity* that provide self-identity and that challenge merely functional or merely subjective vocabularies, merely descriptive or merely playful utterances, all of which amount to disengaged perspectives on social behavior. Nevertheless, hypergoods seem to provide no more guidance than Taylor's earlier reliance upon a language of qualitative contrast. The transitional moment, be-tween self-identity and public existence, the key moment in Taylor's entire philos-ophy of freedom, is filled in with the *self-evidence* of the good, which clouds the picture of how it is the product of agency, how it is shaped by linguistic agents and shapes the perspective of other linguistic agents. Consider the following statement on the hypergood of God or the Good:

> There is no question here of our ever being able to come to recognize [God as essential to our best account of the human moral world] by prescinding from our moral intuitions. Rather our acceptance of any hypergood is connected in a complex way with our being *moved* by it. It is necessary to add 'in a complex way', because we never think of these things entirely on our own and monologically, however certain moral views may exhort us to do so. We may accept something as a good although we are relatively unmoved by it, because at the lowest, we think very little about it and glide along in conformity with our milieu; or because we revere and look up to established authority; or perhaps best, because we choose certain fig-ures as authoritative for us, sensing in them that they are moved by something authentic and great, even though we don't fully understand it or feel it ourselves. But through all these complex chains of intermedia-tion, the connection between seeing the good and being moved by it cannot be broken. (*Sources* 73–74)

This dense quotation indicates the excellence and the limitations of Taylor's posi-tion. As nonprescriptive, nonmonological, intermediating chains of expressions, hypergoods mark a decisive break with narrowly pragmatic or propositional philosophies of language. So too with the picture of the human subject as atomis-tic individual or rationally motivated subject. But what does it mean to be moved by the expression of a hypergood? How do we choose it as authoritative? Taylor speaks of agents' revising of their perspectives and of transitional states of social awareness, but he never offers an account of how a central hypergood reality goes hand in hand with the claim of a particular form of language. And yet without language, hypergoods could not exist at all. Where do recognition of a hypergood and being moved by it meet in the realm of language? We need to determine this meeting point, and, following Taylor, we know that the determination involves situatedness rather than backgrounds and universals. But until we find the deter-mination through language, we remain trapped in the circle Flathman describes: that of dialogical speakers in a nondialogical realm of language.

From the perspective of the literary disciplines, language may be analyzed into finer strands of meaning and structure than are captured by the contrast between expressive and designative functions or between hypergoods and naturalist explanations. These strands do not necessarily inhibit interpretive communities from making normative judgments or detach literary critics from the norms of a wider cultural sphere. Of course some interpreters, for example, Stanley Fish or his antitheorist followers Knapp and Michaels, may be happy with a model of norm making that sees all norms—literary, behavioral, historical, legal—on a single continuum. A greater recognition of discontinuity between these contexts, best theorized in the critical language of the literary disciplines, need not imply a complete breakdown of rational norms or a return to radical pluralism and relativism. The ability to maintain a situated, critical reflection, to recognize the presence of agency in a decision, may require a much more literary view of language, as rhetoric, grammar, sign, or speech-act, each with its own distinct powers and limits as a vehicle *for* critical reflection or *between* reflections. Taylorean agency seems to fall short in its account of how agents may affect the balance between different linguistic properties and how this may in turn shape linguistic practices for other agents and their acceptance or rejection of assertions, judgments, dialogical meanings, even of what they consider to be rhetorical or not in the first place.

How do different elements of language cohere with each other, especially in works of literature? As noted, *Sources of the Self* contains Taylor's first extensive use of and commentary on literary texts. It therefore brings into focus the way some of Taylor's key concepts, like situatedness, take on a specifically literary articulation. But it also indicates how much more work remains to be done in catching up with the level of reading that is now standard in the literary disciplines. A complete review of *Sources* is well beyond the scope of my inquiry into agency. *Sources* is a monumental work that is primarily devoted to a reaffirmation of the concept of the self in the context of the historical moment we call modernism. Without wanting to abstract *Sources* too severely, I think a brief look at the way Taylor treats modernist poetry and imagism (in Rilke, Hulme, Eliot, and Pound) shows that he combines an underdeveloped concept of literary language with his most developed concepts of situatedness. Bringing Taylor's work into the literary disciplines means righting this imbalance.

Taylor's meditation on the meaning of literary modernism begins with an examination of its source in the romantic expressivism that defines his basic terms of reference for literary language. Romantics and modernists—which in Taylor's discourse includes Coleridge, Hegel, Schelling, Wittgenstein, Schopenhauer, and

Heidegger—reject the scientific, or mechanistic, view of the self as a detached, neutral observer. But modernists throw a twist into the expressivist view of language because they are also antisubjectivist, even at times antihumanist (see *Sources* 461). As a criticism of expressivism as mere self-expression Taylor supports the modernist project, but then of course his own view of expressivism, as I have indicated, has little in common with merely subjective or atomistic utterances. The whole complexity of his project has to do with replacing, if not always clearly, the atomistic/communitarian distinction with the expressive act through which the reflective self enters a public sphere of understanding, a sphere which is coherent but not totally describable. For Taylor, the modernist version of this (primarily romantic) act of self-realization is through a strong attachment to the fabric of concrete experiences that redefines the unity of the self in an increasingly fragmentary world. How do we define this new unity without capitulating to the excesses of the postmodernist dissolution of a unified self?

The literary task, according to Taylor, is to find a form of expression that lets the particularity of the world become manifest, in all its new multiplicity, but that also lends it sufficient coherence to be able to support the concept of situatedness. Taylor's answer is to characterize this form as *epiphanic,* a revelation of meaning through juxtaposition. What is most interesting about this form (aside from its symbolic and romantic overtones, which is usual in Taylor's writings) is that the terminology that attaches to it seems to be derived from the earlier terminology used to describe the situatedness of the agent as *between* choices, never radically in one or the other:

> Much modern poetry is no longer descriptive [of nature]. There is no unambiguously defined matter referred to or portrayed. Images are not simply introduced as simile or metaphor to characterize a central referent, story, or object. From the Symbolists on, there has been a poetry which makes something appear by juxtaposing images or, even harder to explain, by juxtaposing words. The epiphany comes from between the words or images, as it were, from the force field they set up between them, and not through a central referent which they describe while transmuting. (465–66)

Once defined, the epiphany accomplishes what situated agency and expressivism had previously: it is constitutive rather than designative; it cannot be controlled but it can shape and direct self-awareness—but all this is now given a distinctly literary articulation. The argumentative twist is that the literary epiphany, so defined, gradually becomes in Taylor's discourse a source of respect for language in and of itself; the epiphanic poetic utterance may not designate or even express anything subjective, but as the historical advent of *die reine Sprache* its very surface quality uneasily squares with Taylor's treatment of it as a medium of self-awareness. That is, Taylorean modernism is a careful and delicate revision of an earlier, expressive phase of language, in turn a revision of earlier nominalism, and the historical logic that holds all this together is the human project of joining into an ever-greater, ever-more-mysterious linguistic communion. What it is impossible for Taylor to think through is the whole modernist interrogation of the surface of language as a deeper interrogation of the model of *interiority* of meaning. Surface awareness of language need not be epiphanic at all but might as easily refer to what we now call the *material* properties of signification, in short, the entire modernist (Saussurean) definition of the sign as tripartite, made up of the material signifier, the conventionalized meaning, and their unity in the sign. That is where the significant debates in contemporary literary theory begin: in questions of degree of conventionality of meaning; in questions of the relative autonomy of the signifying process; in rethinking the entire epistemological tradition of two poles of meaning, inside/outside, in favor of more pragmatic or grammatological models of linguistic communication.

The equation of literariness with the epiphany blocks out this other side of modernity because the emphasis is always upon how the epiphany captures the plenitude of the humanist network of discourse. There is no effort to think through the speaker's basic relation to language as other than revelatory and participatory, even if the terms of the human change greatly in time and place. Betweenness as a cross between the philosophy of situatedness and literary theory does not guarantee a sophisticated approach to the topic of agency because the betweenness seems not to acknowledge discontinuous, conflicting, or incommensurable elements within the construction of a particular language or literary text. In fact, just the opposite: its surface connecting of bits of language is merely a "frame" for Taylor that allows selves to pass, as through a shaping lens, between discourses. The ephiphany, because it is irreducibly poetic and mysterious, contributes to the attack on mechanism and depersonalization: it reminds us, says Taylor, that, "we have to stop seeing language as simply an inert instrument whereby we can deal more effectively with things. It involves becoming aware of what we do with words" (481). Is it really too much to ask the other modernist question about what words do to us? Is that really such a threat to the whole concept of human agency, which needs to be shored up in terms of sensibility, personal experience, vividness, and all the other now-impoverished terms that make up Taylor's vocabulary of literary criticism when he discusses a poem by Rilke or Celan (see 482–86)? The epiphanic element that Taylor identifies comes close to a recognition of the material dimensions of the signifier, but in Taylor's discourse this approximate recognition is immediately recuperated in a way that is faithful to the modernist attack on subjectivism but never dares to put into question modernist theories of textuality. I think the mixture of superb insight and theoretical limitation in the following passage indicates a certain need to reconstruct Taylor's philosophy of language if it is to gain influence upon the analysis of literature:

> The epiphanic power of words cannot be treated as a fact about the order of things which holds unmediated by the works of the creative imagination. That [Pound's] Canto I captures the energy that runs through Homer isn't a truth like that (as we used to believe) Saturn is linked to melancholy or that (as we believe now) DNA controls heredity. Discoveries like Pound's come to us indexed to a personal vision. Indeed, many of the references in the images of Pound, Eliot, and other poets come from their own personal experience. The fragments that Eliot "shores against his ruin" in *The Waste Land* are an idiosyncratic collection. . . .
>
> For this reason, inwardness is as much a part of the modernist sensibility as of the Romantic. And what is within is deep: the timeless, the mythic, and the archetypical that are brought forth by Mann or Joyce . . . may be transpersonal. But our access to it can only be within the personal. In this sense, the depths remain inner for us as much as for our Romantic forebears. . . .
>
> This doesn't have to be rampant subjectivism. The epiphanic is genuinely mysterious, and it possibly contains the key—or a key—to what it is to be human. (481)

Taylor's literary celebration of language as human realization does not address literary theory's delineation of the linguistic structures and forces that have remained hidden by what Derrida would call the logocentric tradition. The only way to get beyond an even greater fissure between human agency and the language of literary theory would be through a much more strenuous effort to situate the perspectives that are presently failing to connect. Within the scene of linguistic recognition we have to allow for a much higher degree of incommensurable meaning without seeking a prematurely expressive harmonization. I would follow Taylor in calling this the shaping of language. I want to go beyond Taylor only in making this shaping much more specific, by finding to the highest possible degree of exactness where the incommensurability of meanings lies, where it can be traced and further articulated.

Alex Callinicos focuses and summarizes this remaining problem in Taylor's work very well in his discussion of "expressivism and the hermeneutic tradition" that begins with Dilthey and Weber, continues in Gadamer and Habermas, and would now include social theorists like W. G. Runciman and philosophers like Donald Davidson and Michael Dummett. What follows is obviously a highly selective borrowing from Callinicos's wide-ranging study.[7]

Hermeneutical social theory differs from strict social science in basing theoretical analysis of agency upon a communicative exchange of understanding between speakers as cultural rather than natural subjects. Rather than offer causal or positivist accounts of human behavior, this tradition turns to concepts like empathy and participation and a fusion of horizons as the basis of cultural inquiry. Much of Taylor's philosophical corpus addresses these debates directly. The basic concern is the first account of the contact between speakers.

The hermeneut wants to give a special place to communicative practices, to make them the most important constitutive events of cultural development. But there always seems to be a large gap between the central definition of what goes into the communicative moment and its general cultural unfolding. It is like the gap, in Taylor's work, between a very well defined contrast that situates the agent in a choice and the apparent emptiness of the contrast on the general level of community norms. Or as Callinicos puts it, "Does the 'triple-H' philosophy of language [Taylor's shorthand for Herder-Humboldt-Heidegger] rule out the possibility of social *theory*? . . . Does it imply that all the investigator can do is to characterize the self-understanding of agents, indeed of necessity relying on the very conceptual vocabulary they themselves use to articulate this self-understanding?" (98–99). To invoke some of the vocabulary Callinicos draws from the hermeneutical tradition, how does a theorist, in search of principles of understanding, generalize immanent understanding? Must this understanding between agents remain tacit, a matter of immediate practices and customs? How does one refute or validate conflicting points of view? or suggestive contrasts or perspicuous contrasts? The vocabulary supports the whole concept of the agent as expressive, but it seems to force the social theorist back into some exterior foundational discourse about human nature, beliefs that support practices, specially applied rules that govern rational communication, the primacy of the designative function, holistic social structures—all that expressivism set out to avoid in the first place. In Callinicos's view, Taylor's emphasis on participation in the community turns out to be a masked form of its complete antithesis, which he polemically dubs "linguistic solipsism":

> Taylor and the hermeneutic tradition generally seem to commit the . . . error . . . of reducing interlinguistic understanding to the understanding of a language by a native speaker. Thus Gadamer treats interpretation as a relation to tradition, which is both continued and transformed in being appropriated. But this "fusion of horizons" seems to assume the existence of a persisting shared culture which unites both the living members of that culture and previous generations. But how does understanding occur when no such culture exists? The problem does not arise simply in the case of interpreting an alien speaker. It may also arise for the historian studying a society different in fundamental respects from his or her own. The hermeneutic tradition seems to condemn us in these cases to a sort of linguistic solipsism, in which members of different cultures confront one another in a relation of mutual incomprehension. Taylor does not seem to deny that we can understand an alien language but he offers no account of how this is possible. (108–09)

The same sort of disguised solipsism would be true of Habermas's theory of communicative action, in which again the central place given to language in the formation of valid social consensus rests on a circular discovery of a foundational source of agreement (normative context, shared knowledge, truthful belief) in the very construction of language itself. How could any speaker, Callinicos asks, understand a false statement in the first place, since that would imply that the speaker is perhaps merely outside, alien to, correct linguistic usage? That is exactly the point made by James Tully in his commentary on Taylor and Habermas (see chapter 1). As in Taylor's account of language, there seems to be an unwarranted, possibly incoherent, assertion that language upholds the community of speakers because language is both immediately understandable and an offer to choose to understand. How can we choose what we have already chosen in having already understood?[8]

I would formulate this agential paradox as an omission: What is left out of the hermeneutical account of cultural knowledge is the phase in which highly reflective agents discover the power either to articulate *claims* upon the meaning of the most central expressive terms in the host culture or to decide which are the central ones.

If radical expression of a decision is incoherent because the whole idea of radical commitment blocks out the alternative the agent has decided against, then generalized acceptance of language as the offer of communication is also incoherent. The agent is pictured as giving assent to an utterance that has already been accepted as a valid communication. On the level of collective social analysis, literary tradition, and the legitimation of norms in law and in approved speech-acts (taking oaths, making promises, and truthful reporting), expressive activity should not sacrifice contradiction and linguistic incommensurability to an implicit idealization of situatedness. The concept of situated, linguistic decision making needs to allow for a certain measure of struggle and competing claims between linguistic actions without sacrificing the goals of consensus and shared understanding.

The point I am trying to make is that the concept of situatedness in theories of language will be lost if it is not sustained by a finer investigation of how claims are imposed, acknowledged, and critically evaluated by speakers. One of the intellectual commitments I continue to admire the most in Taylor's writing has to do with the validation of any vocabulary shifts in the context of "the struggle of daily life, in which individuals and couples strive to make sense of their lives and give shape to their hopes, fears and aspirations."[9] Taylor is addressing specifically the requirement that any theory of historical change through political conflict, especially wars between states, match its explanatory vocabulary about power or justice to as much of the everyday vocabulary of social history as it is capable of retrieving. The matching process is not a matter of metatheoretical analysis of a past event on a grand conceptual scale, a self-certifying of the theory itself, but an effort to keep up the linguistic task of situatedness on all levels of cultural and historical understanding. The prosaic level of understanding is not the only or the supreme context of understanding; it is simply the level at which the multiplicity and inevitable discontinuities within language will resist abstract or generic formulation. The language of marriage, of love, of the family, of labor, of sexuality will count as much as that of the documents referring to military strategy. Without this prosaic dimension of understanding, which will include our own present-day vocabulary, we may think we gain methodological validity, but it will certainly be at the expense of expressive complexity.

Taylor's overview of the point of departure for the disciplines of history and social science fits the literary disciplines equally well, and in my view deconstruction best of all:

> Different languages, and different variants of traditionally recognized languages, are in competition. Their protagonists are in struggle. But there is no single focus, the struggle is carried on in a multitude of different contexts on a great many levels, through the history of society. The reigning language of any epoch is the provisional outcome of this multi-layered struggle as it stands at that moment. (HC 224)

Deconstruction supplements Taylor's view not because it is some abstract theory of difference, conflict, and plurality that leaves us always at the same inert, atemporal point of departure. On the contrary: it refuses to homogenize conflict and difference while it preserves to a much higher degree the tasks of immanent critical decision making between linguistic contexts.

In concluding my discussion of Taylor, I would like to turn briefly to two of his essays on the philosophy of language, "Language and Human Nature" and "Theories of Meaning."[10] I have been suggesting that Taylor's important contributions to the view of agency as situated tend to become weaker as they become broader because his language of contrast fails to build in some of the contradictory linguistic forces discussed in literary theory, particularly by deconstructionists. In moving gradually toward a three-way dialogue among Taylor, de Man, and Cavell, I shall define my own critical stance, which will be developed with reference to theories of textuality in part II of this book. So I want to repeat at this point that my stance depends upon filling in some of the gaps where each philosophical position on language already overlaps but has not been sufficiently recognized.

My effort to draw together Taylor, Cavell, and de Man in no way marks a return to holism, essentialism, or a narrow circumscription of valid utterance. I continue to put forward a concept of situated decision making that attempts to steer between the extremes of relativism and foundational conceptual centers. What seems to inhibit dialogue between these particular reflective agents is a certain failure of recognition, the absence of answerable claims upon each other in spite of their convergence in terms of plurality and antifoundationalism. Taylor's important contribution to the whole inquiry into linguistic agency seems to rely upon only one sort of scene of recognition, that of language as expressivism. Cavell has perhaps gone the farthest in marking the ever-present danger of what he calls, somewhat fancifully, skepticism, by which he means the refusal to acknowledge the claims others impose upon our construction of selfhood. But his offer of a new therapeutic or aesthetic solution to skepticism operates under the extremes of ordinary grammatical expression or highly figurative expressions. These extremes require a finer contrast. Finally, de Man's "grammatization of rhetoric" offers one of the most sophisticated pictures of the precise points of discontinuity and critical choice within language; it is an attempt to break down *language* as a monolithic term for grammar, rhetoric, speech, convention, and literary style. But to complete the circuit of inquiry, we need to speculate about the coherence of the deconstructive agent, to bring the inquiry back to the concerns that Taylorean philosophy raises about our ability to respond to contrary insights through the effort to articulate.

Taylor's essay on language and human nature stakes out the whole topic of linguistic recognition. He prepares us for his discussion of the moment of recognition by rapidly going over the history of theories of language from Neoplatonism in St. Augustine to the scientific revolution associated with Descartes, Bacon, and Hobbes. His magisterial, Hegelian-style overview of the spirit of language in the Western tradition is aimed at bringing us to the romantic doctrines of Herder and Humboldt, where his own views on expressivism merge with the tradition he is narrating, specifically in terms of the recognition of linguistic signification that the romantic philosophers made central to their theories:

> *That* is just the mysterious thing. Anyone can be taught the meaning of a word, or even guess at it, or even invent one, once they have language. But what is this capacity which we have and animals do not to endow sounds with meaning, to grasp them as referring to ["physical phenomena"]?
>
> And this is Herder's point. To learn a word, to grasp that "triangle" stands for triangles, is to be capable of this reflective awareness. That is what needs to be explained. To account for language by saying that we learn that the word "a" stands for a's, the word "b" for b's, is to explain nothing. How do we learn what "standing for" involves, what it is to de-

scribe things, briefly, to acquire the reflective awareness of the language user? (227–28)

The verbal act of signification needs to be grasped in all its specificity, for only by giving it sufficient recognition as a signifying event will we be able to locate and develop reflection and expression. Although this essay does not speak of situatedness or contrastive decision making, similar concerns about agency follow from the effort to conceptualize language through the special recognition of its signifying function, which, Taylor suggests, is all too easily taken for granted. A deeper recognition of language as signification strengthens our capacity to become significant agents for each other. It draws speakers together in ways that the so-called scientific or narrowly designative theories of language as a merely instrumental medium do not.

Since I have been relying heavily from the outset on the immanence of the agent's critical stance in linguistic practices, I am naturally very sympathetic to Taylor's attack upon theories of nominalism and scientism, which view language as an empty medium of signifiers for the meaningful content it serves to transmit. Much of this attack is parallel to the one Taylor makes upon the unsituated agent. Abstractly free agency seems to go hand in hand with a false picture of freestanding language. So in medieval nominalism the insight gained into the organization of signs as a general, conceptual classification scheme of the world's particulars is at the expense of a loss of language as intersubjective participation in a collective worldview. The upshot of nominalism is the advent of the designative theory of language, which detaches the agent from a realm of linguistic participation. Taylor sees a continuation of this tendency in the scientific revolution, in which the emphasis shifts to the sign as a representation of inner ideas which are the main conceptual organizers of perceptual knowledge. As this Western exteriorization of the sign becomes the dominant tradition, language comes to be seen as the "great seducer, tempting us to be satisfied with mere words" (225) instead of the empirical reality they serve to represent. So the task of linguistic theory becomes the control of language's representational function. Either the speaker masters language, makes it designative by "definitional fiat," or the speaker is led astray.

When Taylor quietly inserts the topic of mastery and control into his otherwise conventional history of language, he is pointing us to his real underlying concerns. The linguistic sign as a notational fiat marks the presence of the unsituated speaker: in enslaving language, the speaker is deluded by a false image of autonomy and authority, much like the Sartrean case we saw earlier, which exposed the incoherence of radical choice. The illusion of having mastered language, or having to need to master it, makes it appear as if the speaker could enter and exit the linguistic realm at will, resorting to language to communicate an already formed idea or conceptual framework. This illusion not only gives unwarranted privilege to one particular function, the designative over the expressive; it also obliterates the whole question of how language is constitutive of a wide range of cultural practices, such as the spheres of religious and aesthetic expression, but also political consensus, ethical values, and historical reflection. Changes in these spheres and in their expressive status within a dominant scientific worldview cannot seem very important if they have been reduced to mere individual belief or marginal significance because they lack the controls built into proper linguistic usage.

Taylor's return to the scene of recognition in the romantics is an attempt to see linguistic signification as a situated rather than a controlled linguistic event, as a stance as well as a standing for. Instead of splitting up language into so many primary and secondary functions, Taylor tries to elaborate signification in immanent terms: we shape language continually and are shaped in turn by the whole range of signifying activities we can never hope to dominate completely. Language is not something we enter after we have had a thought or feeling; language is a fluid medium already present in the original signifying gesture. Reflective expression is the process of becoming more and more aware of the exact boundaries and limits of signification. All this is expounded in another one of Taylor's eloquent passages:

> As Humboldt puts it, we have to think of language as speech, and this as activity, not realized work; as *energeia*, not *ergon*.
>
> But if the language capacity comes to be in speech, then it is open to being continually recreated in speech, continually extended, altered, reshaped. And this is what is constantly happening. . . .
>
> But this activity has to be seen against the background of the earlier point about language as a whole. The new coinages are never quite autonomous, quite uncontrolled by the rest of language. They can only be introduced and make sense because they already have a place within the web, which must at any moment be taken as given over by far the greater part of its extent. Human speakers resemble the sailors in Neurath's image

of the philosopher, who have to remake their ship in the open sea, and cannot build it from the base in a dry-dock.

What then does language come to be on this view? A pattern of activity, by which we express/realize a certain way of being in the world, that of reflective awareness, but a pattern which can only be deployed against a background which we can never fully dominate; and yet a background that we are never fully dominated by, because we are constantly reshaping it. Reshaping it without dominating it, or being able to oversee it, means that we never fully know what we are doing to it; we develop language without knowing fully what we are making it into. . . .

Conscious speech is like the tip of an iceberg. Much of what is going on in shaping our activity is not in our purview. Our deployment of language reposes on much that is preconscious and unconscious. (232)

Taylor's eloquence follows directly from the concept of language embedded in his figurative expressions. In order to give due recognition to the agent's effort to signify, to grasp the fact that culture itself is made up of multiple signifying gestures, Taylor reaches for a literary vocabulary. Why? Literary prose serves the goal of elaborating articulate effort without overly specifying meaning. It leaves room for Taylor to invoke "backgrounds," "depths," indeed the human aspiration to create, without sacrificing the concept of situatedness in language, without returning the argument to the categories of mastery/autonomy. Literary expression has sufficient coherence to be considered a genuine articulation, not a merely wanton or irresponsibly playful emotional utterance, but we have all been faced with its so-called aura or mystery, which it shares with aesthetic objects, its refusal to yield a single, definitive proposition.

At what point, however, do aesthetic contemplation and literary expression begin to crack and break up? Taylor's literary-symbolic emphasis works well as a general mode of entry into the domain of signification, but it cannot continue to do all the work of critical reflection he would demand of it. A symbolic attitude toward communication helps Taylor to keep the focus on the total integrity of the signifying process: it has no arbitrary beginning or end; it cannot be controlled from outside the expressive sphere. One gesture of standing for is decisive for all other expressive gestures, in an indefinite sequence. There is no radical, autonomous exit from language. And so in one sense Taylor has inverted the whole notion of expression as purely autonomous, the realm of ideals and imaginary forms, unaccountable to social facts and conditions. I would not want to lose any of this philosophically valuable insight; I can see no point in writing off Taylor's commitment to expressivism or his figurative grasp of it as so much idealistic mystification. That would be a failure to acknowledge the substance of his argument.

But his is not the only attitude that brings us squarely up against the connections among reflection, agency, and a host of signifying practices. We can go much further in analyzing and discriminating the specificity of linguistic signification without necessarily lapsing into metalinguistic radical control or radical detachment from our immanence in language. As Taylor's discourse grows more and more explicitly literary, it quickly loses contact with areas of investigation in the literary disciplines, in which symbolic expressions are no longer seen as the dominant vehicles for critical decisions about linguistic signification.[11]

Taylor argues that standing for confirms romantic theory because it is an expressive gesture saturated with the entire field of linguistic meaning, rather than a single act of designation:

> The traditional view understood art in terms of mimesis. Art imitates the real. . . . The Romantics gave us a quite different conception, by which, in one formulation, the artist strives to imitate not nature, but the author of nature. Art is now seen not as imitation, but as creative expression. The work of art does not refer beyond itself to what it imitates . . . it is itself the locus in which the meaning becomes manifest. It should be a symbol, rather than an allegory. (229)

Against this position, deconstruction has formulated a much greater tension between allegory and symbol, mimesis and authorship, not by denying the central role of standing for or substitution but by seeing the tension as a problem of rhetoric, in the sense of the figural displacement of meaning, instead of unidirectional self-expression. How can this deconstructionist recognition of the role of rhetoric give us a sharper picture of the incommensurability of allegory and symbol? Why do they remain in conflict? and what does this tell us about rhetoric as a shaper of linguistic signification? Taylor rarely touches upon the whole question of figural structures of meaning. And when he does speak of rhetoric it is only in the very limited sense of deceptive public speaking, the art of persuasion (see "Theories of Meaning," in *Human Agency* 266–68); rhetoric reveals at least the inescapably public dimension of language but is not worth considering as the equal of the unproblematic symbol.

In all the topics I am presently outlining, my point is not that Taylor is wrong. Far from it. I simply wish to supplement his valuable insights and show their connection to the language problems in modern literary theory. When he states that the "traffic" between literal and figurative meanings is "two-way" (289) and that religious commands and fiats can never be reduced to strictly literal meaning, I am in complete agreement. But if it is true that literal meaning is not absolutely primary, then we may need to drop the whole notion of the primary, not hypostatize it. We come back to Callinicos's point about a possible strain of solipsism in Taylor's account of situated agency. Taylor has a tendency to gloss over the precise junctures of linguistic conflict and discontinuity that force the agent into critical reflection by finding in them humanity's essential striving for romantic symbol making.

4 Stanley Cavell and the Decision to Mean What We Say

In chapters 2 and 3, I have been developing a view of situatedness in the context of a nonfoundationalist view of society. Situatedness provides an account of the right degree of coherence between an individual human agent and a society of plural beliefs and values. Certain of these values and beliefs place the agent between incommensurable options, and the act of deciding between incommensurables becomes a means of strengthening and identifying the stance of an agent in the midst of plurality. Situatedness is an answer to questions about relativism, holism, and subjectivism and is consistent with important aspects of a nonfoundationalist concept of personhood in a plural society.

I have suggested that a Taylorean language of qualitative contrast supports the definition of situatedness, with the important qualification that it may be further developed through certain aspects of contemporary literary theory. To begin that development, I now require an account of the way agents influence the contrasts and decisions within language for each other. Stanley Cavell's work answers some of these questions and forms a bridge between Taylor and issues arising from pragmatism and deconstruction, which will be taken up in part II of this book.

The plural elaboration of human agency cannot occur without a complexly articulated language of contrast which sets the terms of the decisions the agent constructs and which expresses the conviction and partial identifications the decision produces. Cavell comes into the discussion once we begin to situate agency within the finer degrees of linguistic contrast and discontinuity illuminated by modern theories of literature. *Expressive language* is a term that does not capture sufficiently the norms, values, and claims that speakers impose on each other or shape communally. A simple contrast between expressive and designative functions cannot sustain complex articulation. Although Cavell seems to be working on a nonproblem for most contemporary philosophers—the question of whether to take the skeptic's position seriously—his real object of investigation is the way reflective, expressive agents continue to lose linguistic contact with each other. Human agency, as Taylor shows, does not control all the elements of language. Rather it lies in the ability to articulate identity, consensus, and community, without supposing foundationalist grounds. Furthermore, the agent's expressivism must be immanent to the actual shaping of an ethical identity. Cavell heightens the task of articulation by showing how easy it is to give up mutual attunement, and that the attunement of agents to each other requires some special insights into a theory of language. The linguistic theory Cavell turns to is found in his comments on literature, textuality, deconstruction, and ordinary language philosophy.

Cavell's philosophical position is difficult to summarize because it undergoes continual development and experimentation. His explicit concern is the "threat of skepticism," but the phrase has a rather elaborate meaning for him. If skepticism were as absurd as the way it is often caricaturized, there could hardly be a threat. Cavell takes skepticism seriously because he sees in it more than an epistemological anomaly. In his extended use of the term, skepticism is the ever-present underside of the entire epistemological tradition, beginning with the Cartesian paradigm of constructing certainty out of solitary extreme doubt. His investigations begin where Taylor's leave off, in articulations that fail to reach another speaker, either because the speaker is so certain as to speak past an interlocutor or so doubtful as to become unintelligible. One of his most recent working definitions of skepticism emphasizes this point:

> What skepticism threatens is precisely irretrievable outsideness, an uncrossable line, a position from which it is *obvious* (without argument) that the world is unknowable. What does "threaten" mean? Not that skepticism has in its possession a given place in which to confine and isolate us, but that it is a power that all who possess language possess and may desire: to dissociate oneself, excommunicate oneself from the community in whose agreement, mutual attunement, words exist.[1]

There is no infallible cure for this threat.

Take one of Cavell's chief personifications of skepticism, Othello. His perverse entanglement in doubt/certainty seeks proof all the time, yet is beyond proof. What empirical evidence or valid speech-act could assuage his self-consuming doubt? Has Othello gone off on some false epistemological track because he no longer seems capable of perceiving the truth? Cavell thinks such questions are completely beside the point, since they beg much deeper questions. Cavell (acerbically) likens the framing of the play in terms of epistemological questions to a yokel who rushes on stage to save Desdemona or who switches on the houselights to break the awful moment of wife-murder. Othello is beyond proof, and so he is beyond refutation or explanations of this inappropriate sort. The question Cavell would ask is, What prompts us to answer Othello in the first place, to feel a need to overcome our separation from what we are witnessing, even as we (following the most basic Johnsonian sense of illusion) know we are watching a play? The power of the play lies in its capacity to make intelligible to the audience a profound lack of mutual attunement on stage. The audience is made aware of the threat of skepticism. In fact, the play's portrayal of skepticism renders epistemological efforts to designate incoherent:

> The point is that [the yokel] thinks something is really happening, whereas nothing is really happening. It's playacting. The woman will rise again to die another night.—That is what I thought was meant, what I was impatiently being asked to accede to. The trouble is that I really do not understand what I am being asked. . . . You tell me that that woman will rise again, but I know that she will not, that she is dead. You can say there are two women, Mrs. Siddons and Desdemona. . . . But what you have

produced is two names. Not all the pointing in the world to *that* woman will distinguish the one woman from the other . . . you can't point to one without pointing to the other; and you can't point to both at the same time. Which just means that *pointing* here has become an incoherent activity. (*Disowning Knowledge* 99)

The inability to intervene in the climactic moment of doubt, when Othello turns into tragedy, marks the power of skepticism in general. It is the Othello-like failure to acknowledge another speaker's words and leaves epistemology pointless. If epistemology were sufficient to establish certainty, skepticism would not occur in the first place. It is worth recalling Williams's point that cognition does not automatically bring certainty. Where does the need to feel certain lie in the first place? For Cavell, various degrees of certainty, tragedy, and revenge form part of even our most seemingly ordinary experiences. They belong to failures of mutual attunement: the substitution of failsafe ways of knowing for the much more difficult task of submitting personal identity to the test of social intelligibility. That is Othello's tragedy, and the still-present meaning of the play: the refusal to submit a self-image to the test of mutual understanding.

Like Taylor, Cavell attaches great value to terms like *expressivism, aesthetic understanding,* and *ordinary* vocabularies. He, too, wants to strengthen and preserve communal awareness through a multiplicity of expressive modes. His position differs sharply from that of Taylor and that of his pragmatist critics like Rorty in its assessment of the difficulties that must be overcome to reach mutual linguistic comprehension.[2] Cavell takes us a step beyond Taylor in linking critical decision making to a recognition of much greater discontinuity in language, without seeing the discontinuity as social instability. Discontinuity is not the philosophical problem; it is amenable to ordinary cure. But the establishment of communal understanding requires a greater degree of specification of which elements of language join to form the central terms of expression. This specification also gives a better account of expressive shaping. The complex linguistic decisions the Cavellean speaker must work through to reach the level of highly tuned articulation cannot be carried automatically by the concepts of ordinary language use or aesthetic expression. At the opposite extreme, the skeptic's withdrawal from discourse stands for a ground zero of minimal communicative effort. But these decisions do not hinge upon a simple substitution of the primacy of expression for the designative function of language.

Cavell places decision making about language right at the center of the extremes of skepticism and romantic expressivism but does not suggest that there is one linguistic pathway between them or a hierarchical ascent from poor to rich vocabularies. Ordinary grammar will not rescue the skeptic from the depths; rhetoric will not preserve the romantic at the heights. And he does not associate one linguistic function with more or less intelligibility. What counts is the moment of the decision and the articulation of a conviction that it manifests. But in Cavell's case the terms of the decision begin to approximate very precise shifts between categories of language that resemble the construction of texts within literary theory. By examining the way in which Cavell locates a moment of decision and its particular linguistic form, I can establish a connection between the philosophical issue of situatedness and the way in which literary theorists talk about texts. Cavell's early essay on aesthetic philosophy and literary criticism, with its commentary on the New Critical definition of a text, provides many details about his eventual concern with the threat of skepticism and its bearing upon the construction of the text within recent literary theory.

"Aesthetic Problems of Modern Philosophy" starts with a gentler version of Othello and the yokel.[3] Cleanth Brooks and Yvor Winters are disputing over the "Heresy of Paraphrase." It is a gentle confrontation (in need of a gentle solution) because the issue of skepticism, with its tragic potential, is never raised. Yet the dispute seems to arise out of similar contradictory efforts at designative "pointing": "What, in such an exchange, is causing that uneasy sense that the speakers are talking past one another? Surely each knows exactly what the other means; neither is pointing to the smallest fact that the other fails to see" (*Must We Mean What We Say?* [MWM] 76). For "pointing" read "paraphrasing." Brooks is accusing Winters of placing too much value on paraphrase as a way of getting at a poem's meaning. But Winters is saying nothing of the sort, only that *some* poems can be paraphrased and that these are the better poems for their transferable, rational content, which paraphrase supposedly captures. The skirmish serves to illustrate the sorts of communicative failures that occur frequently in the literary disciplines.

Cavell unravels this forced lack of comprehension between the two critics and finds that both commit the same kind of (little skeptical) error of exaggerating the need for certainty beyond what they already know and agree upon. Brooks and Winters equally recognize that a poem is not identical to a paraphrase, but each seems to insist that his concept of paraphrase is the better theory of poetry. An awareness of the lack of continuity between poetry and critical vocabulary turns into a battle over who has the correct grasp of poetry's real textual structure. Once the process begins, the whole concept of paraphrase, and by extension critical discourse, goes astray. Paraphrase becomes the crux of opposing concepts of poetry and a further source of theoretical disagreement, when in fact it serves very well to point critics to commonly understood features of poetic language.

What *specifically* does paraphrase point to in a poem? That is the real question these critics block each other from answering. The unwarranted leap from paraphrase to theoretical generalization (what is poetry? what is good poetry?) belongs to a muddled effort to make all articulations continuous and definite in meaning. Paraphrase *is* a pointer, even a pinpointer, to certain kinds of ambiguous articulations, but that does not mean it cancels or supports what it points to, that it is the proof of one particular theory. Cavell likens paraphrase to the needle of a compass: "An arrow pointing approximately north is exactly pointing somewhere. One paraphrase may be approximately the same, have approximately the same meaning, as another paraphrase" (76). Approximate expressions of meaning work very well. So what drives a critic to deny the "ordinary contrast between 'approximate' and 'exact?'" What is the critic trying to gain by moving paraphrase from a partial grasp of poetic meaning to an implied doctrine about the exactness of poetic utterances in general?

For Brooks, the limits of paraphrase become a strategic means for holding poems at a distance. Paraphrase can be made finer and finer, but it will never reach the core or the essence of the poem. Cavell advises that this sort of overcorrection "happens with astonishing frequency in philosophy" (77). Because Brooks wants poems to have exact structures but clearly needs to maintain a difference between poem and paraphrase, he inserts into poetry an appreciative but idle set of terms which have no explanatory value. Cavell compares this to philosophies of perception or psychology: we never know the empirical object completely, but we can have practical certainty; we never know another person's feelings, but we can infer them. Practical certainty is often sufficient for ordinary understanding and does not require a grounding in foundationalist theories of perception or meaning.

Similarly, paraphrases express an understanding of poems, and Cavell goes on to show that they converge upon specifically metaphorical linguistic structures. But that does not mean all poems are made up essentially of metaphors or that all poems by definition resist paraphrase. Brooks inadvertently reifies poetry into a holistic linguistic object, cutting it off from ordinary prosaic discourse and thereby turning criticism into a much less shareable, intelligible vocabulary than it need be.

New Criticism has been widely criticized for its emphasis on poetic autonomy and organic wholeness, its separation of poetry from the referential languages of history, science, and sociology. But Cavell is not making yet another version of that old argument against New Criticism. That argument had already reached a dead end in Winters's side of the dispute when he took the counterposition that poetry is defined by its paraphrasable, or "propositional," content. Thus a line like Wallace Stevens's "As a calm darkens among water-lilies" becomes defective poetry, in Winters's views, because it will not translate readily into a proposition. Winters is not so philistine as to argue that propositions and poems are the same kind of language. He recognizes that metaphors, similes, and images are different from literal descriptions. He argues, however, for the centrality of propositional content in any poetry that would claim rational meaning.

Gerald Graff, in defense of Winters, has given the same argument a new lease on life in *Poetic Statement and Critical Dogma*.[4] The Winters-Graff position is always put in the most reasonable terms. It suggests that rational poetry should aspire to making richer propositions about human culture and concedes that its propositional content will not necessarily cover the multiplicity of human cultural endeavors. But the positive equation of paraphrase with rational poetry is just as much overkill, in Cavell's analysis, as the Brooksian equation of poetry with resistance to paraphrase. Brooks's paraphrase holds poetry further and further away from ordinary intelligibility; Winters's paraphrase is much too damning of all sorts of articulations that paraphrase was never meant to relay in the first place. Winters's approach does not work very well on authors like Whitman or Joyce or on Symbolist, Surrealist, or Imagist poetry in general. But that may be because the language developed in such poetry is not what paraphrase is able to point out. The larger, implicit claim, that such poetry therefore provides less social insight, is more disconnected from historical issues, or promotes cultural disintegration, does not follow at all, any more than do the New Critical reverse claims that paradox and irony promote higher cultural sensibility. Although paraphrase is one of the best methods of finding mutual linguistic attunement and is thus an excellent critical device, this debate has forced it into an issue of true and false methods and diminished critical understanding on both sides. Cavell summarizes it this way:"Brooks is wrong to say that poems cannot in principle be fully paraphrased, but right to be worried about the relation between paraphrase and poem; Winters is right in his perception that some poetry is 'formulable' and some not, but wrong in the assurance he draws from that fact" (MWM 82).

Poems are made up of all sorts of language: metaphors, literal statements, generic conventions (which may determine phonological and syntactic features), idioms, and even speech-acts. The attempt to capture or distance some essential core of language overplays the value of paraphrase. Each critic refuses to see paraphrase in the context of truly contradictory modes of expression. It seems as if the recognition of linguistic contradiction is what they find to be threatening, attaching to it accusations of irrationality or critical imprecision. Moving from paraphrasable content to other, nonparaphrasable kinds need not be interpreted as a sudden loss in meaning. It might be a solicitation for another kind of understanding, and there is no reason to suppose that it will not work or that it is in principle less significant.

Mapping the precise areas of conflict and the convictions needed to negotiate them is where mutual attunement begins. In Cavell's view, Brooks's aesthetic contemplation of Grecian urns and Winters's rational attack on disorderly poems begin to evoke the pseudo-assurance of the skeptic, who has turned his back on the task of measuring which articulations claim the attention and expressive capacities of other speakers. As in the example of Othello, pointing or paraphrasing does not constitute an engagement with failed intelligibility. Theoretically, it is a nonstarter. In the Brooks-Winters debate, it is a vicious circle.

Literary theory has a more important role to play in the development of a language of personal resonance than this debate suggests. Cavell's outline of the proper task of poetic expression is analogous to Taylor's: if literary discourse is to mean anything, it will rest on "the ways in which conviction in [judgment] is produced" (93) and also nonskeptically shared. The degree of conviction is what distinguishes it, gives it its wholeheartedness, to come back to Frankfurt's term. Of course this still leaves a lot to be demonstrated. But from the outset Cavell's investigation of these special articulations of conviction shows that intraverbal pointing and designative naming are insufficient means of avoiding the "risk of explicit isolation" (89). Pointing and naming are simply not very articulate devices, in the sense of measuring what exactly is incommensurable in the positions of different speakers. Brooks and Winters do not raise us to this insight because in fact their positions are not as incommensurable as they appear to be.

Brooks's vulnerability to attack has less to do with paraphrase as an abstract problem than with the exaggerated separation it tries to impose between paraphrase and poem. When Brooks tries to keep the paraphrase from actually touching the essence of the poem, he inadvertently makes it impossible to enter or strongly identify with the poetic language, as if it were somehow a critical violation of its fragile, suspended balance of paradoxes and ironies. This sharply limits poetry's direct participation in the process of articulation. Poetry loses its claim upon the speaker's own articulate effort. In this regard, Graff's attack on Brooks seems to have exposed a flaw. Graff writes,

> Brooks seeks to credit poetry with an intellectual substance while averting the reductive implications of equating poetic meaning wholly with a set of stated ideas. But instead of solving the problem by seeing poetry as *both* a means of "testing" *and* "stating" ideas, Brooks indulges in the characteristic either/or of antipropositional theory, counterposing assertion and dramatization as irreconcilables. No one would deny that poetry "tests" ideas or that it deals with the way human beings "may come to terms with" ideas. But the rhetorical strategy in which "testing" and "coming to terms with" line up in opposition to "stating" and "generalizing" introduces a specious and unnecessary antithesis. Ideas, unlike physical substances, are not inert; to "test" an idea is to become committed to some intellectual point of view which emerges from the test. Of course, Brooks has in mind the dialectical qualification and ironic counterthrusts typical of the poetry he most admires, but he forgets that qualifications and revisions do not negate ideas but rather make them more subtle and complex. (*Poetic Statement* 91–92)

I could not agree more. Ideas in poetry are made complex and should not be neutralized in some autonomous, dramatic space. If they are dramatized, it will be like Cavell's reaction to a Shakespearean tragedy, a test of our own immediate convictions and articulate efforts. Brooks uses paraphrase to focus linguistic contradictions at a distance, away from the expressive identifications and contrasts within a community.

When Graff rests the testing of ideas on his notion of paraphrase he robs poetry of its ability to impose a claim as much as Brooks did. Paraphrase is not a test. It is a mode of attunement, only a relatively weak one which is no better than irony as far as the language of an interpretive community is concerned. Graff is right when he says, "It helps little . . . to say that poetry is unparaphrasable, for, in a sense, most instances of language are also. Yet it would be absurd to hold that most utterances are unparaphrasable" (148). Rather than define clearly the commonality of features that poetic and nonpoetic expressions share, which renders them often paraphrasable without loss of intelligibility, he attaches the much greater but weaker thesis that most utterances are paraphrasable because they are "conceptual." We inhabit the Graffean world through our concepts, beliefs, customs, social institutions, and the conceptual medium of paraphrase is what links them all together. Of course, as he says, paraphrase is modest and cannot give a total picture of all these conceptual links between utterances. But this qualification misses the deeper layer of argument Cavell has tapped: utterances that express convictions and shape dispositions are not abstractable as generic concepts. Graff's modest proposal is fundamentally the mimetic-designative theoretical position, which refuses to test the ways speakers in fact impose claims upon each other. The total ungraspable meaning is no more substantial than the Brooksian core or essence. We do not need more paraphrases and more descriptions of poems. We need more immanence and situatedness. Why this persistent fear that this much more arduous critical engagement with texts is too unstable and irrational? Graff and the rationalists in general are victims of the skeptical fear of language itself, what Taylor terms the fear of its seductive power, which they assume will rob the critic of epistemological reliability. Language, when mentioned at all, is radically impoverished as a medium of agency and decision making as long as it is conceived in this subservience to epistemology.

Taylor and Cavell show that the need to master language, to set limits on its contribution to knowledge-testing, already betrays a skeptical suspicion of other speakers' expressive intelligibility, a refusal to recognize speakers who are not carriers of concepts. There is no testing, however, without a finer awareness of how articulations are shaped and shared communally. Articulations produced by what I am calling convictions are no more monolithic or totalizable than "predication, assertion, belief, fact, and knowledge"—the terms upon which Graff rests his whole theoretical position. There is some absurdity in rationalist theorists paying their modest respects to language because it seems less real than referents. No one would go as far as denying the existence of the referent for the sake of language itself. But it does no good to argue against reduction unless propositions propose understandings we share, accept, or reject. Are these actions any less real?

I am saying that Graff's account of paraphrase does not enable us to take the next step. Perhaps it is too modest after all.

Compare Cavell on paraphrase. He begins along the same lines as Graff but veers sharply in another direction. Most ordinary utterances do not invite paraphrase. True enough. But this does not imply, as Graff would have it, that all we need to do is specify the conditions for paraphrasability, as some normative function of language which draws together all utterances on a continuum of progressive understanding from poem to speaker to context to social framework. Cavell's analysis of paraphrase holds to the original insight that it is pointing out a particular kind of utterance, that it is invoked under special circumstances, without going as far as saying that it is capable of focusing the basic concepts of an entire order of propositional knowledge. Although Cavell is even more concerned than Graff or Winters or Taylor with the risk of speakers going astray through overevaluations of the importance of one category of language, he refuses to assume a safe return to linguistic holism. If paraphrase is a reliable pointer to a linguistic particular, then why assume it is a generally reliable guide to the way we interpret language?

The limits of paraphrase, which everyone seems to recognize, might indicate specifically *discontinuous* utterances. Broaching these discontinuities, which in no way implies a complete breakdown of intelligibility, fundamentally alters the kinds of articulations produced by agents because it cuts both ways. Not all discontinuities, once recognized, *need* to link in order for language to refer or to perform speech-acts. And those that do establish links will be specifiable now as *claims,* specific interventions in the linguistic field that shape other speakers' responses. Paraphrase is a false critical method if it is used to substitute weak connections for relatively trivial discontinuities—which impose no answerable claim—and if it further inhibits the broaching of those discontinuities which situate speakers in truly decisive expressions. Cavell limits rather than extends paraphrase in order to make both operations clear.

What does paraphrase point to after all? and what exactly are the discontinuous elements in language? The answers are not very deep; they belong to ordinary usage. If someone says, "Juliet is fourteen years old," it would not make sense to try to paraphrase the statement. Maybe the person addressed does not know any Juliet or that she is the name of a character in a play or what the significance of being romantically awakened at that age might imply. Yet none of these extensions of the statement requires paraphrase. The content of the statement belongs to a larger network of information, but it is not relayed by trying to find new words or expressions to make the meaning any clearer or more compelling. The same would be true of idiomatic statements, which sound much odder but also are not extendable through paraphrase. Cavell offers these comic examples: "Someone might actually fall flat on his face, have a thorn in his side, a bee in his bonnet, a bug in his ear, or a fly in his ointment—even all at once" (MWM 80). Who would offer to paraphrase all this? The meaning of these idioms might be explained by talking about psychology, mood, and behavior. In fact, they could be interpreted literally, as real events happening all at once.

But idioms, literal statements, and true, justified knowledge of fourteen-year-old adolescents in love do not require paraphrase. Speakers may need to know the right conditions for making use of an idiom. And on many occasions they may want to think about whether or not a statement should be taken literally, if for example someone utters, "Sufficient unto the day is the evil thereof." That is a serious challenge to some people's deeply held beliefs. There is no gain in communication or conviction, however, if speakers try to point out the meaning of what they have just uttered by paraphrasing it.

Idioms, expressions of faith already established in the speaker's mind, and descriptive statements will not become more or less literal or contextually appropriate by being translated into new words. They already draw upon a wide range of ordinary beliefs and attitudes or forms of life that have achieved the acceptance of the ordinary. The *language* that holds these together and makes them communally and commonly understood imposes no special claims on the speaker's ability to articulate. Thus it should not be made into the primary vehicle of expressive language. It will not serve to measure conflict and conviction at a deeper level of social norm making, where greater decisions and interventions are required. In fact, literal language suggests the speaker's freedom to "*put [a] thought another way,* and perhaps refer you, depending upon who you are, to a range of similar or identical thoughts expressed by others. What [the speaker] cannot (logically) do . . . is to *paraphrase* what [he] said" (78). To come back to Graff one last time, language that has been approved as literal and conventional already has been *tested,* which is not to say that it is primary or governing or designative in any simple sense for all articulations, but only that it cannot be rendered more complex.

Cavell's delineation of expressions which do call for paraphrase makes no attempt to continue along a single linguistic axis. Quite the opposite. Paraphrase occurs in response to extraordinary linguistic usages, such as metaphors. When someone says, "Juliet is the sun," paraphrase is exactly what is called for in extending the sentence's meaning:

> I shall *not* try to put the thought another way—which seems to be the whole truth in the view that metaphors are unparaphrasable, that their meaning is bound up in the very words they employ. (The addition adds nothing: Where else is it imagined, in that context, that meanings are bound, or found?) I may say something like: Romeo means that Juliet is the warmth of his world; that his day begins with her; that only in her nourishment can he grow. And his declaration suggests that the moon, which other lovers use as emblems of their love, is merely her reflected light, and dead in comparison; and so on. In a word, I paraphrase it. Moreover, if I could not provide an explanation of this form, then that is a very good reason, a perfect reason, for supposing that I do not know what it means. Metaphors are paraphrasable. (And if that is true, it is tautologous.) When Croce denied the possibility of paraphrase, he at least had the grace to assert that there were no metaphors. (78–79)

Paraphrase and metaphor are joined here with much greater precision than we have seen before. In fact, this is the first connection drawn between paraphrase and a specific linguistic structure. Cavell is simply asking us, in the first instance, to pay attention to when we resort to paraphrase, to trust our knowledge of its use rather than setting out its conditions a priori under the rubric of paraphrasability. The parenthetical remarks in the quotation go even further: paraphrase does not contextualize or analyze metaphors. That would be giving it too great a role. It approximates metaphors, points them out. But it has no general critical function to perform, although it does force speakers to understand it in its own terms. Paraphrase's limitations are just as important as its elaborations of the speaker's understanding. It does not have the power to turn metaphors into literal statements. Paraphrase is an acknowledgment of discontinuity within language, since it does not work for other kinds of expressions and is not perfectly assimilable with the metaphors it unpacks.

Cavell's acute recognition of this linguistic discontinuity neither implies radical dislocations of meaning or the play of textual difference, nor supports grand efforts at delineating the relative autonomy of poetic utterances in relation to ordinary speech. The specific disjunctions and switchings within expressions count as *critical* articulations insofar as they are contradictory, but few are or can be made so. Paraphrase leads us to this moment but provides no method or stance beyond that. After a metaphor has been pointed out, it is still up to us to determine its meaningfulness and expressive value, what it is trying to assert as a connection. The difficulty is that there is no perfectly continuous means for doing so in terms of one kind of language.

Discontinuity poses no threat under ordinary circumstances: *we don't have to decide* what is literal in order to interpret and use most literal statements or jokes or idioms, or to read many poems, or to hear the voice of irony in a novel. The ordinary discontinuity of utterances, the fact that we can make perfectly good sense of them without immediate resort to interior acts of conceptual paraphrase, does not support the hypothesis of unconscious structure or of an always-operating structure of beliefs. Decisions that work through complex linguistic articulations do not necessarily link up with a single structure of beliefs or interlocking levels of meaning.

Most utterances do not demand critical interpretation because they impose no claims, create no conflicts. The fact that metaphors do takes Cavell into the questions of decision making and mutual attunement. But that does not mean metaphors have unique powers to raise these questions any more than their paraphrases do. It is only a beginning for the task of connecting human agency to a much richer theoretical language of contrast. Cavell puts it this way: "To give the paraphrase, to understand the metaphor, I must understand the ordinary or dictionary meaning of the words it contains, *and* understand that they are not there being used in their ordinary way, that the meanings they invite are not to be found opposite them in a dictionary" (79).

Perhaps the contrast between ordinary and extraordinary use is formulated a little too hastily, since it is probably never a strict case of one or the other. (At other times, Cavell will argue that ordinary semantic usage does not contrast with anything at all.) What he wants to get at is found in his neighboring citations of William Empson's writings on metaphor: a "pregnancy" of meaning that is forceful and persuasive because of the "psychic tension" that produced it.[5] These exotic terms indicate the real nature of the break with the ordinary.

Metaphorical assertions rest on a very complex layer of conviction; to understand them is to be drawn, partially, into another speaker's wholeheartedness. I realize that Frankfurt's word is no clearer on its own than Empson's, but at least it recalls the nature of the arguments we are considering. Poetics may view metaphor as a distinct linguistic structure or as an ornament of style. And linguistic-poetics may go a little further in placing it within a larger cognitive domain of sorting the world by comparisons and likenesses. The philosophers and literary theorists whom I follow, however, would not attach such large structural connections to individual metaphors, since the tension they contain does seem to call for a perspectival shift, but not along special cognitively tested lines.[6] Cavell comments on the nullity of the difference between metaphorical and literal truth:

> Theory aside, I want to look at the suggestion, often made, that what metaphors literally say is *false*. . . . But to say that Juliet is the sun is not to say something false; it is, at best, wildly false, and that is not being just false. This is part of the fact that if we are to suggest that what the metaphor says is true, we shall have to say it is wildly true—mythically or magically or primitively true. . . . Then what are we to say about the literal meaning of a metaphor? That it has none? And that what it literally says is not false, *and* not true? (MWM 80)

I would summarize these questions with one more: What causes speakers to become situated between literal and figurative meanings? That is what Cavell seems to be pointing to, with no implication attached that such a moment of situatedness is paradigmatic of language in general.

To answer any of these questions about metaphor is to express truth as a matter of conviction: Juliet *is* the sun, not for everyone perhaps, not as a rule of interpretation, but also not as a wild statement radically outside normal discourse. The more we understand the metaphor, the more we adopt the stance of the speaker, the articulations that are consistent with and expressive of it, perhaps beginning with weak paraphrases. Theoretically, however, the understanding does not belong either to literal or figurative, designative or expressive, ordinary or extraordinary language.

Taylor, we recall, reached too hastily for the literary answer to the false primacy of literal meanings and thereby lost a sense of how such apparently wild statements could count for us. Cavell, as I am reading him, is providing the missing linguistic details of the whole concept of situatedness without actually talking about it. Metaphor does not shape language; only human agency can do that. But it is one way of situating the agent between different semantic registers (here roughly captured in the contrast between ordinary and extraordinary), where expressive decisions can be critically enacted and supported. Of course the difference need not consist of semantics; it might be performative or rhetorical or a mixture of the three. Does Romeo's trope belong exclusively to one of these categories?

Yet the categories do exist, and to assimilate them completely would be a folly I would not attribute to Romeo. Furthermore, to recognize these differences theoretically is no purchase on criticism, and criticism may be based on a limited theoretical awareness of betweenness or difference (a now-fashionable term). I would not want to call Romeo a fictional representation of a literary theorist either. His love language is created for him because he exists only insofar as he is posited as a lover. The decisions that formed his love and its expression are assumed.

There is a limit to the decisions that agency can withstand and still remain coherent. What matters, for the moment, is the difficult task of filling in those decisions. The centrality of decision making to Cavell's entire position is made clear in another, more recent essay, "Being Odd, Getting Even," which concludes with a self-quotation from yet another essay of his:

> Accepting [Carnap's] "thing-world" is just accepting the world, and what kind of choice do we have about that? . . . And what kind of choice do we have about accepting a form of language? We can accept or reject whatever in language *we* can construct. . . . If we can't *decide* that (we will say that) the things of our world exist, shall we say that we *believe* they exist? That is something a philosopher will say in the course of that rehearsal of our beliefs with which he begins his investigation of their validity as a whole. But that rehearsal does not *express* belief in anything; it contains no claims. Or shall we say that we have *faith* that the things of our world exist? But how is that faith achieved, how expressed, how maintained, how deepened, how threatened, how lost?[7]

I think that Taylor could not put it better. To finish my previous point, we can believe in Romeo and his world only by affirming his love language, more specifically the kind of metaphor he uses to tell us about Juliet. Although the metaphor demands a complex awareness of the difference between literal and figural language, it does not resolve itself as the cancellation of this difference, and it does not aspire to a complete interpretation of the conditions of love (any more than *King Lear* or *Othello* does). We cannot rewrite the play, or the metaphor, entirely in our most central terms, which today are perhaps largely Freudian, more brutally parental and sexual than astronomical. The play does not exist unless we accept its form of language as a given, but as we use it to deepen or to abandon the central terms of our language of love we will be faced with ever-greater decisions about which language claims central authority in our lives.

The basic point about such language is that it is always plural or at least never homogeneously literal, designative, or figurative. Without that plurality, there would be no way to gain or to shape or to maintain a social identity. It has been suggested that if there were no novels no one could fall in love (though I suppose Cavell would argue that tragedies teach us how we fall in love with ourselves). The plural nature of language opens the connection between Cavell and de Man. It would be perverse to ascribe the same philosophical projects to Cavell and de Man, but it does seem worth investigating whether we can further refine our concept of decision making and the plurality of language by comparing them. De Manian deconstruction, in my view, is just such a refinement, rather than a groundless textual play of difference for its own sake. Cavell dismisses deconstructionist decision making because it seems to have no impact on the way that human agents express themselves.[8] Does it claim anything more than that meaning is multiple or indeterminate? I would agree that deconstruction, were it thus, would not be much of a criticism of anything. But clearly that is not the position I am arguing in this book.

Cavell's analysis of metaphor and the grammar of paraphrase recognizes that the elements of language are, to some extent, discontinuous. But when it comes to putting this insight into philosophical terms—like skepticism or the expressivist rejection of analytical philosophy's attachment to propositional semantics— Cavell simply puts a check on further theorizations about language. Once the speaker is tuned into the expressive literary sphere of language, Cavell's concern is how this tuning may be maintained and strengthened so as to capture the claims that speakers make upon each other. It is like moving from paraphrase to aesthetic understanding to Freudian transference, as his essay on the politics of interpretation suggests. Specifying the claim that a particular linguistic form has and specifying further that this form is largely *literary*, not the sort of ordinary language which never tests the speaker's hidden levels of skepticism, is Cavell's major contribution to contemporary philosophy of literature.

Cavell's entire philosophical project powerfully indicates the limited value of the simpler pragmatic answer to skepticism, which merely offers the "normal, probable, and ordinary" as the cure for skepticism, thereby disregarding how any speaker could have suffered profound misattunement in the first place.[9] This would be like saying to the neurotic, "Your discourse is abnormal and doesn't count." But how did that happen in the first place? and can it be turned around to bring that person back into interpersonal attunement? Telling the neurotic to be pragmatic or sensible will fall on deaf ears. The neurotic is perhaps a clearer example of difficult misattunement than the lovesick speech of a Shakespearean character, say Othello rather than Romeo, because it is easy to overlook Othello's misattunement in the name of literary greatness. After all, is he not supposed to be tragically destroyed (a topic I discuss in detail with reference to Empson in chapter 6)? And the point is obviously not to equate poetry with neurosis. The point is that Othello's language measures our own linguistic attunement, draws us out of our potentially skeptical egocentric assurance that we do not depend on other speakers' expressions for part of our personal identity.

Cavell recognizes that deconstruction is not the same thing as skepticism precisely because its concerns are with linguistic structures, metaphorical versus literal meanings, discontinuities between grammar and rhetoric—the concerns which he says his auditors were rightly hearing in his comments on deconstruction during the lecture which was subsequently published as "Being Odd, Getting Even." But deconstruction cannot assist his project if it keeps upsetting the literary moment of expression, the decisive moment of attunement, with some blanketing invocation of the undecidability of any meaning.

In my view, however, deconstruction can be used to build up Cavell's position, just as Cavell can be used to build up Taylor's. The term *decision* is the red herring here. When the Cavellean speaker enters discourse in a decisive way that will seek the acknowledgment and the answering of others, shape a vocabulary, or find the central terms of reference, the agency that goes into the decision is surprisingly transparent in terms of language. Out of what language of contrast is the decision constructed? Instead of contrast, Cavell offers a quasi-sublime gesture of pulling oneself up by one's bootstraps, an Emersonian act of self-creation. It is highly poetical, as readers of Cavell will know, and once under way concerns itself with loss, affect, and faith. It has the sort of claim and force that was absent from Taylor's picture of the scene of linguistic recognition as the signifying gesture, yet it seems consistent with Taylor's principle of situatedness as against immutable hierarchies of meaning or foundationalist concepts. But as a matter of agency, Cavell's greater recognition of the discontinuities within language that must be overcome is surprisingly uncritical. The (sublime) speaker moves between ordinary grammar and poetic expressiveness but seems not to be engaged in the construction of the choice of levels. Cavell writes as if there is one global decision to overcome skepticism and enter language at some newer and higher plane of sense. It is like Taylor using expressivism to establish situatedness for agency and then leaving the whole topic of literature, rhetoric, and semiotics on the sidelines of the self's deepest spiritual sources. Cavell also establishes an expressive, extraordinary, nongoverning space for language, in a culture bound by pragmatism and skepticism, and then leaves the critical analysis of literature or metaphor back in the world of Emerson, Poe, and Thoreau.

Deconstruction, as I see it, is the most precise analysis of the multiple features of language that need to be decided. It maintains a kind of Taylorean situatedness because it uses a language of contrast to embed the speaker between incommensurable meanings and values; it does not attempt to synthesize them dialectically or simply describe them as given, unchanging structure. And it shares with Cavell the specification of the most significant literary forms of language without attaching any troubling concerns to the discontinuity of most ordinary uses of language. But because deconstruction's language of contrast is finer and its recognition of discontinuity greater (than the ordinary, the paraphrasable, and the metaphorical), it involves a proportionately higher degree of incommensurability of meanings before it may situate the reader. If deconstruction is indecisive it is not because it is a priori committed to meaninglessness; it is because the terrific critical effort that goes into mapping the precise moment of conflict between the elements of language is the construction of a decision. The decision will be taken, to be sure, but it will not be uniformly upward in the direction of the sublime or of aesthetics, or between the designative and expressive polarities of the real. Deconstruction offers a high degree of situatedness, which comes directly out of the finer texture of the critically determined choices to be faced in language. And it expands the Cavellean insight into the discontinuity of language, but not by working up the distinctions between the ordinary and the sublime, the prosaic and the poetic, the grammatical and the rhetorical. Instead, it pinpoints, with more accuracy than any other rhetorical analysis of which I am aware, the central terms or tropes or structures that immanently constitute the claims of a *text*.

I would like to see Cavell's commentary upon de Man as a passageway into the kind of deconstruction I am proposing.[10] Cavell deals specifically with de Man's essay on semiology and rhetoric and begins his commentary on deconstruction by being intrigued by it. De Man's interest in the difference between constative and performative utterances and between referential and nonreferential statements sounds familiar to a student of J. L. Austin:

> [De Man] appears to take [these distinctions] to turn on whether a use of language refers to something outside language, something in the world, and on whether a use of language has some actual effect on others. But to defeat the idea that constative and performative utterances differ in their responsibilities, or responsiveness, to facts and to distinguish among ways in which words may have "effects" or "forces" just are Austin's purposes in arguing against positivism and the later Wittgenstein. (192)

But the distinction as a whole is not inherently purposeful or philosophically deep. The question remains: What good can you put it to? Putting it into the service of undecidability is not very good. Cavell asks whether there really is an "aporia" between constative and performative language, any more than between knives and forks, just because someone *could* spear with a knife or cut with a fork?

As with Williams or Taylor, the philosopher in Cavell wants to know which hypergoods are to count and how they are to count in people's lives before he is willing to take seriously different tools for spearing those hypergoods. Does it matter that some grammatical forms—for example, the interrogative "Isn't the weather glorious?"—function rhetorically as praise? On the level of formal linguistic analysis, Cavell finds nothing very exciting in deconstruction, and I would have to agree because the formal distinctions can be rapidly decided under ordinary circumstances.

Serious engagement with deconstruction begins with the utterances whose purpose is none other than to define human identity in language. The example is still a comically trivial one: Who is Archie Bunker? But the terms of Cavell's answer to de Man's reading of the now infamous line, "What is the difference?" indicate a deeper conflict in purpose. What does it matter if this utterance is seriously asking about the different style of lacing one's shoes or saying, rhetorically, that lacing does not matter one bit? Cavell says,

> Archie's question is a hedge against assertion, and like "Isn't the weather glorious" it is a statement that asks for a response. But while the difference between asking "What's the difference?" and saying, for example, "It doesn't matter" is that the question asks for a response, it may be that Archie at the same time does not want a response from his wife. This would

show an ambivalence that many would take as the commonest characteristic of marriage, or of a comic marriage. But that is a fact about some Archie, not about the inevitable relation between grammar and rhetoric. The moral of the example seems to me to be that there is no inevitable relation between them. This seems to me the moral of ordinary language philosophy as well, and of the practice of art. Put it this way: Grammar cannot, or ought not, of itself dictate what you mean, what it is up to you to say. (194)

Cavell's moral indignation at de Man's exploitation of this banal fragment of language targets the deconstructionist's apparent disdain for human agency, for the way speakers need to author their meanings and the way they demand a response from each other. The act of expression and the response it entails are Cavell's highest purposes. Once authorship and art are in question—and marital comedy is definitely a matter of art for Cavell—ordinary distinctions no longer apply, for in Cavell's view we are then reaching out for conviction, for the hope of connectedness to other speakers through an exalted, revered, redeemed language, which, if we are lucky, brings us back into the ordinary with a new aura, as suggested by Heidegger or Emerson or Thoreau (see 195–98). For Cavell, domestic comedy is one of those areas in the culture with the highest mixture of ordinary aura and traumatically skeptical lovers who refuse to acknowledge their dependence upon each other.

But this heavy response to de Man's (undoubtedly ill-chosen) example has the air of someone talking right past deconstruction, like Winters and Brooks talking past each other about cores and essences. As I read the logic of de Man's example, the whole distinction between the ordinary and the elevated is recast, not so as to disable agency but so as to locate it, critically, in what Taylor calls the surface between the elements of language. De Man's purpose is not inferior to Cavell's. He is not concerned with an abstract distinction between grammar and rhetoric. His little example of the crossing of grammatical and rhetorical features, which could be clarified by the context that makes it ring with humor and irony, is a pointer to what sorts of literary structures occur in literary texts. Cavell, in this particular case, first isolates the elements of language as constative or performative in order to find a point of contact with deconstruction, but as soon as he detects a little rupture in the fabric of the ordinary he seizes it either as withholding communicative effort, as nascent skepticism, or as a demand for a response, the acknowledgment of attunement. That seems to be the only decision offered by the rhetorical question. But for de Man the act of deciding begins with constructing the terms of the interpretation as between different linguistic pathways. Perhaps these pathways are not clear from the little example; they certainly grow stronger in the course of his essay as a whole. Where the missing terms of the Winters/Brooks debate were easily supplied from ordinary language philosophy's distrust of the vocabulary of essence, in response to deconstruction the ordinary understanding between comiclike husband and wife seems entirely beside de Man's point. De Man is working on an entirely different problem that in the long run perhaps situates us to a more complex degree than Cavell does. The inert distinction between grammar and rhetoric in the abstract takes on life as it is repeated and revised through ever-more complex stages of the de Manian analysis, whereas Cavell leaves us stretched between domestic comedy and Heideggerean revelation.

De Manian deconstruction is not a dialectical theory of language; there is no effort to synthesize the ordinary and the sublime, a point I return to in my chapter on de Man. But it offers critical coherence and agency by continually reconstructing the terms of difference that it first establishes as the *decisive* ones, especially in the most complex literary sources. Cavell's emphasis on the claims of language, and his broad distinction between those utterances that are claims and those that are ordinary, moves in the direction of deconstruction once we get past Cavell's own poor characterization of the topic of indecision.

I said earlier that deconstruction involves a language of contrast. But the decisions invoked within the terms of the contrast do not yield an objectivist set of rules or grounds. In that sense deconstruction shares with Rortyan neopragmatism a nonfoundationalist approach to history and culture. What it can do is expressed in generally sound terms by Rorty:

> The world does not speak. Only we do. The world can, once we have programmed ourselves with a language, cause us to hold beliefs. But it cannot propose a language for us to speak. Only other human beings can do that. The realization that the world does not tell us what language games to play should not, however, lead us to say that a decision about which to play is arbitrary, nor to say that it is the expression of something deep within us. The moral is not that objective criteria for choice of vocabulary are to be replaced with subjective criteria, reason with will or feeling. It is

rather that the notions of criteria and choice (including that of "arbitrary" choice) are no longer in point when it comes to changes from one language game to another. (*Contingency, Irony, Solidarity* 6)

Most of the points in this book are consistent with Rorty's statement, with one important exception. I maintain that choice does matter when it comes to changing language games and that language games, even as programmed vocabularies for holding beliefs, are not perfectly interchangeable. What I want to show after a discussion of philosophers like Cavell, Taylor, and Williams is that language games converge around what literary theorists have been trying to specify as texts, and further that the circulation of these texts in a plural culture requires certain acts of decision making that shape personhood. Taylorean situatedness, for example, rejects the arbitrariness of meaning without sacrificing the task of deciding which language is authoritative for the speaker's identity. But we know from pragmatists like Rorty that the results will not decide what is essentially and universally *human*. Perhaps it is better to look upon these decisions as the negotiation of linguistic junctures and switches which constitute some of our most complex forms of life.

Plural Theories of Literary Texts **PART TWO**

5 Determining a Literary Text

A philosopher like Stanley Cavell turns controversies within literary theory into concerns that touch upon human identity and community. These concerns include self-esteem and skeptical defensiveness, ordinary understanding, and sublime expression. Many of Cavell's concerns mesh with a nonfoundationalist approach to the study of literature as defined by pragmatists like Rorty and Fish.[1] Pragmatists attempt to avoid a generic, universalist vocabulary of essence, beauty, *truth,* epiphany, and canonicity. That sort of vocabulary appears to justify the study of *etc.* literature by appealing to some ground which would vouchsafe literature's existence or value. Criticism and interpretation are then defined as the least distorted approximation of the work of literature in relation to one of these grounds. In the writings of contemporary pragmatists, however, literary works do not need to be justified, and interpretive activity does not need to be validated or falsified. Pragmatists look upon literature less as an image of reality, a fiction, or an artful vehicle and rather more as a tuning instrument. The criticism of literature becomes the development of a vocabulary of shared speaking contexts, richer descriptions, and a recognition of how local academic communities and contingent reading experiences can be valuable without being grounded in the traditional language of romantic psychology or methodological validity. The work of the pragmatists, therefore, falls within the Cavellean trajectory that moves criticism away from paraphrases of poetry and dramas (whose odd diction is usually more in need of paraphrase than the diction of novels) toward appropriation and the merging of literary utterances with the speech activity of readers, as if poetry were recharged with readerly meaning, which Harold Bloom calls misreading.

A nonfoundationalist approach to literature can arise from several different sources: a rejection of aesthetical and formalist means of detaching literature from its immediate interpretive context; an epistemic (and somewhat circular) debate about the possibility of objectivist criteria for interpretation; or a debate about the priority of designative or referential linguistic functions over semiotic or emotive functions. In this book, pragmatism and nonfoundationalism have their sources in the basic recognition that we live within a deeply plural society. By "deeply plural" I mean that the slender threads that connect academic communities of learned readers will produce an extremely varied and rich set of interests among readers of literature and the resonant vocabularies they develop to articulate and strengthen those interests. These interests include popular forms of cultural expression, the emergence of marginalized groups contesting canonical Western philosophical, religious, and ethical norms, and the large-scale vocabularies that address the fate of the nation-state, international justice, and political histories. In recognizing this plurality and the multiple articulations of identity that are already upon us, pragmatists are better positioned to take up philosophical issues about language, ethics, tolerance, and communal coherence without attempting to fit this plurality into a search for universal foundations or a hierarchy of norms and values.

The implications of this nonfoundationalism are becoming increasingly clear. In the absence of a core or true inner self, personal coherence is a matter of adjusting to a plurality of language games, or what Rorty calls vocabularies. The multiple pictures of belief and conduct which literature affords us are not reasons to behave one way or another or partial glimpses into a singular social fabric. These pictures can be shared, expanded, made familiar, worn out, and reused, however. And the study of literature can contribute a great deal toward that particular social good. Pragmatists like Rorty and philosophers of language like Taylor and Cavell see works of literature as focal points of multiple, participatory vocabularies rather than as secondary imitations of life.

But once the activity of interpretation has shifted from foundationalism to dialogism, certain tasks associated with conviction, satisfaction, and self-reliance require new forms of expression. Interpretations now must exist as collectively shared forms of speech. Even if it no longer makes much sense to see some interpretations as more or less subjective than others, how do we cope with the feeling that our interpretations nevertheless must count for other readers? Even in a pragmatically constituted interpretive community, isolated, failed, and insignificant interpretations are always possible.

In the chapters on Taylor and Cavell in part I of this book, I considered the types of decisions about identity and value that would situate an agent in a nonfoundationalist society. Situatedness after the end of foundationalism relies upon a Taylorean view of the contrasts presented and adopted by an agent in language. But *language*, in fact, proves to be a crude term for the specific interplay of signs, tropes, performatives, and grammars which articulate contrasts and decisions. Stanley Cavell's analysis of metaphor and paraphrase attempts to specify which moments within a linguistic matrix constitute the claims of one speaker's convictions upon another. A specification of the linguistic structures and acts of decision making that would constitute a claim upon the values and convictions of the community seemed to be absent from Taylor's philosophy of language, leaving him with a rather symbolic view of literature's mysterious ability to capture personal and social experiences. Taylor looks upon the resources of language as a means of overcoming the atomism/communitarianism distinction in social philosophy. But lacking a clear specification of linguistic claims, he leaves a blank in his account of how personal decisions may shape the language of the community.

Pragmatists like Rorty and Fish also have specific views about what holds a person in place after the collapse of foundationalist discourse. The particular advance brought by the work of Rorty and Fish at this stage in my argument is a strong recognition of literature's role in the formation of community and identity. Taylor provides a substantial connection between language and identity in order to account for situatedness but does not seem to develop this connection within works of literature. Pragmatists like Rorty and Fish make extensive use of literary works and are prepared to a much greater degree than Taylor to treat them in nonuniversalist terms.

The nonuniversalist terms which Rorty and Fish use include *irony, metaphor, antiformalism,* and *familiar vocabularies.* Each of these terms is meant to suggest degrees of overlap between different and sometimes incommensurable vocabularies. Familiarity and adoption by speakers are the main criteria for assessing the importance of vocabularies or the need to shift between them. By invoking these terms I do not suggest that they can be easily transposed into a discussion of the claims and incommensurables that would be required in a full-blown theory of literary structures and meanings. But at least they point pragmatist critics in the right direction. They allow pragmatists to look for connections in the construction of literary utterances, personal identity, and social practices. The specific nature of the inquiry is an advance upon a generalist inquiry into the status of literature in relation to global terms like history, society, or self.

Within the specific play among reader, the work of literature, and the concerns of a particular interpretive community, the pragmatist position emerges at its strongest and most influential. The particularized and detailed redescription of a work of literature is what distinguishes pragmatist philosophers most sharply from hermeneuts, whose language seems by comparison generic and abstract, no matter how great the philosophical goal of concretely situating the reader. It is precisely this gap between the goal of situatedness and the theoretical vocabulary of literary studies that leads me back to the pragmatist writers at this stage. For the pragmatist, there is nothing to be gained from a purely theoretical study of literature. There are only measures of personal and communal change brought on by the adoption of a plurality of vocabularies, with literature affording a greater measure of plurality than most forms of ordinary discourse. For my part, I would seek in the pragmatist focus on difference, plurality, and change specific moments of contrast or, more difficultly, decision making in the face of incommensurable options that could be adapted to Taylor's account of what situates an agent. This task would involve respecting the pragmatist's awareness of pluralism without accepting some of its paradoxes, like the radical split between public and private concerns or the complete absorption of all interpretive moments into immediate social context and customary practice.

In part I of this book I questioned whether pragmatism's picture of nonfoundationalist conviction contained a sufficiently refined theory of language. In part

II, I am returning to this question through a specific engagement with the differences in language within works of literature. What, if anything, distinguishes the language of literature from the host of other language games it draws upon and returns to in ordinary social discourse?

The answer to this question is what gives the notion of *textuality* its distinction and importance in the remainder of this book. I have purposely kept the term *text* out of play thus far in order to obviate its use as a synonym for *literature* or *discourse* or *vocabulary* or *language*. In my view, deconstructionist and poststructuralist literary theory enters a mutually modifying relation with pragmatist and expressivist philosophies of language through its development of a theory of textuality. The determination of a piece of language as a text may be linked to the specification of the sort of language that situates a human agent in the midst of plurality, but the actual task of determination in the work of a deconstructionist like de Man or a poststructuralist like Jameson is as important as the specification of a moment of choice in the work of Charles Taylor or the specification of what counts as a linguistic claim in the work of Stanley Cavell. I do not see a theory of textuality as another version of hermeneutical holism in which all social phenomena become "textualized" or as a nonfoundationalist vocabulary that makes it easier to talk about beliefs without confusing them with epistemic grounds or referents.[2] While it is true that textuality is closely bound up with issues of reference, and while it is also true that the term has been stretched far beyond anything specific to literature, an attempt needs to be made to preserve some specificity for the term if it is to do the work I intend in this book.

I would follow a deconstructionist like Paul de Man in looking for a determination of textuality within the range of complex linguistic structures that involve figural meanings as much as ordinary grammatical or logical ones. The point of such complex structures is to determine both the degree of commensuration possible between them and what these different degrees of commensuration imply for the production and distribution of resonant languages. In order to avoid certain confusions at the outset of part II of this book, I shall try to clarify several important consequences of this approach for the chapters that follow:

1. Lack of commensuration is not an abstract principle that can be applied to or forced upon any work of literature as if it were a universal linguistic principle akin to a Saussurean theory of a sign. If textuality involves an exact determination of certain forms of language that cannot in the final

analysis be commensurated, then it is important to realize that this determination must be actively constructed, in the manner of a Taylorean choice. It cannot be arbitrarily located on the assumption that it must already exist in the work of literature. The determination involves pinpointing a linguistic crux that may shape a larger pattern of discourse, but without the determination the task is an inert act of criticism.

2. Lack of commensuration among all the elements of highly articulate utterances goes hand in hand with a recognition of the plurality of discourses at large but should not be confused with an endorsement of pluralism for its own sake or with an effort to relativize values and beliefs according to particular or local interests and communities. I follow Taylor in seeing a link between the articulation of a pattern of values or beliefs that may never reach final commensuration and the process of becoming situated in a complex social sphere. Determining which utterances deserve to be considered textual is linked to finding where one stands.

3. The determination of textuality is what distinguishes the contribution of each of the critics examined in the remainder of this book. This task of determining the textual is what Empson, Fish, Jameson, and de Man all have in common; it is what distinguishes their approach to literature from that of a philosopher like Taylor and from other literary theorists. But the determination and construction of a linguistic moment that may be defined as textual is also what connects their work to Taylor's philosophy of situatedness. In the first instance, the determination of textuality may be compared to the determination of incommensurable choices, a nonholistic approach to social identity and coherence, and a recognition of an ongoing plurality of discourses in culture and society. But in the next instance, the determination of textuality is a special advance upon hermeneutics and pragmatism; and it is an advance that emerges from the disciplines which are closely connected to the study of literature. The determination of textuality as in the work of the four theorists studied in part II of this book gives philosophical significance to Anglo-American literary theory since the New Criticism. Their work helps define a place for literary studies in a nonfoundationalist view of personhood and community. What makes literary theory as a distinct inquiry into language important?

4. A theory of textuality has an important role to play in a pluralist and nonfoundationalist philosophy of literature precisely because it resists to a high degree a generic, abstract formulation. Perhaps the circulation and adoption of the term *text* belongs to the emerging discourse about a postmodernist society. At present the term has a flexibility that appears to be suited to a plurality of interests, much like the popular usage of terms like *deconstruction* and *poststructuralism*. In this book, however, the resistance of *text* to a generic definition goes in the opposite direction of precision, limitation, and an economy of expression.

Not all works of literature need to be defined as texts, and a determination of a particular web of utterances as textual does not cover all the meanings and uses that may be found in one community's canon or multiple canons of literature. Furthermore, writers who produce poems, plays, novels, autobiographies, letters, documentaries, historical narratives, literary criticism, bibliographies, encyclopedias, and scholarly monographs rarely see themselves bound up in theories of textuality. But then again, they may, as writers, not see themselves as philosophers either, part of whose work is to shape a language for personal identity and present the means for both recognizing and coping with social pluralism. The literary theorist's language of textuality is what bridges the gap between multiple patterns of discourse, which Taylor, Rorty, and Cavell all acknowledge as the pattern of literature, and the crucial determination of key utterances which have a claim upon personhood and situatedness. Not all forms of expression need to be called texts, and the term *text* should not be applied to anything that loosely lends itself to interpretation. The whole point of the philosophy of situatedness as expounded by Taylor and the claim of literary language as expounded by Cavell is to avoid hermeneutical holism.

5. How should one read literary theorists, therefore? Where do their expressions about the value and meaning of different works of literature fit between the ordinary and familiar language of everyday experiences and the unusual, figural language of the poets? The answers to this question are multiple and can be given only in the terms by which a literary theorist actively constructs a speaking position as *between* different features of language. What matters to a grasp upon textuality, just as to a grasp upon

Taylor's language of contrast, is the quality of determining linguistic difference. The more determined the linguistic difference that is being bridged, the more likely that the textual insight will lead to an articulation of important, but not totalizable, relations between human agents. As Martha Minow and Martha Nussbaum note, particularity of expression is discovering where one stands in a web of social relations. These determinations do not stand on their own, however. As Cavell urges, they must be made to count and be rearticulated, just as we already know that works of literature must be rearticulated in order to contribute to thoughts about ourselves.

This definition of situatedness does not emerge at the expense of plural values and identifications as discussed in part I with reference to philosophers like Frankfurt and Williams. To bring all these concerns together without reifying textuality into fixed structures that correspond to fixed categories of speech activity, we need to follow the examples of textual determinacy in the work of literary theorists like Empson, Fish, Jameson, and de Man. The order in which they appear does not reflect a progression toward better theory but rather greater and greater efforts toward the determination of textuality. The measure of greater determinacy is equivalent to a measure of deeper situatedness.

6

A Dialogue between Common Attitudes and Private Romances: Cavell and Empson on *Othello*

I have been arguing that the determination of a segment of language as a *text* is necessary to the pragmatic task of circulating and critically adopting works of literature in a deeply plural society. I have also been arguing that these pragmatic tasks are deeply connected to personal individuation and communal identification and, further, that these connections give the study of literature importance as philosophy increasingly sheds foundationalist epistemological principles. At this point in my argument, the exposition of these concerns comes to rest largely on actual examples of textual determination, for these immanently illuminate, as Harry Frankfurt would say, the ways in which a textually determined language situates readers of literature. By using the term *situatedness,* I continue my efforts to build up Charles Taylor's language of qualitative contrasts in relation to the task of individuating oneself in a deeply plural society.

First among the questions that begin an inquiry into the determination of textuality is, How should readers respond to a work of literature or to a writer who appears in an already highly determined literary context? for example, Shakespearean tragedy? By now, it is clear that the term *text* in this book has nothing to do with formalist or classical definitions of Shakespearean tragedy as they may be found, for instance, in the common vocabulary of Shakespearean literary critics or literary historians. *Text,* henceforward, does not mean the determinacy of Shakespearean drama or poetic writing by virtue of its lofty iambic pentameters and Elizabethan diction, five-act structure, and use of popular and heroic stereotypes, nor its mimesis of universal tragic flaws. Formalist definitions of *textual* properties fall outside the pattern of inquiry of this book. By textual, I refer back to the sorts of questions that Stanley Cavell poses about Shakespearean tragedy. His approach to Shakespearean tragedy clarifies the relation between an agent's decisive articulation of forms of language that impose claims and demand acknowledgment and the forms that are already present through the agency of a writer like Shakespeare.

In *Disowning Knowledge,* Cavell attempts to define Shakespearean tragedy as the verbal enactment of the process of loss and restoration of contact between the isolated (in his jargon, skeptical) individual and his community. Tragedy is the product of verbally enacting that isolation and restitution, below the surface themes of family relationships, romantic love, heroic statesmanship, and human affect used by various tragedies to stage the enactment. The verbal details of the enactment, not a universalist concept of the Shakespearean account of human nature (or inversely, the supposedly ideological bias of Shakespearean insight), need to be carefully determined, repeated, and grasped by successive audiences.

Cavell's analysis of what makes a Shakespearean tragedy count and work touches on the determination of textuality as I intend to define it in the rest of this book. In a way that parallels his inquiry into paraphrase some twenty years earlier, Cavell attacks the incoherence of literary criticism that would point at the reality *and* the illusion of a tragedy, as if it were fixed in meaning or dramatic space and merely waiting to be turned into propositions that could be independently tested over time and experience. The incoherence lies in attesting to the pervasive claim of interest in the power of Shakespearean tragedy along with the feeling that its characters, language, and formal structure are obviously distant and outside normal experience. Cavell's effort to reenact the meaning of tragedy without resorting to paraphrase might be mistaken for a pragmatist readerly-response to literature. Does not Stanley Fish remind us that texts exist only insofar as they are read and that there is no such thing as an independent, freestanding textual object in the first place? More needs to be said about Fish's argument, which is the subject of the following chapter. But one immediate difference between Cavell and Fish is that Fish's radically pragmatic position does not explain very clearly what, if anything, determines a reader's response to a tragedy as opposed to, say, a comedy, a romance, a farce, or a melodrama. If the interpretive community and the text are one, how can one be seen as influencing the other? Cavell shares with Fish the avoidance of a false reification of a text as an inert object of *separate* interpretive practices, which he would see as yet another version of the epistemic/skeptical incoherent use of illusion to map reality, and of doubt as the invocation of failsafe certainty. But he differs sharply from Fish because he recognizes from the outset the specificity of tragedy. That recognition gives me an opportunity to indicate the *limits* rather than the sheer plurality of meanings which follow from the right orientation into the problem of determining a text. It is this orientation that I began to sketch, very abstractly, in the previous chapter.

It would be too much to say that William Shakespeare consciously thought through the philosophical problem of skepticism and used it to create tragic plays of enduring fascination. And it would be too much to say that Shakespeare thought through a particular theory of textuality as the basis of tragedy writing. But if we are to avoid reducing tragedy to the immediate interests of different postmodernist interpretive communities or to an abstractable set of propositions about the real properties of human nature, then we must ask what we are responding to in the language of Shakespeare when we find it both familiar and distant. It does seem reasonable to assume with Cavell that, though the diction and thematics sound distant to contemporary audiences, the language of Shakespearean tragedy is sufficiently determined by the problems of isolation and community to continue to count in today's pluralized society, in which at least part of the experience of locating oneself lies in locating certain strands of language as they emerge between discontinuous social contexts. Shakespeare does not give us an image of pluralism, any more than he gives an image of an epistemologist working on the problem of skepticism. But perhaps he found tragic material in the discovery of solitude, multiple and conflicting interests within the social matrix, a combination of irony and conviction in strong personal identity, and he was able to articulate a language that could put these materials into partial commensuration and contrast with each other. Insofar as that language may be accurately determined and responded to, a reading of Shakespearean tragedy is not an exercise in literary revisionism or in literary theory, but what I am describing as the determination of textuality. Again, not every single passage in a play will have a "textual" status, paradoxical as that may sound. But then not every utterance produced by a speaker in the course of a day will reflect a holistic hermeneutics. Tragedy lies in the textual cruces that determine expressions of loss of linguistic attunement, communal restoration, and personal individuation. To grasp these cruces we have to know what counts about our language games, as we respond to the work of the Shakespearean play.

My reliance upon Cavell to provide the right orientation for the task of textual determination is unavoidably qualified by his own reliance upon the topic of skepticism. In order to limit the relevance of skepticism as it may bear upon tragedy, I am juxtaposing Cavell's analysis of *Othello* with Empson's analysis of Shakespeare's use of the word *honest* in the play.[1] The juxtaposition is far from being an arbitrary one. For one thing, Cavell admires Empson's way of handling literary metaphors. Like Cavell, Empson does not attempt a paraphrase of Shakespearean tragedy but rather seeks to locate in the play the actual shaping of meanings that bear upon ordinary usage. Their analyses of *Othello,* therefore, differ sharply from the practices of any school of literary interpretation that continues to rely upon propositional translations of the play's meanings.

Empson's analysis of the word *honest* qualifies Cavell's emphasis on skepticism, however. In fact, their readings of Othello's tragedy are practically antithetical to each other. As Christopher Norris notes, the larger purpose of Empson's verbal analysis of a keyword like *honest* in the play is to dismantle the entire concept of the tragic:

> Words like "fool" and "honest" have a down-to-earth quality of healthy scepticism which, Empson argues, permits their users to build up a trust in human nature based on a shared knowledge of its needs and attendant weaknesses. "Dog" is the most cynical of the family, a rock-bottom term of mutual disillusion, yet at the same time a "hearty" recognition of mankind's common predicament.
>
> There is not much room in this rationalist outlook for anything in the nature of a "tragic" philosophy of values.[2]

In the confrontation between Empsonian honesty and Cavellean skepticism we are not faced with a true versus a false reading of the play, where ultimately one critic's theory of tragedy cancels out the other's. Rather, we are dealing with contrasting constructions of the play as a text in which the issue can be settled only according to different degrees of situatedness. That is what gives Cavell's and Empson's opposing definitions of the tragic the kind of philosophical interest that is palpably absent in the opposition between Cleanth Brooks and Yvor Winters. I suggested that Shakespearean tragedy continues to count and work among present-day readers because it is still part of the language that we use to individuate ourselves and position ourselves in a plural matrix of values. This matrix cannot be thematically extracted and paraphrased but is rather immanently illuminated in the play's language. As Cavell suggests, the determining of a linguistic claim is also the discovering of one's own language of convictions and ability to reach attunement with other speakers. This process of attunement is plural and flexible. The quality of determining the degree to which characters are tragically misattuned from each other is instructive for audiences facing the same personal conditions. Cavell and Empson take up these issues in just the right way, by actively reconstructing portions of the play which would seem to have the greatest contact with a reader's or viewer's own task of individuation. The difference between them is in degrees of situatedness that emerge from their constructions. As I mentioned at the conclusion of part I, Cavell's construction of a language that would situate a person occurs somewhere between sublime utterances of great conviction and ordinary experiences which are familiar and domestic. Empsonian honesty is a reconstruction of human individuality that would situate readers of Shakespeare in ordinary circumstances without having to pay the price of tragic skepticism. Which is preferable? The answer cannot be given in the abstract. It requires that we follow their constructed determinations of the key utterances of the play. These determinations are what I am calling texts. Because Cavell has been discussed at length in a previous chapter, I shall focus on Empson first, especially on his claims that Iago as the voice of honesty has had the most important influence on the reception of tragedy into the world of everyday experience. Following my discussion of Empson's determinations of honesty as the textual base of the play, I will return to the issue of Cavellean tragedy as it is focused on Othello and Othello's endurance in our contemporary propensity for skeptical individualism.

It is very curious that Shakespeare develops the word *honest,* which directly connects an ethical norm with a way of speaking, through one of the most recognizable vice-figures in English drama, Iago. Iago's "honesty," Empson argues, marks a crucial historical evolution in the word, standing midway between an earlier code of honor and trust and a subsequent discovery of what Empson calls the "Independent Self." Iago's honesty seems to be necessary to the realization of significant differences in human personality and disposition and perhaps to the location of this realization in an awareness of personal psychology, but it also seems to verge on a potentially tragic cult of egoism and selfishness which carries the sense of being honest first and foremost about one's own impulses and desires with a consequent loss of trust between individuals.

What centers upon Iago, therefore, and the extensive discussion of *honest* that is the keystone of Empson's *The Structure of Complex Words* is the development of new social relations between speakers. Is the new order progressive and antichivalric or sinister and skeptical? What are we to make of Empson's conclusion that Othello's suicide rests not on his discovery of Desdemona's innocence but on the collapse of Iago's honesty? Apparently Empson would argue that the fundamental crux of the play rests on the complete destruction of an earlier code of honor which, somehow, Iago's peculiar honesty partially supports. According to Empson, without Iago Othello has no characterizational claim to existence.

Empson does not follow Bernard Spivack's dominant line of inquiry into Iago as a personification of evil.[3] A fixed morality of good and evil is largely irrelevant to Empson's investigation of what continues to count for contemporary readers who are confronting Shakespeare's use of *honest*. But does Empson go too far in seeing *Othello* as a rationalist study of the ethic of mutual understanding and support?

Before I turn to a fuller examination of Empson's reading of *Othello,* I would like to emphasize that the collapse of mutual understanding into tragic personal delusions remains an essentially linguistic problem in Empson's discussion. On that point, his approach to Shakespearean tragedy complements Cavell's. There is no way to prevent this collapse by disproving the evidence, by dismissing the charge against Desdemona, or by attempting any explanation simply outside Empsonian linguistics. It is like Cavell's example of the yokel who rushes on stage to Desdemona's defense, or the child whose fears are quieted by being told that it is just a play, or the sudden illumination of the house lights that breaks the play's spell without canceling its meaning.[4] Such refutations of the play's events amount to a virtual negation of theater itself, and with it what Cavell calls the honest response that the play is demanding.

Empson's reading of the play deserves consideration in the context of my project because it insists that the study of a complex word like *honest* reveals the precise enactment of an expressive language which belongs to individualism. Whatever is troubling about the play must be seen in relation to the problems of articulating the gradual separation and differentiation of personal identities within a social world that can no longer be given as an unchanging hierarchy of class and position. For Empson, *Othello* is about a new way of openly articulating private meanings, about the public honesty (real honesty, not ironic honesty) that belongs to a particular concept of individuality. To listen to the language of the play is to become aware of honest communications as the voice of a new individualism which mixes doubt, self-esteem, conflicting loyalties, dependencies, and a sense of personal merit. Empson looks upon human individuals as they emerge and shape each other against the background of these as yet incoherent strands of personhood. Individual articulations, from the microlevel of conversation up to the level of implied doctrines and normative assertions, are exchanged and altered through the discovery of new forms of linguistic agreement. The further implication of the theory is that in time key individuals, like Iago, come to typify larger structures of human identity. Iagoism as a mode of expression is social insofar as it draws upon the semantic background of *honest,* but it is typical insofar as it focuses select features of that plural background of meanings and values.

Such a reading far excels a number of traditional interpretive approaches which cannot get inside the play precisely because they fail to reconstruct the language of the play, be it through Iago's honesty or Othello's skepticism.[5] For Empson, the question of Othello's bombastic-sounding rhetoric would never arise. Rhetoric is never merely egotistical, a vanity of words, because that would leave unanswered the question of why we are paying attention to the language in the first place. Similarly, the assumption of the autonomy of literary conventions, in the treatment of Iago as the personification of evil, implies a severe limitation of literature's expressive participation in ordinary social discourse.

Cavell's perspective on Shakespearean skepticism is the truly challenging alternative to Empson. For Cavell, *Othello* is about the historical emergence of the isolated, profoundly uncertain, vengeful individual, who is unable to value others. In tracing Empson's analysis of linguistic structures of honesty, which form the basis of speakers' mutual understanding, I shall try to discover why a large gap remains between Empsonian honesty and the Cavellean denial of the importance of other people. Through denial, Cavell is able to touch upon the same concern as Empson, the emergence of the conflicted, uncertainly situated individual. To enter into dialogue first with Empson and subsequently with Cavell, one needs to enter the play *Othello* in their way. We listen to *Othello* when we engage in an active determination of the play's honest or skeptical language of personhood in relation to our own.

For Empson, Iago wins the approval of the audience once honesty serves as a basic social norm, but that does not mean he is truthful or praiseworthy. The issue has to do with the way meanings gain normative values in Empsonian semantics. Iago does not exemplify some normative value already at work in Elizabethan vocabulary, but rather the way in which norms are built up. In its pre-Shakespearean phase, according to Empson, honesty is used to praise someone; it belongs to a courtly or chivalric discourse in which praise is a common form of address. But in the dozens of mentions it receives in *Othello,* Iago is clearly not being praised; in fact, part of Desdemona's noblesse is revealed in her patronizing attitude toward Iago, in her praising him like a good, common rogue or dog. If Iago reflects some normative honesty and so deserves our approval, it is not because he is praiseworthy, but because he is reevaluating a more basic level of honesty, one closer to the minimum standard of assumed truth telling, which as a norm is not especially praiseworthy in and of itself. Many pre- or non-Empsonian readings of the play founder at this level in an attempt to substitute psychological motive for these discursive restructurings of honesty. Characterizational accounts of the Iago-Othello relationship provide poor explanations of the way they honestly communicate with each other.

A. C. Bradley and F. R. Leavis, for example, in their opposing ways, search for the motives that drive Iago and Othello. Iago is a good companion, loyal and steadfast in his duty toward Othello, but so roguish and average that he does not merit appointment to higher military status and is passed over in favor of the more chivalric Cassio. Iago then gains his motive for revenge, his envy of Cassio, and his secret hostility toward Othello. His revenge runs out of control, however, confirming his base character (Leavis) and thus his relative lack of didactic, literary value, or the revenge becomes fascinating to watch in and of itself as it unfolds (Bradley). On the next level of analysis, we may consider the destruction of Othello as tragic because of the defeat of the code of honor, regardless of whether he or Iago is chiefly responsible for it. There are many variations on this interpretive theme. But what if the elaborate honest exchanges between Iago and Othello are an attempt to mark the emergence of a new, postchivalric mode of speech of a very different tragic nature, in which truth telling and deceitfulness, and the older honorable code of behavior which has become vulnerable, are not at issue. Or, to put it more accurately, what if *honest* as a normative term for truth and praise is being restructured as the expression of a norm based on individualism? There is nothing to approve in Iago's dishonesty. But there is something basic to the construction of a community in the doctrine of individualism and its expression in ordinary speech, what G. K. Hunter seems to be getting at in his metaphor of a social fabric of small assents at work in the play.

Honest individualism has its own ethical paradoxes and dilemmas, of course. For one thing, *honest* must carry the implication of truth somehow, but truth has shifted from faith in mutual understanding to protecting, defending, and exploring a new sense of self. One can honestly shelter oneself, maintaining an honest reserve, or one can be honest in the company of one's fellows, like honor among thieves. The fundamental ethical paradox, for Empson, is that the "the selfish man *is* the generous one, because he is not repressed" (192). Selfishness has a "natural ease" which, Empson suggests, evolves into the cultural stereotypes of the Enlightenment Noble Savage or the Victorian Gentleman. The normative element rests on the resolution of the contradiction within individualism so as to make individualism typical, the "measure of all things." As Empson puts it, the typical individual man can "recognize and fulfil both his own nature and his duties to society" (196); his impulses do not lead him away from socially constructive behavior.

The concept of honest individualism allows Empson to determine the peculiar contradictions of Iago's speech which remain hidden to critics who would separate psychological character from literary expression. One of the chief tasks Empson sets for himself is to make Iago plausible, typical of a new individualism in which we all share. But why is Iago the typical case, instead of poets like Herbert or Pope who extend the use of the word *honest*? Why not make Gay's dramatic rogues the type of honesty? All of them take second place to Iago, who gets the pivotal chapter of Empson's book on complex words. How does Iago become the measure of all things in the play? Supposedly, it is because he shapes the new doctrine of individualism by reconciling its inner contradictions in a decisive way. After Iago, there is no turning back to honor. He presents no ideal worthy of emulation, but somehow we all become like Iago in our inner lives; he is our new average, as Wyndham Lewis noted. Iagoism has to do with discovering, checking, and releasing impulses as we try to gain new forms of social intimacy and mastery between our much more spontaneous, unpredictable, and natural selves.

Although he never asks us to approve of Iago's immoral behavior, Empson seems to think Iago's dialogue draws upon the vocabulary of honesty in actual speech, so that we have to work through Iago's speech, like him or not, in order to socialize ourselves. Consider Empson's unpacking of the densely honest discussion of Cassio held by Othello and Iago in act 3, scene 3, the discussion in which Iago supposedly begins to win the strategic upper hand. Cassio has already been dismissed for drunken brawling, has lost his precious reputation. But now Iago discovers a further slight he must pay back in learning for the first time that Cassio had played the go-between for Othello and Desdemona, even as Desdemona now is playing the role for Cassio. Once again, Iago is made aware of his social inferiority, of his exclusion from the confidential circuits of the higher nobles. And so he begins to capitalize on sexual innuendos about Desdemona's fidelity, sowing doubt in Othello, presumably, and assuaging his own injured feeling. It is a spontaneous turnaround: Iago must cover his injury instantly, if his own honesty, or fellow feeling for Othello, is to be credible, and this involves a rather complex posture of reserve which becomes increasingly important in the course of Empson's analysis. Iago's curious reserve, his deliberate hesitation in pouring poison into Othello's ear, becomes the resolution of his inner contradictions and his typifying gesture for winning approval. Iagoism is crucial, Empson says, because it is the first successful resolution of "being ready to blow the gaff on other people and frank to yourself about your own desires" (221). The whole point of Iago's honesty is that he does not blow the gaff, ever; he simply gives the impression that he could dismantle the pseudohonorable love of his betters in one stroke, but what he does instead is recode their behavior in terms of honest/false confidence in their knowledge of each other. Just how far can this recoding go without becoming implausible either by reducing Othello to a fool and thus canceling the tragedy as such or making Iago more convincing than he really is? Empson appears to choose the latter. Here is Empson's construction of the first key text of honesty:

Oth.: *Is he not honest?*   (Faithful, etc.)
Iago: *Honest, my lord?*   (Not stealing, etc. Shocked)
Oth.: *Ay, honest,*   ("Why repeat? . . . ")
Iago: *My lord, for aught I know* . . . ("In some sense")

Iago: *For Michael Cassio*
  I dare be sworn I think that he is honest.
Oth.: *I think so too.*
Iago: *Men should be what they seem,*
  Or, those that be not, would they might seem none.
Oth.: *Certain, men should be what they seem.*
Iago: *Why then, I think Cassio's an honest man.* (221–22)

Empson suggests that the point of the dialogue is for Iago to praise Cassio for being "frank about his own [sexual] nature," his youthful vigor, but simultaneously to condemn him for letting others see this, for lacking in public decency, as for example in the intrusions of Bianca which come later. Iago thus appears to understand Cassio's nature, one man to another, but as a more skilled and mannered gentleman, he has the honor not to discuss Cassio's behavior in too much detail. Thus, "Iago can hide what reservations he makes but show that he makes reservations; this suggests an embarrassed defence—'Taking a broad view, with the world as it is, and Cassio my friend, I can decently call him honest'" (222). To understand Iago is to accept this view of human nature while leaving room to criticize, with tolerance, those whose nature interferes with proper appearances in public. The honest thing to do is to lean on this common wisdom instead of prying into people's private affairs. The wild effect of the exchange, then, is for Iago to shift the feeling of candor from Othello and Cassio onto Cassio and himself, leaving Othello in doubt about his previously reliable romantic confidant. And with the sexual twist, there is further room for doubt regarding Cassio's real motives in the proximity of women. Cassio's natural honesty is in conflict with a woman's honesty, her chastity. Finally, Empson suggests that the whole dialogue is englobed by a heartier, manly honesty, or fellow feeling, built up between Iago and Othello as they seem to share a mutual distaste for annoying sexual implications in the midst of their official business. This man-to-man honesty, this serious attitude toward business at the expense of sexuality helps to explain Empson's conclusion that Othello is ruined by his discovery of Iago's falsehood, not Desdemona's.

Implausibility does not intrude into Empson's reading of the passage because he discovers (imposes?) so much semantic complexity. He reaches deeper than G. K. Hunter's contrast between the words *be* and *seem* in locating Iago's efforts to shift the entire semantic register of *honest* from honorable, trustworthy, and puritanical to trust in conflict with sexual knowledge. (It is useful to keep in mind Bradley's point that Iago suspects that he has been cuckolded by Othello; trust and sexuality never stabilize in any pairing of the play's characters.) But there are difficulties in the values Empson works into his discussion.

We must recall that the major task of Empson's reconstruction of Iago's speeches is to establish their plausibility. Empson wants Iago to share a level of intimacy with Othello: he is warmly, appreciatively filled in as a character in spite of his lack of truthfulness. Iago is a bit of a poet in that he cannot be said to have lied when he has affirmed nothing, and yet something of typifying significance clearly has been valorized: his reserve, the last vestige of honor that attaches to basic, minimal honesty.

On the theoretical plane, Empson usually argues that minimally defined norms, for example, "Honesty equals not lying," can be valued by speakers only if special circumstances warrant it. If everyone basically tells the truth all the time, then one does not earn praise for conforming to this assumption. Looking at the special acts of approval, then, becomes the key to discerning the more complex values at work in social discourse. In the fragment of dialogue just considered, Iago wrests an appreciative, approving use of honesty as "faithful, worthy of special confidence" from Cassio onto himself. But here the special circumstances that warrant the word shift have a twist: approval rests upon a pseudohonorable distaste for the vulgarity of sexuality, a nascent puritanism, which begins to take over the mutually supportive/destructive relationship of Iago and Othello. Perhaps we may now call these characters individuals in their isolation, interdependence, and defensiveness and in their effort to be hardy with each other, but it is not at all clear what exactly is of typical value about all this. How does this sort of speech situate a reader or viewer? Cavell will call this sort of individualism a fatal trap, worst of all in its deep sexual horror. Empson seems content with this state of affairs—he will go on to argue for Iago's purity—as long as the language of the play seems to work, to get the messages across from character to character, even if we miss many of the implications of the words in any given exchange.

The failed coherence of the individual, or the independent self, and a normative set of values is the problem that emerges in Empson's approach. And that indeed should be the problem in situating ourselves in relation to a Shakespearean tragedy. But how do we solve it? Cavell's discourse about individuals calls attention to the task of submitting oneself to communal intelligibility. Evading that task leads easily to a skeptical denial that others really count for oneself. Iagoism's reserve works because it can be filled in in many ways by the background meanings of the word *honest*. But as a nonassertion, lacking the test of common intelligibility, it leaves us to decide whether to approve it as honor or reject it as wounded ambition. Though seemingly rich in semantic play, this decision is really a very narrow one in terms of ordinary feeling, as can be seen in the sexual cost it imposes even in Empson's utilitarian acceptance of human impulse.

Two further examples from Empson's discussion reinforce this point and inadvertently begin to reduce the tragedy's expressive activity. Of course that is Empson's intention, the virtual cancellation of the tragic mood of the play's conclusion, but it is a step that needs to be taken with Cavellean caution. The first concerns Othello's supposed humbling before Iago's purity when he confesses to Emilia that it was "My friend, thy husband, honest, honest Iago" who informed him of Desdemona's falsehood (see Empson 226 on *Othello,* act 5, scene 2). Empson says that the line mixes horror with a "hearty use" of the word *honest*. There is no irony in calling Iago honest at this point, as if Othello is feeling the full measure of his deception. Just the opposite: there is a horrible realization, but it lies in a final acceptance, even an agreement, with Iago, the supposed element of heartiness or fellow-feeling. As in the dialogue concerning Cassio, Othello continues to feel a prudish disgust at sexuality and finds support for this aversion in Iago's analogous misogynist position. Thus the horror is not a truth retrospectively revealed about Desdemona but a confrontation, still shared by Othello and Iago, with the inherent awfulness of female sexuality. Cavell makes the same point about an underlying sexual hysteria in Othello's character, and Peter Stallybrass points out Desdemona's victimization as woman. The peculiarity of Empson's reading, however, lies in the way he attaches the positive values of shared understanding, mutual feeling, and common value to Iago and Othello by negating sexuality. Empson's semantic analysis of *honest* opens new affective possibilities in the word but closes down its tragic potential. What sort of human individual would actually talk in this way? What sort of individuality is dependent upon such a misdirected horror?

Empson never asks these questions because there is no tragedy in this horror; it has been displaced by the heartiness he would uphold. To hear Othello's lines as tragic an audience would have to allow for the possibility that an individual's utterance comes from somewhere deep in the state of individualism, of aloneness, self-recognition, affirmation of self. Othello, it is true, is affirming something. But he may be affirming something about his own lack of sexuality and clutching onto

Iago so as not to expose it. The emergence of individualism in feelings of doubt comes much closer to Cavell's general account of what the Othello-Iago relationship is all about in the first place. Empson will allow Othello to perform his individual reconciliation of horror with heartiness, in itself a very plausible human reaction formation. But as soon as Empson adds that Othello thereby submits himself to a clearer, purer, ideal view of love without sex, he leaves us to wonder about the normative background these lines are supposed to evoke. Iagoism has become the background, the type, the measure, the average that defines Othello.

In Empson's final phase of interpretation Iagoism takes over Othello completely, or so Empson reads the double negation of honor and honesty in the lines Othello speaks before his suicide: "But why should honour outlive honesty? / Let it all go." Empson's reading deserves to be quoted in full because it offers itself as the only explanation of the "force of the question":

> Outlive Desdemona's chastity, which he now admits, outlive Desdemona herself, the personification of chastity (lying again, as he insisted, with her last breath), outlive decent behaviour in, public respect for, self-respect in, Othello—all these are honour, not honesty; there is no question whether Othello outlives them. But they are not tests of an idea; what has been tested is a special sense of *honest*. Iago has been the personification of honesty, not merely to Othello but to his world; why should honour, the father of the word, live on and talk about itself; honesty, that obscure bundle of assumptions, the play has destroyed. (229)

Since Othello's honor does not depend upon Desdemona's chastity, which, in Empson's view, is a minor form of honor specifically attached to women, it can outlive her. By contrast, male honor by this time is so intertwined with the male honesty typified by Iago that it cannot survive Iago's destruction. This quasi-homoerotic, sacrificial reading (does the father have the right to outlive the son?) is the closest Empson comes to admitting a tragic mood. The reading is a remarkable summation of the play: the ambiguous reserve noted in the dialogue about Cassio gradually fixes itself as a hatred of sexuality, which then becomes the source of reciprocal male understanding, and finally the measure of honor's faint historical afterlife, soon to reach extinction. Something has misfired in the course of honesty's structure of commonly shared meanings. Although the theory is telling us that we have reached the fullest articulation of feeling, that we can speak more honestly about ourselves once we are freed of honorable reserve, the vocabulary that pours out has very little force; it makes practically no claim upon our attention, except perhaps as a semantic puzzle. Does this sound like the voice of an emergent individualism, even as it marks the collapse of personification?

Another historical version of this new language of individualism may be found in Stephen Greenblatt's reading of *Othello* as an exercise in self-fashioning.[6] Identity and a framework of social discourse involving the church and human sexuality are dialectically related in Greenblatt's discussion, with an odd lack of expressive substance, similar to what I am noting in Empson. For Greenblatt, Othello comes "dangerously close to recognizing his status as text" (238), specifically the church's texts against adultery within marriage (i.e., being too lustful toward one's wife). And Iago becomes the "principle of narrativity itself" (236) who gains persuasive power over Othello through his learned, casuistical manipulation of the church's doctrines. This complex, interesting effort to situate a self in some larger field of (always repressive?) discourse begins to sound as strained as Empson's male bonding of Iago and Othello. *Othello* becomes either a study in male fellow-feeling or a study in the male self's exploitation of its own field of sexual discourse. Empson and Greenblatt seem to agree intuitively that the play is about something new in the concept of the individual self and that this conception rests upon the peculiarity of the Othello-Iago relation. But both seem to undermine the category of the individual self they seek to reveal to us, either as inevitably misogynist in what it actually puts into practice in its new expressive activity or as abstractly "textualized" (a fate worse than being sexualized?).

The strength of Stanley Cavell's reading of *Othello* lies in the expressive agency of individualism, which he too sees as the problematic new discovery of the Shakespearean period and which he calls skepticism. Cavell's reading of the play differs from Empson's in one striking interpretation of the significance of Iago's honesty:

> However far he believes Iago's tidings, he cannot just believe them; somewhere he also *knows* them to be false. This is registered in the rapidity with which he is brought to the truth. . . . I am not claiming that he is trying not to believe Iago, or wants not to believe what Iago has told him. . . . I am claiming that we must understand Othello, on the contrary, to want to believe Iago, to be trying, against his knowledge, to believe

him. Othello's eager insistence on Iago's honesty . . . is not a sign of his stupidity in the presence of poison but of his devouring need of it . . . that the idea of Desdemona as an adulterous whore is more convenient to him than the idea of her as chaste. But what could be more terrible than Desdemona's faithlessness? Evidently her faithfulness. (133)

Cavell removes two problems that have been hampering interpretations of the play: the implausibility of Iago creating all of Othello's doubts; and Iago as a spokesman for some normative, puritan contempt of female sexuality. For the first time, a powerful element of denial is revealed for our consideration, and this allows the play to claim a tragic effect. Cavell does not see tragedy in the destruction of chastity, but in Othello's refusal to accept it; Iago and all his schemes support rather than challenge this refusal. The reason Cavell explicitly terms this denial rather than accept Empsonian reserve is that it requires a deliberate effort, complete self-investment. Othello must do the work of denial, and in this Iago really provides very little help. Far from rationalizing the destruction of Othello in the emergence of Iagoism, one historically eclipsing the other, Cavell asks us to listen to Othello's voice, a voice that has become very difficult to hear because we have indeed become too Iagoish, too caught up in our own little fantasies of individual social position and unable to recognize the poverty of our desire compared to the individualism that Othello expresses.

Othello is the beginning of individualism in his doubt, uncertainty, lack of perfect knowledge. Cavell suggests that, philosophically, Othello is in the spirit of Descartes rather than of Montaigne. In Descartes, the dilemma is put this way: "If I were . . . the author of my own being, I would doubt nothing, I would experience no desires, and finally I would lack no perfection."[7] The Cartesian self is the tragic self because it is driven by an insatiable need to authenticate its own existence epistemologically but finds its epistemology limited, open to doubt; it discovers its own insufficiency in reason. The tragedy is heard in these lines Othello utters:

> By the world,
> I think my wife be honest, and think she is not,
> I think that thou are just, and think thou are not;
> I'll have some proof . . .

> (act 3, scene 3, quoted in Cavell 389–92)

For Cavell, the word *honest* is not part of some network of chastity, honor, and impulse upon which the meaning of the utterance draws. Cavell reads these lines as the expression of "possibilities that reason, unaided, cannot rule out" even as Othello seems to admit that he is beyond the aid of reason. Desdemona's honesty is not susceptible to visual proof. The farcical manipulations of the hand-kerchief and the comic scenes of eavesdropping already indicate the poverty of "proof" in face of the skeptical individual's insatiable demand for certainty. These lines become intelligible to us when we begin to see that Othello's doubts depend not on Desdemona, an insight Empson seems to have intuited from his own angle, but on a refusal to see Desdemona for herself. Her honesty and chastity would expose his *lack* of perfect individuality, would tie him to her, would impose a much greater demand on his psyche. The skeptic, argues Cavell, prefers to accept doubt as the assurance of individuality rather than to submit to the test of another person's affection. Hence we have Cavell's suggestion that Othello is refusing to accept Desdemona's chastity rather than her adultery. To accept Desdemona is to submit one's all-consuming doubt, the perverted assurance of one's proper individuality, to dependency on another person, to the acknowledgment that there are other individuals, rather than the endless retesting of the object world of epistemological sense experience. This is also why Othello seems to put Desdemona to the final test as if she were an object, a piece of stone. His violence toward her is directed as if toward a product of *his* artistry, the necessary violence the sculptor wreaks upon the inanimate object to make it mean something for himself. Tragedy at least discredits skepticism's self-destructive victory over its own accumulated doubt and denial of human otherness.

Skepticism consumes language's attunements in the form of epistemological doubt, which in effect circumvents the possibility of being answered or challenged by another speaker; the only response it seeks is one from the object world. I repeat (from part I of this book) Cavell's presentation of his own battle against the encroachment of skepticism in all forms of life:

> What skepticism threatens is precisely irretrievable outsideness, an un-crossable line, a position from which it is *obvious* (without argument) that the world is unknowable. What does "threaten" mean? Not that skepticism has in its possession a given place in which to confine and isolate us, but that it is a power that all who possess language possess and may desire: to dissociate oneself, excommunicate oneself from the community in whose agreement, mutual attunement, words exist. My work begins with philosophical defenses of the procedures of ordinary language philosophy,

of appeals to the ordinariness of our attunements in words as responses to the skeptical threat. (Cavell 1987: 29)

In a recent essay in the volume *Reconstructing Individualism,* Cavell carries forward his philosophical attack on skepticism in a discussion of Descartes and Emerson on the need to perform oneself linguistically into individuality, the challenge Othello has warded off as a threat. Cavell's verbs of individual performance include *subjecting, mastering, obeying,* and *deciding* the meaning of words that become expressive of human individuality. This kind of Emersonian self-reliant individualism is linked to a sublime theory of poetic language as being especially elevated and worthy of attention, so that individuality is not turned completely inward, like Othello's, where it would become tragic. But is the language of individuality necessarily sublime? Does it have to command, obey, submit, and create to become authentically itself? Is romantic poetry the only way out of tragic personal delusion? Although Cavell seems to be more in touch than Empson with the nature of tragic utterances, he is not necessarily advancing any better ethic of individualism. Empson makes *honest* a term of dense relevance to ordinary speech, (inadvertently) typical of a strain of misogyny within post-Elizabethan English literature. But Cavell, recognizing the tragedy of failed sexual intimacy between husband and wife, does not offer any better final outcome, since the horror of sexuality is made to serve as a reminder of an ongoing excommunication from a discourse of trust and mutual acknowledgment. Elsewhere in his essays on skepticism Cavell shows an interest in combining the language of Emerson with that of Freudian therapy. Will reading Freud make our lives any less tragic than will reading Shakespeare?

At the outset of this chapter I suggested that the determination of textuality is linked to the situating of oneself in a plural matrix of value and beliefs. I do not wish to conclude that the opposition between Cavell and Empson on the meaning of Shakespearean tragedy is a direct example of the situatedness I am trying to define in relation to a highly determined work of literature, like a tragedy. I do not think *Othello as a text* presents readers and viewers, specifically male ones, with a choice of becoming either a typically Iagoish personality or an Othello stretched between sublime superiority and pathetic inadequacy. I do think, however, that it is necessary to work through the sorts of arguments put forward by Cavell and Empson in order to clarify the relation between situatedness and the determination of a text of tragic language. Cavell and Empson limit each other's position, and marking that limit is actually closer to how I think tragic language, once it has been genuinely determined in a Shakespearean text, situates readers and viewers.

Empson and Cavell are equal in their efforts to respond to a language that is determinedly tragic. Their different approaches, either the normalization of tragedy as the advent of a new fabric of honest if not trustworthy communication or skeptical inversion and danger, recognize crucial elements of uncertainty and misalignment between very distinctly etched human figures on the Shakespearean stage. It is probable that elements of communicative uncertainty and wavering trust similar to the ones mapped by Shakespeare exist in everyday human communication in societies in which Shakespeare continues to be read. Perhaps Freud, if not Shakespeare, provides our current familiar vocabulary for acknowledging this probability. A pragmatist like Rorty might see the issues around tragedy as the last "ordinary vice" (Judith Shklar's term) of a liberal culture: our propensity to be cruel toward people we do not understand. My largest claim would be that in order to grasp the occurrence of these odd and harmful communications, it is better to follow the determinations of meaning and patterns of utterance of Cavell and Empson than the rather more generic vocabulary of hypergoods (Taylor) or public goods and private idiosyncrasies (Rorty). For if highly varied and plurally constituted human individuality is a feature of our modernist and postmodernist lives, then failures and dependencies of linguistic attunement and the ethical relations that accompany them will operate through a nongeneric, highly determined vocabulary. Perhaps that is one of the tasks that sophisticated feminist theorists are presently engaged in when they protest against pseudo-objective social science and monolithic definitions of personality structured along a simple binary axis of gender. In this chapter, Empson's and Cavell's different responses to an undercurrent of tragic communication between individuals indicate what an encounter with that sort of vocabulary might look like. To the extent that a concept like tragedy refers to a highly determined form of language, the work of Cavell and Empson remains of paramount importance. Neither gives the definitive reading of a Shakespeare play. Both keep alive a sense of tragic language as part of risks and failures of highly skeptical individuals who need to affirm contact with each other from time to time. A concern with tragic language may impinge rarely upon readers of literature. Certainly when it does, it is not because someone needs to theorize a concept of tragedy as an ontological feature or as the essence of modern society. That might just as easily turn tragedy into something banal, as I think Milan Kundera shows in a novel like *The Unbearable Lightness of Being*. I think that the highly determined responses of Empson and Cavell show that when tragic language does impinge upon readers of literature it will be related to moments when they are being asked to decide how much or how little of themselves is required to maintain trust and confidence. Probably it is not too much to say that such decisions will occur within a field of sexual discourse. To reenact these sorts of decisions, repeating what Empson and Cavell have re-enacted upon Shakespeare, is to follow a highly determined path of linguistic situatedness that cannot be put in abstract, universalist terms. In that sense it is the individual in the web of a certain language game, rather than what literary critics rather less precisely define as the concrete universal.

A canonical work of literature is not identical with a work of philosophy dedicated to the abstract articulation of a concept of situatedness. Shakespeare is not Hegel. Therefore to identify oneself in the name of an author like Shakespeare, as Cavell seems to have done, is to overextend the general significance of a linguistic insight into tragedy. That is why I continue to admire the precision of his insight into what drives tragedy, when it occurs, but feel uncomfortable with his return to the general issue of skepticism and the romantic language of the sublime as deep sources of individuation in our culture. Works of literature are idiosyncratic, as Rorty suggests, which means that they are very well suited to the task of exemplifying multiple connections between human agents, when they are critically appropriated and repeatedly determined by a plural readership. But, by the same token, equally important insights arise from other determinations of tragedy and sublimity and from authors like Hegel rather than Shakespeare. These determinations, found in the work of Stanley Fish on *Coriolanus* and of Jameson and de Man on, respectively, the textual properties of Hegelian expressivism and the Hegelian sublime, must be given their due.

7 Stanley Fish and Coriolanus: The Force of the Interpretive Community

The writings of Stanley Fish provide the clearest exposition of contemporary pragmatist thought in relation to the discipline of literary studies. Perhaps no other critic in North America has had a greater influence in replacing formalist theories of the text with a highly plural discourse about human agency and works of literature as they are circulated within "interpretive communities." In recent years Fish has extended his earlier antiformalist position by recasting the entire concept of a literary text in terms of pragmatist nonfoundationalism. At this point, Fish is the leading voice of the movement known as New Pragmatism.[1] His writing, unlike that of the other critics examined in this book, does not require preliminary contextualization in the vocabulary of nonfoundationalism. It rather assists my ability to use a pragmatic vocabulary to discuss other issues in contemporary literary theory. The following are some of the tenets of New Pragmatism that have replaced formalist discourse in the literary disciplines: theory *is* practice;

there is no text apart from collective acts of interpretation; there is no literal language that stands apart from actual linguistic usage; any use of language has a rhetorical aspect in that meaning cannot be separated from expressions of the personal values and beliefs of particular speakers.

Fish's antiformalist position on the use of language is comparable to Taylor's philosophy of language in at least one respect: the tenets of New Pragmatism cannot be followed as if they were abstract controlling principles for a theoretical discourse about literary texts. Rather, Fish's writings reach for perspicuous formulations of what constitutes actual practice. In their specification of interpretive practices, the New Pragmatists approach the concept of situatedness. Theoretical claims which attach to the description of a practice are occasioned only by the need to address objections put forward by foundationalist opponents of pragmatism. Fish shares with other theorists and philosophers grouped in this book the belief that finding oneself within a practice of interpretation turns foundationalist arguments about relativism or subjectivism into a nonissue. The force that maintains interpersonal agreement about verbal meaning or that prevents the arbitrary imposition of meaning is embedded in the very performance of the act of interpretation. At a higher level of practical insight, universalist and foundationalist assumptions and metatheoretical statements about literature in the abstract are dissolved in favor of local, contingent, communal norms that make up literary studies and, according to Fish, legal studies, social science, and historiography. The vocabulary of each practice may illuminate issues that arise within neighboring practices, but Fish would maintain the pragmatist's awareness of plurality and refuse any attempt to homogenize or hierarchize the vocabulary of different practices in relation to each other.

The energetic output of essays by Fish, Walter Benn Michaels, Steven Knapp, and Barbara Herrnstein Smith, supported by the philosophical writings of Richard Rorty, now serve as basic reference points within a complex network of institutionalized duties and procedures associated with literary studies, in new areas of multidisciplinary research, in definitions of original scholarship and interpretation, in the way qualifications and standards are changing within the university-based discipline of literary studies. Some of the energy that appears to have driven the emergence of New Pragmatism lay in the specific way it overturned the influence of the New Criticism. New Criticism built its pedagogy and view of language on poetic meanings and structures that seemed irreducible to propositions and referential statements. New Critics admitted that these poetic meanings and structures were not completely detached from ordinary usage and that they existed in tension with semantic reference. But their purpose in analyzing different degrees of semantic tension in poetry was to see how far poetic language could establish an autonomy or distance from a basic level of ordinary verbal meaning. Poetic tensions in meaning defined a semantic core which came about by words turning inward upon themselves, picking up resonances and polysemy from each other and thus coming into existence, autonomously, as "verbal icons" and "structures."[2]

Fish's break with New Criticism became decisive for contemporary interpretive practice because it avoided the inverse hypothesis that new critical word direction could be turned outward again, so as to regain literature's referential and social dimensions. Unlike Gerald Graff, who steps into the vicious circle of trying to reparaphrase what New Critics had ironized,[3] Fish radically questions whether any verbal categorizations stand in some temporarily unspecified remove from the social sphere of practices, norms, beliefs, and interpretive communities. That is not to say that reading literature is immediately equal to studying military history or analyzing the international flow of capital or raising ecological consciousness. Literary criticism does not join directly in social criticism or shape political events as soon as it abandons formalism. It is not even very clear to what extent contemporary novelists, poets, and dramatists shape such events, though they certainly may shape the vocabularies that are part of such events.

Antiformalism in Fish's writing is not a simple rejection of formalist tenets as being too indifferent to social change. A partly expressive view of agency is carried forward by New Pragmatism because it denies that language exists unless it has been intended or actualized by a speaker in order to communicate a meaning or perform a conventionalized task.[4] Literal versus metaphorical meaning is an untenable verbal distinction once the autonomy of any semantic context is put into question. Theory, as a set of independent principles or methods that would govern a separate sphere like practice, meets the same fate. When formalism is overturned, it cannot be because expressive agents have moved out into some broader social or political context; it is because *the actual practice of interpretation has grown stronger* in its ability to articulate the position of the speaking agent. Instead of calling for a committed criticism within the discipline of literary studies, in the manner of Graff, Fish tries to develop and extend the purview of the literary interpretive community by further "pragmatizing" Habermasian discourse theory or the peer-review process or the relation between gender issues and

institutional authority.[5] None of these would be seen as matters of special principles, foundational concepts, or issues of intrinsic merit or as governable from
some critical vantage point above or outside the immediate expressive forms
which constitute each evaluative discourse. Fish calls neutrality the fallacy of
"critical self-consciousness."

Once we find ourselves on the pragmatist pathway into Fish's works, new concerns and objections come into view, and this chapter will for the most part
address them. In part I of this book, I said that an attack on the notion of reflective
consciousness or self-consciousness was linked to the effort to situate human
agency. I argued that the concept of situatedness lies in determined expressions of
convictions and identity. According to Taylor, that determination is closely linked
to the *nonradical* formation of crucial decisions about enacting oneself in a plural
sphere of discourse in which perfect commensuration of values or objective criteria are no longer in play. I have been linking Taylor's account of the positioning of
an agent, in the decision making that constructs a language of contrast, to some of
the ways in which literary theorists situate readers and speakers by determining
linguistic contrasts of meaning as texts. How well does Fish's picture of an actively
interpreting human agent allow for the construction of a language of choice? How
does Fish determine a concept of textuality, granting that he knows this determination will not be given in terms like *formalism, subjectivism,* or *relativism*. In
asserting a link between multiple interpretive practices and communal norms as a
source of textual determination, does Fish also help to determine further what
sort of texts situate human agents? Is there an equivalent in New Pragmatism to
the expressive level found in the vocabulary of Taylorean hypergoods? or Cavellean skepticism?

   In asking these questions, I am trying not to beg them. Fish's writings occupy
a vital place in any nonfoundationalist effort to connect human agency, plural
convictions, and specific linguistic practices. But by now, it should be clear that
my approach to the particular insights and difficulties brought to light by each
critic is to measure the determination of textuality in relation to the determination
of situatedness. To proclaim them as one and the same thing, right from the outset,
impoverishes the process of textual determination, even if it is fair to say that the
fusion of textuality and situatedness is what is sought in the final analysis.

   Although Fish is an important exponent of one of this book's three philosophical pillars, his authority cannot be invoked with complete confidence be-

cause his actual determinations of texts do not immediately settle these questions. Fish's proclamations in the name of the New Pragmatism need to be balanced against his best determinations of certain forms of language as texts and his use of textually determined utterances as the scenes of coherent decision making. Fish does not need to be refuted, but the limits of his pragmatic discourse need to be carefully measured if we are to avoid what Callinicos calls "linguistic solipsism," the taking for granted of what one has set out to show. Fish's use of key terms like *agency, situation, performance, community,* and *text*[6] seem very strained at times, although they do serve to point literary criticism in the right direction. To the extent that New Pragmatism reinforces the critique of universalism and foundationalism, as in an essay like Fish's "Consequences" (*DWCN* 315–41), it keeps the focus on local, communally shared practices which steer the discourse about literature away from hierarchical or holistic reasoning. But the short-circuiting of the vocabulary of practice and an overestimation of the performative nature of communal language may inadvertently curtail the development of the agent's situatedness.

The negative knowledge that no gap for abstract theorization exists between rhetorical utterance and human agency may limit Fish's inquiry into the specific relation between a given literary text and the interpretive community. The limitation may be seen in the constricting formulations of interpretive practice that appear in Fish's writings once he begins to challenge the traditional interpretive vocabulary of critical consciousness or literature as representation or as mirror of society. Once we view the interpretive practice of literary studies as a direct entry into a wider field of linguistic articulations, we need to carry through all the way and develop the language that shapes and holds the expressive identity of agents in these various, sometimes conflicting collectives. Fish uses the concept of community and situatedness to dismiss the problem of relativism, arguing correctly that it is a problem only if an agent really could inhabit two radically different perspectives at once.[7] But he could be seen as relativist himself in the deeper sense discussed by Bernard Williams (see part I, 31–33): the dissolver of all conflict and difference between norms and expressions under a monolithic definition of communal practice.

How does an agent, in Fish's view, recognize the claim of, decide between, and contribute toward one interpretation or another? A multiple view of literary textuality makes it possible to pinpoint the source both of Fish's constrictive mode of expression and what is genuinely valuable in his presentation of the nonfoundationalist position. The remainder of this chapter is devoted to an elaboration of the value and the limits of Fish's work, but first I wish to call attention to a couple of the constrictive articulations that it is my aim to surpass. One of them appears in a recent essay by Fish in *Profession 89,* entitled "Being Interdisciplinary Is So Very Hard to Do." The essay is a version of the argument that Fish employs against relativism and formalism in that it attacks the whole idea of a human agent working in some unspecified linguistic space, here placed between disciplines. Being interdisciplinary, for Fish, is another illusion of detachment or neutrality which ceases to exist as soon as the agent speaks within an interpretive practice. The agent always must be seen to speak from a position within the norms of a particular discipline; when changes do occur, it is through the effort of one discipline colonizing or rhetorically usurping the vocabulary of another (as Fish also argues in his essay "Change," *DWCN* 141–60). But the whole idea of speaking with conviction instead of with reflective distance results in a peculiar loss of articulation. In the essay "Being Interdisciplinary," he writes,

> While some agents confine themselves to the horizons of a particular profession, others situate themselves in the wider horizons of a general cultural space and therefore manage to be at once committed and not committed to the labors they perform. It is the latter group that keeps faith with a higher vision by not forgetting "the forces and factors" that underlie and give point to local urgencies. . . . They remain aware of "the reader's and writer's immersion in a network of social forces that both grant and limit the possibility of intellectual authority" . . . and unlike their less enlightened brethren they resist the tendency of any "regime of truth" to deny its "constitutive dependence on what it excludes, dethrones, and replaces". . . . That is, they contrive to practice a particular craft without buying into the claims of that craft to be self-justifying and autonomous and without allowing the perspective of that craft to eclipse the other perspectives that would come into view were the craft's demands sufficiently relaxed.

The question is, as it was before, is this a possible mode of action? Again the answer is no, and for reasons that will become clear if we rephrase the question: can you simultaneously operate within a practice and be self-consciously in touch with the conditions that enable it? The answer could be yes only if you could achieve a reflective distance from those con-

ditions while still engaging in that practice; but once the conditions enabling the practice become the object of analytic attention (against the
background of still other conditions that are themselves unavailable to
conscious inspection), you are engaging in another practice (the practice of
reflecting on the conditions of a practice you are not now practicing), and
the practice you began to examine has been left behind, at least as something you are doing as opposed to something you are studying. Once you
turn, for example, from actually performing literary criticism to examining
the "network of forces and factors" that underlie the performance, literary
criticism is no longer what you are performing. (*Profession* 20)

The sound alone, if not the sense, of this quotation alerts us to the fact that
something has misfired in Fish's statement about practice. Assertive as the vocabulary of practice may be, there is something oddly inarticulate about it. What Fish
says about the impossibility of joining noncommitment and the experience of a
practice's claim upon the agent is true. But to develop the points about situation
and performance in the quotation, we would need to know how an agent contributes to the construction of choice between different, competing, or even antithetical practices. Otherwise, all we have is the negative knowledge that judgments are
never weighed with complete independence from our actions and utterances.
Contingent shifts of practices no doubt play a large role in the choice of which
author becomes the subject of an essay in literary criticism, which methods the
critic identifies with, which university's norms shape a critic's career development.
According to Rorty, giving up the search for epistemic foundations and justified
beliefs means committing oneself to the contingent nature of the interpretive
practice that becomes a source of personal identity and group solidarity. But I
would continue to question whether contingency and the radical negation of
theoretical reflection provide a sufficient vocabulary for sustaining a nonfoundationalist discourse about agency, conviction, situatedness, and expressiveness.
How does Fish locate the decisive moves within a network of interpretive practices that define the coherence of a speaker's identity? Without that coherence, the
word *practice* becomes just a synonym for the plurality of interests that already
abound in communities of skilled interpreters.

In contrast to Fish's picture of an agent embedded in practice, I refer to my
discussion in chapter 3 of the Taylorean account of agency, which argues against
the *incoherent* picture of agency as centered by the terms of a decision at the same

time as it "radically" drives the winning outcome. Rendering Fish's agent in more coherent terms would not mean a return to the foundationalism he rejects, but it also would not lead to the radical cancellation of different perspectives, incommensurable values, and the construction of choice in the very act of linguistic articulation. A notion of agency that is at work in each and every utterance, speech-act, rhetorical gesture, and response to a literary work presents a radical pragmatist model of multiple, discontinuous microagents bundled together within a minimalist definition of selfhood. Coherence must be found in the decision-making process which transects the public, private, moral, and institutional spaces an agent may partially inhabit and influence. If an utterance about the importance of a particular work of literature cannot be assessed objectively by pretending that it comes from outside an interpretive practice, neither can it be sustained and articulated if it stands in relation to nothing other.

Fish rarely examines the use of language to construct a decision. In an earlier essay on Milton, in which he coined the phrase "interpretive community," choice is elided in the very act of recognizing a position within the community: the only proof of membership in the community is "the nod of recognition from someone in the same community, someone who says to you what neither of us could ever prove to a third party: 'we know.' I say it to you now, knowing full well that you will agree with me (that is, understand) only if you already agree with me" (*Text* 173).[8] In many ways, Fish's earlier work in *Is There a Text in This Class?* shows his lack of articulation of choices that are constitutive of personhood and of an expressive language that sustains important choices in a deeply plural public sphere. In his recent *Doing What Comes Naturally,* Fish seems to take for granted the functioning of interpretive communities, and in particular, the "performative" language of force that sustains them. *Doing What Comes Naturally* sets out to correct the remaining foundationalist errors in a wide variety of academic interpretive practices and institutional norms. As I have already said, there is much value in that project. But the definition of a language that binds speakers within an interpretive community does not seem to have progressed much beyond his analysis of performative utterances first elaborated in *Is There a Text,* in particular in a pivotal essay titled "How To Do Things with Austin and Searle" (197–245). That essay, in turn, is based on a special type of interpretive contextualization of Shakespeare's *Coriolanus,* a play which exemplifies for Fish the exact performative procedures that determine acceptance by and exile from a community of speakers.

Like Empson and Cavell, Fish turns to a particular study of a Shakespearean tragedy because it seems to be determined by certain types of utterances that apply to a larger network of linguistic uses and meanings shared by all speakers to greater or lesser extents. And as Empson and Cavell see *Othello*, Fish sees *Coriolanus* as a complex pragmatic utterance that works and whose work must be reenacted by contemporary interpretive communities. That is what the play is about, to the extent that one can use the preposition without implying an immediate act of reference. The placement and displacement of Coriolanus within the Roman community obey the same linguistic forces that operate in any interpretive community. Therefore, Fish's essay is not a reading of the play, not a formalist or objectivist study of authorial meanings, but an analysis of its linguistic force, a specification of its key pragmatic utterances.

Fish differs from Empson and Cavell, however, in showing no interest in the fact that he is using a tragedy to map the nature of performative language. Although his use of the specific tragedy entitled *Coriolanus* is consistent with the nonfoundationalist approach of other philosophers and literary critics, his use is much more radical than Cavell or Empson's. The problem is not in using a work of literature to talk about issues of communal language. In many ways, direct use of literature is preferable to acts of interpretation that would justify themselves on the shaky grounds of method or propositional content. From a radically pragmatic perspective, using the text to illuminate something particular about the language of communities is the only issue worth debating. And it is extremely difficult to deny Fish this prerogative without tampering with the clarity of his nonfoundationalist approach.

Nevertheless, in narrowly determining the text of a Shakespearean tragedy to a point where *tragedy* ceases to have any meaning at all, Fish's pragmatism may be too radical to shed any light on the development of a language of situatedness. While the language of situatedness has no final or ultimate form which could be used as a fixed measure of the philosophical weight of radical pragmatism, we know from Taylor that problems of incoherent articulation are likely to arise from too radical an equation of personal language with community and choice. Does a text, as defined by Fish, *situate* interpreters in specific interpersonal language games? Or is *text* rather a veiled term for certain linguistic fiats which render a speaker's position an incoherent mixture of assertive force and inarticulate meaning? Fish relies on terms like *community, practice,* and *recognition* to account for the situatedness that is required for nonfoundationalist discourse. But his use of a

Shakespearean tragedy shows certain problems in his radical concept of textuality.

For Fish, the question of textuality is absorbed completely in the bounds of each interpretive community. Thus the tragic obstacles in the Shakespearean drama which Empson and Cavell locate in the failed reconciliation of the languages of individuality and community give way in Fish's analysis to the performative force of being inside or outside the language games of a community or a practice, but never between them. Therefore, at the exact moment Fish determines the central force of the play in Coriolanus's performative act of banishing all of Rome from himself, he portrays Coriolanus as the exemplary agent of all interpretive communities. But in belonging to a tragic hero outside the language of a community, Coriolanus's utterances lack a definition of situatedness.

As a small example of the radical overvaluation of performative utterances, leading up to the more complex case of *Coriolanus,* consider Fish's declaration at the conclusion of the "Consequences" essay: "Theory's day is dying; the hour is late; and the only thing left for a theorist to do is to say so, . . . and, I think, not a moment too soon" (341). As the *declaration* of the end of something that never properly existed in the first place, the force of this utterance does not rest on a refutation of some global concept of theory. But neither does it indicate anything deep about Stanley Fish's expressed beliefs about the profession. Fish's utterance is important and deserves serious discussion precisely because of the nature of its force. The declaration—"Theory is over now"—is certainly arbitrary, but it gains a good deal of illocutionary force, a nod of recognition and agreement, because it is a performative. If Fish were advising or urging or warning us to abandon theory, the force of the performative utterance would be weaker. Any one of these speech-possibilities is no less complex to define and evaluate, and discriminating their various forces is an equally important critical task, but they lead us away from the specification of the declarative form. Fish owes his confidence as a situated speaker to his faith in the most binding speech-act conventions, those with the force of a grammatical imperative. The socially defined conventions of certain speech-acts determine their illocutionary force. All the speaker must do is execute them properly, and this execution, as Fish (following Austin and Searle) has labored to demonstrate so often, is beyond personality.

Fish does not see his assertion of the end of theory as a fiat or as an appeal to his honesty as a commentator upon institutionalized practices; the authority of the utterance derives strictly from the imperative force that is invoked by a well-executed declaration. To declare that something is at an end and have the utterance make sense and take on force, the content of the declaration must be implicitly agreed upon in advance. The declaration sanctions the fact that the community has ceased to speak the vocabulary of "theory-as-detachment." As the speech-act theorists remind us, proof and compelling arguments have nothing to do with the objectivist search for what is independently true or false. There may not be any independent countervocabulary of theory. That is true enough. But what community are we bound to or do we recognize, in hearing Fish's utterance as a declaration? What takes the place of theoretical vocabularies? And what work do they do? If all the declaration does is remind us that we are embedded in conventions, why then do some have more force than others? As Taylor notes, by a radical account of choice all values and beliefs are equally incommensurable. Fish's presentation of radical choice in the language of performative utterances may be able to fend off the criticisms of subjectivism and relativism, but beyond that, radical choice remains a condition of "inarticulacy" (Taylor).

Radical choice and inarticulacy, I suggest, are exactly the outcome of Fish's speech-act analysis of *Coriolanus,* and by analogy the outcome of the radical pragmatist position. Fish's nonfoundationalist approach to the play does display a remarkable degree of textual awareness, however. As I said earlier, Fish avoids giving an arbitrary-sounding reading of the play. He does not appear to rewrite its language radically in terms of the interests of Marxist theorists of the play, like Brecht, for example, or of psychoanalytical critics who might interpret Coriolanus's behavior as narcissism. The strict and careful isolation of the performative moment in the play is an act of textual determination, for it locates a linguistic crux whose reenactment is the only possible source of the play's hold upon an infinite variety of interpretive communities. Fish links performance, textual insight, and community in the task of determining that linguistic-performative moment. In a narrow sense, Fish's limiting determination of that crux may have greater appeal to many readers as compared to the approach of Empson and Cavell, since it establishes a communally shared insight into the play's language without demanding an experience of tragic misattunement between individuals. By the standards of radical pragmatism, the critic has no business setting out essential values and experiences that define tragedy. If we are not going to talk in terms of foundations of interpretation, then the community must be allowed the greatest degree of freedom in adapting Shakespeare to a variety of interpretive interests. Thus Fish gives no account of the specific conflicts between plebeians and patricians, Romans and Volscians, or even, ironically enough, what drives the community to consume itself, the cannibalism Cavell elaborates in the play. But he does attempt to show a link between a text constituted around performative utterances and those utterances by which human agents are bound to communal linguistic practices. Whatever objections to Fish may arise, we should not allow the determination of a performative link between text and community to be broken. But if the link displays the incoherence that Taylor attaches to radical choice, then we must modify Fish's radicalism without giving up its best pragmatic features.

Critics' continual efforts to get past Fish by returning to the neutrality argument do not provide the sort of modification I am going to suggest. Criticisms of Fish made by Jonathan Culler, Robert Scholes, and William Ray all seem to miss the point of Fish's reliance upon Austin and Searle's account of speech-acts.[9] The intentionality of a forceful utterance, strictly speaking, is knowable only through conventional agreements and, as Austin has said, reports nothing deep about the subject's mind. Neither Austin nor Searle would base his insights into performatives on the muddled area of speculation about perlocutionary forces, the influence certain speech-acts might have after they have been successfully executed. Fish is faithful to Austin's insights when he focuses on linguistic force rather than on the structural properties of language and looks pragmatically at language to see what work it actually does to support everyday interpretive practices, without some deep revision of the theory of intentionality or signification as a consequence. That is perhaps the primary reason he dispenses with a Cavellean sort of inquiry into a tragic state of mind behind the language of a Shakespearean tragedy. But we must recall that Cavell is also a student of Austin and knows that limits are as important in ordinary language philosophy as precision. In avoiding arbitrary speculations on the meaning of tragedy in favor of specifying the play's performative force, Fish is very likely overextending the limits of one category of language. His failure is not a theoretical one about language in general, but rather a radical failure to accept the limits of his approach. This is where the slippage in Fish's position occurs.

Austin said that performative utterances brought to light a new set of questions: "What we need besides the old doctrine about meanings is a new doctrine about all the possible forces of utterances."[10] The status of the performative utterance outside the epistemology of linguistic reference was clear, but many of these forces remained ambiguous, except where the convention was fully defined, as in getting married, or where it derived from an explicit performative verb, for example, *command, urge,* or *apologize.* Fish seems to recognize Austin's point about speech forces, but he does not respect Austin's caution about their ambiguity. Austin thought he had revealed something in speech that epistemology had covered up, but he insisted that the grammar of his subject had barely begun and that only a few illocutionary forces were categorizable because only a few had achieved widespread social approval. Austin writes, "Social habits . . . may considerably affect the question of which performative verbs are evolved and which . . . are not" (245).

Fish's essay on *Coriolanus* takes as its immediate object the highest claim that could be attached to performative utterances in a world in which they never carried the slightest ambiguity. As a speech-act play, *Coriolanus* "is about what the theory is about, language and its power: the power to make the world rather than mirror it, to bring about states of affairs rather than report them, to constitute institutions rather than (or as well as) serve them" (244). As an allegory of the banishing of literary theory the play's fundamental speech-act, Coriolanus's "I banish you," becomes a crux for assessing the validity of Fish's particular brand of pragmatism. How can Fish attach so much clarity and importance to a speech-act that is fundamentally incoherent? Rather than solidify the norms of the community, Coriolanus's utterance has an inverted imperative force: it goes against the community, yet it invokes, as a command, the greatest degree of linguistic force. How can Fish tolerate such incoherence in an example that is supposed to be paradigmatic for the operation of interpretive communities? Illocutionary force, the power in language that Fish says is the only quality susceptible to common description, appears in the most unsituated context imaginable. So when Fish thinks that he can keep to the use of this force (now that he has brought it to the surface in all its purity) and drop the unnecessary baggage of literary theorizing henceforward, he is radicalizing beyond reasonable limits the significance of his discovery.

   In his attempt to clarify the unique force of Coriolanus's use of the performative verb *to banish,* Fish first isolates those speech-acts that Coriolanus successfully performs, all of which serve to maintain his proud independence from the plebeian community. He excels at refusing and promising because these mean being true to one's own word (see *Text* 211). But even the most minimal form of dependence or obligation discomforts him, no matter how transparently procedural in nature. Fish writes that Coriolanus's "language is (or tries to be) true not to publicly acknowledged realities but to the absolute values he bears in his breast" (206)—a doomed effort at independence. Coriolanus resists procedure because, Fish argues, he is fully aware of its powerful force, its capacity to give meaning to his actions and his language by the standards of a public sphere he rejects as unworthy of this personal merit. His belief that it might be possible to avoid public behavior and rest aloof on one's inner strength sets up his tragedy.

At first, Coriolanus resists the deliberate strategy of entrapment practiced by Sicinius and Brutus by trying to speak ambiguously. When approached by three citizens in act 2, scene 3, he is told that the ceremonial price of the consulship he properly deserves on his own merits is to ask it "kindly." And he does: "Kindly, sir, I pray, let me ha't." But "kindly," in true speech-act fashion, reports nothing about Coriolanus's psychological desire to become a consul, nor does it express his sense of personal desert (concerning which he always speaks of his wounds). As Fish says, the word means "both properly and in accordance with nature" (206). Which sense is Coriolanus using? As a polite formalism, "kindly" would be a trivial expression of the intention to request something, since there is no urgent force attached to the request. (Compare his reference to the old man in Corioles who once used him "kindly" and whose freedom he requests in the strongest possible terms from Cominius, a request so strong it approaches the "force of a command" as Fish notes, *Text* 207.) If in accordance with nature, then what is kind between Coriolanus and the plebeians is so general as to be innocuous. Because there is an ambiguous split here between the form of the request and its weak/strong force, the tragedy's prototheorists of interpretive communities, namely, Brutus and Sicinius, must specify with greater precision Coriolanus's obligation to the citizens, above and beyond what he may have promised his ambitious mother, Volumnia, who hungers for family honor via the success of her son. They stir up the citizens to an awareness that Coriolanus has used them scornfully, and they now seek to pin him down, via speech-act theory, to a verbal commitment whose authority cannot be evaded.

And Fish follows their path, seeking to specify the constitutive powers of all speech-acts and rescue this power from the theoretical abuses of Wolfgang Iser, Richard Ohmann, and even, ultimately, John Searle. For all these critics have failed to recognize that illocutionary force may not govern literary interpretations, that it is not literary theory but rather the fundamental prerequisite of all interpretive communities.

The process by which Coriolanus's independence is tested is inexorable. He cannot will a simple request from the plebeians, consequently becomes the center of the uneasy peace between the patricians and plebeians, and is then banished by the latter even as he fails to honor the former. Oddly, however, as absolute expression of his independence, he exclaims at the pitch of the controversy, "I banish you!"—which statement, Fish says, is outside the precincts of speech-act conventions yet somehow disruptively forceful as a function of the "kind of act banishing is." Coriolanus is outside institutional life because his exclamation is largely void in content (how can he banish everyone else?). The exclamation confirms the quest for complete independence in his behavior but also points out its social impossibility. If Coriolanus's utterance had linguistic force, the world would become completely relativistic. Fish says, "What Coriolanus does opens the way for anyone who feels constrained by the bonds of a society to declare a society of his own, to nominate his own conventions, to stipulate his own obligations" (216). Yet Coriolanus's utterance somehow manages to function like a declaration. If Coriolanus's utterance were entirely void he would be a solipsist, talking to himself, perhaps irrationally. His declaration irrevocably alters his ability to remain in his community. In effect he banishes himself, and his departure begins to expose the military and political weakness of the Roman state.

Declarations, according to Searle, "bring about some alteration in the status or condition of the referred to object . . . solely in virtue of the fact that the declaration has been successfully performed," and they always imply a special authority on the part of the speaker (quoted in *Text* 214). For Fish, this means that "declaratives create the conditions to which they refer . . . and testify to the power of language to constitute reality" (215). Coriolanus's act of counterbanishing demonstrates, for Fish, the fundamental, declarative, or constitutive, nature of all social institutions, not so much in its affirmation of an institution, but in its sheer, isolated force that makes possible all institutions in the first place. The double structure of declarative utterances—their linkage of reference to creation, first-person grammar to social stability—is operative in Coriolanus's utterance prior to any world he might imagine he fits. I quote Fish once more: "What brings about the state of affairs in which a declarative utterance is endowed with its intended force? The answer is, another declarative utterance, and it is an answer one would have to give no matter how far back the inquiry was pushed" (216).

Fish's location of a crucial, if ambiguous, declaration at the heart of the play's tragedy is a determination of what I would call textuality. The focus upon Coriolanus's declaration is by no means arbitrary, and the way it shapes the issue of communal acceptance and rejection, without invoking tragic affect and psychological intention, gives the declaration significance for different interpretive communities. Whatever interests may be brought to bear on this play, some account must be given of this special utterance because there is no text of the play without it. Nevertheless, Fish's own commentary on this crucial utterance is incoherent, and that is because it is too radical in extending the force of the declaration to all constitutive linguistic events. Coriolanus's act of banishing has real consequences but is impossible to normalize. It declares—and thus creates—a new, irrevocable situation but makes the alteration of a situation a matter of radical fiat. It brings to a climax the constraints of speech-acts but voids their relevance.

These moments of inarticulacy, which I have noted in Fish's comments on interdisciplinary research or on the word *text* itself, arise only as long as he insists on the purity of a performative utterance's force. But the concept of force is insufficient; it cannot explain away these contradictions and leaves Fish in the odd position of trying to maintain a theory of interpretive stability in the face of ever-more-radical pictures of changing events within the community.

It might be better to follow Austin, and Austin's student Stanley Cavell, and admit that some utterances must remain ambiguous in force, especially those in Shakespeare's *Coriolanus*.[11] *Banish* is a verb that expresses the force of an approved linguistic mechanism of exclusion, and Fish's effort to give it special constitutive force for any interpretive community extends its range beyond anything sanctioned by Austin or Searle. It is remarkable to compare Fish's essay on *Coriolanus* with Cavell's, because everywhere Fish finds greater determination of speech conventions Cavell finds deliberate ambiguity, loss of expression, Coriolanus's inability to articulate. His position is fundamentally "maddening" because every expression of the impossible desire for complete self-sufficiency is misconstrued by the public as an act of withholding participation. For Cavell the play is about the incompatibility of public and private meanings, which we have seen him place at the center of all Shakespearean tragedies. When Cavell encounters the odd moment of mutual banishment in the play, he sees nothing of performative interest about it. It is a merely formal articulation of the deeper failure the play is about, which concerns the characters' several skeptical fantasies about the production of words, "of the value they have when and as they occur." To refuse entirely a discussion of value is a refusal to "interpret our relation to this play, which means . . . to understand what a Shakespearean play is" (Cavell 156).

Such an act of interpretation does not fall into the vicious circle of substituting meaning for force or perlocutionary for illocutionary force. What makes Fish's and Cavell's interpretations of the same play unrecognizable to each other has more to do with the way each sees speakers entering and exiting the social sphere of speech, or entering and exiting a Shakespeare play. These acts of recognition do not depend on the (false) specification of a single analytical pathway, like the referential axis or the performative axis or the rhetorical axis, which would suggest that different interpretations might complement each other when put into the context of language as a whole. On the impossibility of that holism, or the context-neutral carving up of language, Cavell and Fish no doubt would agree. But what makes the play *tragic* in Cavell's view is the inversion of linguistic agency, the inner directedness of the characters' speech into fantasies, unintelligible expressions, self-consuming artifacts—all of which starves the community of dialogical contact:

> What preserves a tragedy, what creates the effect of a certain kind of drama, is the appropriation by an audience of this effect, our mutual incorporation of its words. . . . A performance is nothing without our participation in an audience; and this participation is up to each of us. . . .
>
> The play presents us with our need for one another's words by presenting withholding words, words that do not meet us halfway. It presents us with a famine of words. (168)

The performative layer of language upon which Fish rests his larger pragmatic claim for the functioning of interpretive communities elides the act of participation in favor of a radical picture of the already embodied, already situated speaker. For Fish, a famine of words might appear to be an odd metaphor but could never exist in principle. But the deeper issue raised by Cavell is the connection between participation in the community and the decision by which words are incorporated. I have treated some of the specific forms of decisive enactment in my discussions of Cavell and Taylor. I keep returning to Cavell because he reminds us that the majority of expressions in circulation will not be decisive or tragic, but that the agency that sustains one in the language *community* is formed around those special expressions and not on radically pragmatic mechanisms which render choice incoherent.

Earlier in this chapter, I suggested that, in using the concept of the interpretive community to disarm the threat of relativism, Fish perhaps unwittingly perpetuates relativism in a deeper form, as a course of action that is without any ethical direction. Jeffrey Stout describes this kind of relativism as follows: "You can produce any mapping of a text you please, even the most arbitrary, but you will not thereby have shown that *interpretation* is essentially arbitrary or radically indeterminate. You will have shown only that abstracting from interest and purpose altogether produces mappings that are good for nothing."[12] In radically equating interpretation with performative force, or at least letting anything go once there is a performative bond between speakers in place, Fish does what Stout describes: he maintains that interpretation can be anything, as long as it is a public product, but the product itself is curiously abstract in the end rather than deeply situated in an awareness of plural values and interests.

When Fish attaches the strongest force to declaratives he falls into an old fallacy described by C. L. Stevenson before the advent of Anglo-American speech-act theory.[13] Stevenson suggests that when we use the word *good,* we really mean "I approve this; do so as well." This was Stevenson's attempt to put morality on a sound pragmatic footing by emphasizing transactions between speakers rather than the existence of self-standing, intrinsic goods. So too, Fish declares that *text* is a meaningless literary term if we attempt to construe it foundationally, and that it really means "I approve this interpretation. Do so as well." We do so if we assume that the hidden imperative force works. But if we assume that it works radically, with the same degree of force each and every time, then we may find ourselves speaking like a Coriolanus, sure of our own meaning but completely unsituated in the public discourse around us. That is perhaps why Cavell attacked Stevenson's ethics as more modern skepticism, because all that made a statement ethical, from a grammatical perspective, is a reason for getting what we approve done by another person. As Cavell so aptly characterizes it, Stevenson is talking about the grammar of a statement's force without any sense of the person being addressed (see *The Claim of Reason* 284).

Stanley Fish's pragmatism is an important contribution to the development of a nonfoundationalist approach to literary studies. Many aspects of his antiformalist vocabulary for discussing literary texts have shifted attention to interpretive practice and the kind of linguistic situatedness that would answer concerns about relativism and subjectivism. But his pragmatism has a radical strain which needs to be resisted. I have argued that the most radical elements of his pragmatism may be found in his particular use of performative utterances to determine texts in relation to interpretive communities. That performative utterances constitute texts alongside communities of interpreters is open to question. The statement "Theory is dead" or "I banish all of you" means nothing without the radical fiat "approve my utterance." Once the radical edge is taken off linguistic fiats, it may be possible to preserve Fish's insights into the communal determination of texts without turning the plural interests of different communities into arbitrary interests in particular works of literature.

8 Fredric Jameson's Dialectical Semiotics

In the last chapters of this book I consider two critics who offer the most advanced and complex discussions of textuality in North American literary theory, Fredric Jameson and Paul de Man. In juxtaposing them in the final stage of my argument I do not intend to oppose Marxist literary criticism to deconstruction or discuss in general terms the issues which attach to each critic's school. The writings of these two critics bring to completion the project of this book in their own respective efforts to place large humanistic issues, usually derived from the tradition of European philosophy and social theory, into relation with a highly determined concept of a literary text. The textual determinacy of their writings, which might be fairly characterized as poststructuralist, surpasses that of the other philosophers and critics studied in this book but is not antithetical to the issues that arise from those critics and philosophers. Throughout this book I have been arguing that definitions of situatedness, agency, and conviction, which arise in humanistic philosophers like Taylor or Cavell, need to be put into a mutually modifying relation with the best insights into language that have been emerging from the literary disciplines. Jameson and de Man, to the extent that I am able to modify their remarkable determinations of textuality, assist the articulation of what situates agents.

Of course Jameson and de Man explicitly challenge numerous humanistic assumptions. Which means that in modifying the insights of these writers in the context of certain issues from the philosophy of language I must guard against completely distorting their respective positions. Marxists, by definition, assume that humanism cannot be dissociated from ideological illusions that arise from the historical conditions of late capitalist societies. Deconstructionists, and perhaps de Man in particular, seem to reduce the expressive capacity of language to a set of issues around epistemic error, aporia, and blind or arbitrary impositions of meaning upon the great works of Western literature. Impatience with this sort of approach is evident in Cavell's comments on de Man, which I discussed at the end of chapter 4 (though recent books of literary theory have attempted some sophisticated reconciliations of deconstruction with humanism).[1] Therefore in this chapter and the next, I shall attempt to deal with the issue of antihumanism first and then proceed to the quality of Jameson's and de Man's definitions of textuality, which I assert to be consistent with the best humanistic features of the philosophers and critics studied in the preceding chapters. The real issue for humanism is not to be found in essentialist or foundationalist pictures of human nature and selfhood but rather in highly determined vocabularies, such as may rise in textualist studies, which shape an agent's stance amidst a plurality of language games.

For Jameson, the issue of textual structure and determination is linked to the larger historical progression of *dialectical* analysis. With the possible exceptions of Bakhtin or Lukács, Marxist literary theory up to the time of French structuralism and poststructuralism has not looked to literature as a historical or political force. Instead, literature offers expressions of human aspiration or perhaps reflects ideological contractions, but at best it functions like a mirror of history rather than a motor principle. Jameson's writing combines a strong commitment to the fundamental principles of Marxist analysis with a mastery of the complex theories of literature which have evolved outside the Marxist tradition. The link between the two is found in a deeper articulation of the underlying dialectical nature of human history. Dialectical reason continues to evolve as social and historical conflicts become ever more layered and multiple. Its strength lies in the search for totality and universality of understanding among widely divergent groups, which cuts across national and cultural boundaries. In moving across cultures, it differs from Western liberalism by refusing forms of understanding which are uncritical or based in such assumptions of neutrality as tolerance, fairness, or legal rights. Liberalism is already too implicated in the contradictions and forms of oppression which have arisen in contemporary economic relations between nations and in their class structures. Just as dialectical reason continues to offer a challenge to liberal pluralism, cultural relativism, and liberal individualism, so it challenges any notions of literature as static utterances, idealized views of humanity, or aesthetic products which give pleasure and contemplative peace.

But how exactly does dialectical reason enter into and shape literary analysis? And once it does, what are the implications for theories of literature? Jameson's work answers these two questions, and it does so by finding dialectical principles at work in the actual structure and production of literary works. The dialectical approach is what gives Jameson's analysis both its precision and its characteristic eclecticism and search for ever-greater syntheses, between for example American New Criticism, medieval exegesis, postmodernism, and French poststructuralism. The dialectical moment occurs as a totalization of specifically laid out contractions and incommensurables at the core of influential works of literature or cultural sign-systems or writings about cultural organization and production.

Like Jameson, I have been arguing in favor of an approach to literature that combines a precise delineation of textual and linguistic structures with larger patterns of language use that bear upon issues in ethical situatedness, pragmatic pluralism, and the formation of interpretive communities. Jameson's writings examine contradictions, incommensurable values and meanings, and linguistic structures in works of literature and then situate the reader by positing dialectical syntheses which lead, eventually, to larger historical insights as the contradictions take on larger and more complex forms. Through dialectical analysis, literary texts unfold both large patterns of historical change and the narration of that change. Contradictions on the microlevel of textual analysis translate into the "political unconscious" of the reader and then into "totalizing" narratives of human history.

There are two basic differences between Jameson's approach and the one I am putting forward, however. First, the final emphasis on totalization and universality as the ultimate horizon of history is fundamentally at odds with the plural self which I describe in the writings of Harry Frankfurt and Richard Rorty. The emergence of a plural self capable of coherent functioning in discontinuous social contexts is part of the historical period I would characterize as postfoundational-ist. So there is a major philosophical difference between Jameson's Marxism and my pragmatism. Second, dialectical analysis challenges deconstruction not on the grounds of humanism or in its resistance to deconstructionist nihilism, but be-cause it yields an equally fine and precise determination of textual features and argues that these features can be used to map entire areas of social contradiction, symbolic production, and cultural value.

At this point, the normal procedure would be to compare and assess Marx-ism, deconstruction, and pragmatism in terms of their respective concepts of personal identity, social progress, ethical value, and so forth. But that sort of procedure is one of the things this book is trying to avoid. Instead, the real con-nection between textual determinations and the situating of human agents has to occur through particular acts of analysis and through detailed readings. On that level, Jameson is remarkably adaptable to the approach of this book, since his dialectics provide exactly that level of precision and detail in broaching the con-nection between specific textual cruces and larger philosophical generalizations. In this book, texts answer texts: Jameson's carefully wrought determination of textual structure has to be reworked from within if the dialectical approach is to be negated or modified. Toward that end, I shall trace and then deconstruct the key elements of a dialectical theory of textuality, beginning with Jameson's own acknowledged debt to the first synthesis of structuralist theory and Marxist phi-losophy, the writings of the French philosopher Louis Althusser.

The most significant and controversial developments of scientific or structuralist Marxist theory emerged in two works by Louis Althusser: *Pour Marx,* a collection of essays written between 1960 and 1965, and the first volume of *Lire le Capital.*[2] For Althusser, structuralism does not alter Marxism but, rather, provides the opportunity to reawaken the original spirit of Marx's later writings, especially *Capital,* which already contains and surpasses the structuralist attack on human-ism and empiricism. According to Althusser, Marx had to overcome the humanis-tic concerns of his earlier writings, such as *The Economic and Philosophical Manuscripts of 1844* and *The German Ideology,* in order to develop what was truly original and revolutionary about the scientific laws of production and their relation to cultural history. The fate of Althusserian Marxism in the last twenty-five years has been closely bound up with acceptance or rejection of Althusser's revisionary reading of *Capital* as setting the stage for a truly scientific understanding of the entire concept of production as the transformative law of all social activity, from the most material economic activity to the cultural practices of literature, law, and family life, which Althusser has dubbed the functions of the Ideological State Apparatus.

For Althusser, the Marxist concept of production contains the most revolutionary aspects of the entire theory. It defies analysis and understanding within the narrowly classical theories of economics, psychology, and epistemology which immediately preceded it and which it attempts to surpass completely. Althusser distinguishes Marx's contribution to the concept of production from the tradition of Hegelianism on the one side and from pure structuralism on the other. Hegelianism had already put forward the total mediation of the given world to the critical, ever-developing human subject. If production were synonymous with mediation, there would be nothing philosophically new in Marxism. Althusser's writings would fit into Marx's own characterization of his relation to Hegel as the inversion of dialectical idealism into dialectical materialism. But for Althusser, the difference between Hegel and Marx lies precisely in Marx's realization that the process of mediation could never be completed in the name of the human subject, that reality and subjectivity never reach a state of identity, as they are meant to in Hegelian logic. The forces of production perform the transformations of the world and its multiple articulations. Production is the underlying real base of culture, but it can be apprehended only through the filter of ideology. The burden of Marxist analysis, therefore, becomes the effort to *determine or specify with ever-greater precision the nature of productive activity without ever being able to put it into the terminology of appearances or conscious reflections.* That terminology would harken back to the earlier Hegelian phenomenological project. The forces of production generate *effects* within the organization, or a *Gliederung* (*Lire* 56) of society as a whole, in its institutions like the church, the legal system, and its aesthetic products. But these effects are not direct *results or expressions or appearances* of the same forces of production. In fact Althusser asserts that art, theology, literature, and family life need to be determined according to their own laws of production which are not governed by or identical to the production, in the ordinary sense, of goods and commodities. The inevitable gap between the real base of production and its ideologically inflected apprehension brings Althusser into proximity with the discourse of the structuralists.

Structuralism provides Althusser with a terminology for analyzing ideological and symbolic modes of apprehending production without having to resort to
the classical phenomenological lexicon. Without directly supporting the Marxist
concept of labor as radical transformative actions upon nature and our own
human identity, structuralism, from a strictly linguistic angle, puts into question
the link between *appearance* and meaning, subject/object epistemology with its
accompanying metaphors of mimetic or reflective representations of the world,
and the aesthetic terminology of formalism, organic unity, and the objectlike
stability of given works of literature. Althusser's work raises basic questions not
only about Marxism and literary analysis, but also about the value of literary
insights and readings in general as a form of critical theory. Will an extremely
sophisticated theory of production kill the revolutionary spirit of Marxism by
turning it into something like applied hermeneutics or semiotics? Or is a postclassical, posthumanist analysis of what determines things like literature and
ideology a means of giving Marxism a new lease on life, especially by taking it past
vulgar materialism and empiricism?

The answer to these questions takes on very specific rather than global formulations in Pierre Macherey, Althusser's disciple, and Jameson. Each writer has
understood very well the consequence of Althusser's critique of appearance and
reflective models of understanding. If production does not take on a straightforward ideological expression, then it must be determined through its *problématique* and its "mode symptomatique" (see *Lire* 24–25). The *problématique* poses
for critical analysis the inevitable gaps and absent explanations which indicate the
presence of an ideology. The quality of the determination of ideological presence,
which is never finalized, is what gives the method point and substance.

As an indisputably powerful determination of literary structures and symbolic meanings, Althusser's Marxism goes beyond the mere application of Marxist tenets to literary texts. Althusser's concept of production reshapes the terms of
inquiry into literature. For example, Macherey advocates an analysis of literature
based on structure, but one that cannot be mistaken for mere form or derived
from a special category of authorship: "The problem . . . is that of the structure
. . . from which the work derives, its determinateness. But the notion of structure
is misleading in so far as it pretends to show us . . . its intelligible image. . . . If we
are to make sense of the concept of structure it must be with the recognition that
structure is neither a property of the object nor a feature of its representation: the

work does not derive from the unity of an [authorial] intention which permeates it, nor from its conformity to an autonomous model."[3]

The link between structure and determinateness is all-important. Macherey bypasses all surface qualities of a literary work which could be confused with mere formalism. Structure is the final shape of a narrative or poem or tale which determines the ideological matrix of the author's culture. Labor, for Macherey, is the actual effort to reach a structure by wrestling with ideological material. Structure is not in any way external to the meaning of a literary work; it is immanent in the work itself and it cannot be related to the culture at large by the trope of structure as a mirror of reality. According to Macherey, Balzac does not mirror Paris; he fictionalizes Paris as a complex system of relations. The meaning of Parisian images is in the Balzacian labor of drawing connections, in the gaze and pursuit of objects out of which Balzac determines the conditions of city life. By contrast, when Lenin attempts to give a strict Marxist reading of Tolstoy's nostalgia for the peasant, he fails (see 105-35). Lenin's historical analysis of false class complicity between the aristocracy and the peasantry is not matched by an equal level of insight into Tolstoy's writings. Lenin continues to talk about Tolstoy's writings in terms of their reflections and expressions of contradictory social conditions. Their accuracy is set against a yardstick of true or false class consciousness. From that theoretical perspective, Tolstoy's ideology consists of falsely admiring the peasant from the perspective of the aristocrat. Macherey, however, looks for contradiction at the ground level of what determines the production of Tolstoy's narrative in the first place. The historical deficiencies of Tolstoy's novels arise from deficiencies within the ideological material that Tolstoy is working upon and shaping in determinate form for analysis. Macherey's approach takes us back to the detailed investigation of the silences, gaps, and absences within the structure of Tolstoy's writings.

Jameson's contribution to the school of Althusserian analysis is located in his most important theoretical work to date, *The Political Unconscious.*[4] Like Macherey's *Theory of Literary Production,* Jameson's book is constructed out of a lengthy theoretical first chapter followed by specific interpretations of different writers' ideological values (Balzac, Gissing, and Conrad). Jameson's theoretical chapter takes for granted the contribution of Althusser and Macherey to literary theory. It assumes a critique of "expressive totality" (or Hegelianism) and a method based on the specification of the literary text's ideological "symptoms" and "absences."

But at the same time Jameson adds a new dimension to the Marxist-structuralist project. Jameson takes Macherey's concept of structure and gives it a thoroughly dialectical treatment. He follows Macherey's approach to Balzac in looking for an ideological structure in literature rather than a direct relation of contradiction between author and social context. But the symptoms and structure undergo dynamic modification. Jameson maps contradictions and oppositions through different levels of textual organization, often in the form of Greimassian rectangles and allegorical levels of meaning. Almost any unit of textual meaning, from style to point of view to characterization, can be put into a dialectical process of constant transformation; and these transformations, in turn, become maps of contradictory but connected levels of ideology.

By finding a more dynamic principle at work in structuralist analysis, one richer in contradiction, Jameson attempts to link systematically sign and symbol, rhetoric and praxis, immanent critical interpretation of a literary work and the work's material, historical context. That means that the individual work of literature or the individual author cannot be seen as a synecdoche that illuminates the whole social fabric. But the individual work can be seen as a critical, dialectical shaping of the historical moment, or class consciousness, or as an image of social reality insofar as its own contradictions, gaps, and absences point to a truth about the human condition in history. Jameson's is a subtle and difficult project, one that has an important bearing on the issues which this book defines. He goes far beyond either a straightforward expressivism or a static form of structuralism. His dialectical analysis of literary texts seems to build up even further the situatedness of the human agent, in a way that parallels my own effort to take Taylor's language of contrast a step further.

Before getting down to the technical aspects of Jameson's argument, I would like to define a little better how the concept of universality fits into his theory of literature. Dominick LaCapra and Paul Smith note a strain in Jameson's utopian objective.[5] Smith speaks of holism in Jameson as well as of totality, which is Jameson's own term (and which acknowledges the continuing influence of Lukács upon him). Smith captures very well how some concept of totality is central to Jameson's Marxism:

> Fredric Jameson makes holistic claims for narrative when he suggests that narrative functions to anneal imaginarily the contradictions which any social totality suffers from and wishes to cover over.

. . . however, the logic that brings him to his consequent recommen-
dation—that we ought, then, in the interests of social change, always be
guided by a vision of such totality—seems strange. Social change of the
radical sort which Jameson champions is surely and sorely inhibited by
such a submission to dominant conceptualizations. . . .

Perhaps the best indication of the theoretical implications of his holistic stance is that he is led to posit that a utopian or holistic longing is as it
were natural to what he calls "humankind" and is thus to be found embedded in *any* ideological system. (91)

Smith's sensitivity to the topic of domination leads perhaps to a rather hasty
equation between social totality and oppression, one that Jameson would surely
reject out of hand. But Smith is right to probe the implications of totality for a
concept of embedded criticism. He finds that when Jameson takes up Lévi-
Strauss's analysis of Caduveo art among the native population of the Amazonian
rain forest, a specific analysis of forms of oppression is elided under a " 'full'
subjectivity (often with an underbelly of blocked awareness—what the social
scientists call unconsciousness) which it *presumes* and employs in the maintenance of juridical social relations" (93).[6] With the outcome of the dialectic known
in advance, a future utopian horizon or a posited unconsciousness of the past
serves as background for any contradictions in the surface phenomena of society.
The textual criticism that determines the place and content of the contradiction
does not seem to reach the human subject's "political unconscious" (Jameson).
Why does dialectical semiotics provide highly determined gaps of meaning only to
fill them with an unconscious plenitude of historical narrative in the minds of
individually oppressed human subjects?

LaCapra's treatment of Jameson expresses similar reservations, and he puts
them even more sharply than Smith:

Jameson never attempts to bring into focus the problems generated by the
fact that Marxism has two foci for presumably "totalizing" accounts of
history—one "ideologically" narrative and the other "scientifically" dialectical. But that there is a diacritical gap between these two processes is
crucial to his account and to some of the partially unexplored questions it
raises.

Indeed how precisely the gap is spanned but never closed by critical
thought that demystifies ideology and engages practice is never really ad-

dressed by Jameson . . . for he insists that a centrally totalizing hermeneutic subsumes other modes of interpretation. (239)

LaCapra's own commitment to the Marxist research program makes him sympathetic to Jameson's deep attachment to the principle of totalization. Nothing could be worse than the sacrifice of dialectics to narrow interests and deceptive particulars.

Having noted a fundamental problem in Jameson's blending of dialectics and unconsciousness, Smith and LaCapra stumble when it comes to the articulation of the dialectic. Smith answers Jameson with more individuality of political resistance; LaCapra tries to consider seriously textual "dislocations" in the manner of Jameson but feels uneasy about the possibility of indulging in a lot of technical phraseology at the expense of ordinary consciousness. Smith and LaCapra give general indications about the problem of totalizing all critical insights in the name of dialectics, but the gaps and difficulties they point to could never be resolved by being for or against totality *in principle*. The best way out and beyond these problems might be to specify, as sharply as possible, how dialectical reasoning comes to be imposed upon the features of language framed by structuralism. Dialectical semiotics is a powerful methodological ally of the Marxist critique of expressive totality because it is a method that need not resort to consciousness, phenomenological intuition, or collective experience and feeling to explain social contradiction. Jameson maintains a Marxist commitment to the infinite growth of the human being, to the language of desire and imagination, without necessarily putting that language into humanistic-sounding terms.

Jameson calls dialectical semiotics the final transformation. The shift from a logical system of meaning based on binary opposition to a moment of contradiction and negation recurs in Jameson's adaptation of A. J. Greimas's "semiotic rectangle" and the rectangle's own companion text, Lévi-Strauss's study of the social-sexual contradictions of the Caduveo Indians of the Rio Paraguayan basin. The cluster occurs first in his Marxist study of structuralism and Russian Formalism, entitled *The Prison-House of Language,* published in 1972, whose final page speaks of Greimas as the one leading the way toward a genuine structuralist hermeneutics. It occurs next in his influential study of narrative, *The Political Unconscious,* published in 1981, in which Greimas seems to have lost some value as an intellectual leader but in which his semiotic rectangle still establishes what

Jameson calls the "terms or nodal points implicit in the ideological system" unrealized in surface expressions:

> Appropriated, or perhaps indeed, misappropriated, by a dialectical criticism, Greimas' scheme, constructed by means of purely logical or analytical negations, by its very exhaustiveness opens a place for the practice of a more genuinely dialectical negation in the tension between the realized and the unrealized terms; what for Greimas is to be formulated as a structural homology between the various levels on which the semiotic rectangle reproduces itself, for us on the contrary becomes powerfully restructured into a relationship of tension between presence and absence. (48–49)

Last, in April 1987, the University of Minnesota Press published an English translation of Greimas's *Du Sens* with a foreword by Jameson. In the foreword, Jameson returns to the originality of Greimassian semiotics, which typifies the important contribution of semiotics as a whole within Marxist thought. This originality once again lies in semiotics' nonphenomenological approach to meaning. Jameson quotes Jean Petitot-Cocorda on this crucial point: in Greimas, "meaning is by definition nonobjectifiable. Meaning is not a phenomenon available to the senses. *Qua* meaning it is imperceptible" (ix). In this difficult and strenuously argued foreword, semiotics is sharply distanced from the epistemology of Marx, Hegel, and Heidegger, and from the "reification of words" in Wittgenstein. In each of these three texts on Greimas, the only comparable thinker as far as Jameson is concerned is Lévi-Strauss.[7]

   Once meaning cannot be causally or phenomenologically specified, the concept of ideology changes too. As in the *Prison-House* book and the *Political Unconscious,* the foreword to the translation immediately considers the way Greimassian semiotics puts ideology into a new dialectical perspective. Speaking of the Greimassian seme, the basic place of meaning, which can never reach full or stable definition, Jameson goes on to say, "This is why I have also felt that some enlarged version of the traditional concept of *ideology* (which plays only the most limited and mechanical role in Greimas's texts) might well be appealed to at this point, both as a way of specifying the nature of these semiotic analyses and operations and also as an occasion for evaluating them and suggesting their wider implications" (xiii).

   Jameson's joint references to Greimas and Lévi-Strauss, spread over fifteen years of intellectual development, define his effort to put ideology on new conceptual footing which rests on the priority of dialectics over semiotics. In 1972, Jameson recognizes that Greimas's fourfold structure of opposition and contradiction in the semiotic rectangle is a refinement" upon Lévi-Strauss's description of the Caduveo's body painting, already assumed to be some sort of adornment.[8] (In the original text of *Tristes Tropiques* Lévi-Strauss goes as far as treating the lines as a sexual stimulant, a makeup, confirming the erotic reputation of the Caduveo women.) The asymmetrical patterns with which the Caduveo women adorn the faces of their people is treated as an imaginative solution, on the level of the signifier, of some underlying sexual division within the culture. As mere surface, the body writing is unintelligible, mysterious, difficult to *perceive* coherently. But the intense organization of the signifier as such, the actual lines, axes, and curvilinear edges, begins to make sense as a resolution of social conflict, namely, the severe prohibitions against sexual contact between members of the different classes within Caduveo society. The social conflict becomes the signified of the independently organized signifiers. But much more than intelligibility is confirmed and made manifest. A new semiotics is simultaneously established. The old hypothesis that binary opposition between signifiers was necessary to the construction of cultural signifieds takes second place to this new discovery. To be sure, Lévi-Strauss strongly emphasizes the binarism of Caduveo culture: face painting for example is also the essential definition of human nobility in opposition to the world of beasts, unadorned creatures. And Lévi-Strauss has no trouble extending the axis of opposition: an abbreviated list would include figurative drawing and abstraction, angle and curve, geometry and arabesque, line and surface, border and motif, symmetry and asymmetry (see *Tristes Tropiques* 191).

From top to bottom, Lévi-Strauss sees binarism at work in Caduveo culture, except on the most essential level of man and woman, where a great divide exists that is very difficult to cross and that he does not find in the organization of the neighboring Bororo villages. The dialectical moment enters the discussion when Caduveo body writing goes beyond binarism. Here is Jameson's paraphrase: with Lévi-Strauss we "slip almost insensibly from the concept of the signifier as a series of binary oppositions to that for which the signifier is an attempt to *resolve* such oppositions, now thought of as contradictions" (*Prison-House* 161). Lévi-Strauss now begins to see, literally to visualize and imagine, the body writing as a dreamwork, a form of resolving contradiction, not an independent axis of signification in the service of the culture's pride, its nobility, its hierarchy, all of its supposed folly which he associates with the Aliceworld of Lewis Carroll. These lines deliberately drawn at asymmetrical angles across the human figure define a hierarchy of leisure, beauty, and art but also point to a desire and a dream for sexual union, which has been forbidden. And more than that: it is an unconscious dream made visible through semiotic analysis but still hidden from the Caduveo themselves.

If we follow Lévi-Strauss we progress in our insight into Caduveo culture because we see that surface opposition is only a mask for repressive contradiction. Jameson goes much further, however. He seizes this moment in Lévi-Strauss as the exact crossover point between mere opposition and dialectical contradiction. He immediately connects Lévi-Strauss's analysis with Greimas's rectangle precisely because the rectangle includes both opposition on the horizontal axis and contradiction on the vertical one.

In Greimas's classic essay "The Interaction of Semiotic Constraints," which expresses a debt to the work of Lévi-Strauss, a recognizable cultural norm, matrimony (or grammar for that matter), is defined against an opposite, or contrary, the prohibition against incest, and against a negative "below," something neither prohibited nor normal, for example female adultery.[9] Finally, to complete the rectangle, a fourth term is posited, which is the negative of the contrary: a relation neither forbidden nor abnormal, male adultery.

The use of the semiotic rectangle becomes serious when we are discussing ideology because Jameson deliberately pushes beyond the *virtual* status which Greimas had given it. Greimas writes, "The terms of the social model have no 'objective' content." If we apply the grid to England we find the space of prohibition includes homosexuality, but in the case of the Bororo, the sexually healthy neighbors of the Caduveo, homosexuality is in the same position as male adultery, neither prescribed nor prohibited, merely possible (94).

My point here is that the fourfold elaboration of the rectangle is no more than what Greimas claims it is, virtual, like the images coordinated in the lens of a telescope, which are not really there in the way a carving, a painting, or a piece of body writing is there. The virtual status of the rectangle is what puts it beyond intuition and beyond totalization, although it must be emphasized that the virtuality of the representation is assumed to be caused by a real existing referent in the social world. The values within the virtual image are relational, never fixed. It should in principle give access to the sort of ideological awareness Jameson thinks lies beyond reification or mechanical explanation. Caduveo art, for example, should not be read as a literal transcription of pain or pleasure, nor should it be reified into a proper solution to sexual conflict. At best, as Jameson repeatedly says, it offers a symbolic resolution (though as William Dowling has recently argued, the term *symbolic* remains uncomfortably ambiguous, somewhere between the imaginary and the real). But the way Jameson treats the joining of the axes of opposition and contradiction seems to conform to Lévi-Strauss's original emphasis on a dream state, a mental shift from motivated contradiction to apparent resolution.

Jameson's dialectical treatment of semiotic structure becomes entangled in the issue of human unconsciousness when he treats the points of negation on the lower level of Greimas's rectangle as if they were contradictions. But Greimas, and indeed his first English editor, Ronald Schleifer, are quite explicit about the *privative* nature of this level.[10] The lower level is not defined as being in conflict with the upper but only as the space of what the upper is not, as what is absent or outside the level of contraries. As Schleifer puts it, the first level sets up an opposition between things that are equipolent, nontransferable, like the grammatical opposition between the imperative and the subjunctive. But the lower level of negation is what falls outside the basic opposition, such as the interrogative or the indicative. These are defined not as contradictions of the imperative or subjunctive (which do contradict each other), but by the absence of the first contradiction.

I admit this leaves a lot to be explained. I am not setting out to cancel Jameson's dialectic by returning to some proper understanding of Greimas. All four terms of the rectangle must stand in some relation to each other, and specifying these relations is what gives Jameson's construction of a text for interpretation its remarkably high level of determination. But Jameson's invocation of a background structure which manifests itself in various ways, that hovers between presence and absence, or that makes absence itself, the very category of the Greimassian privative, a reciprocal partner of presence, complicates and confuses the *virtual* status of the rectangle. To give Greimas's own example, much of the time that we are using the rectangle, we are dealing not with green lights or red lights, but with yellow lights: noninterdictions and nonprescriptions in our cultural codes of behavior. Jameson's dialectical transformation of the semiotic rectangle treats absence as repression, reciprocity as contradiction, and the virtual as a hidden clue to the actual when we cannot be entirely sure that we have the right actual there in the first place.

Jameson's repeated appropriation of Greimas in Marxist studies of literature and historiography neglects to consider the virtual status of symbols of ideological conflict. In *The Political Unconscious,* Jameson calls the Greimassian rect-angle a symbol or a graph—a very interesting error in my opinion. As symbol, the semiotic rectangle is merely thought but at least political thought because it deals with contradictions. Jameson is not sure Greimas can explain history or describe the world but at least he gives one moment of cognition, and as this moment dissolves into a narrative impulse it helps us think the possibility of change from within what Jameson calls our "ideological closure." Exactly the same point is made in the foreword to the new English translation. Filling in the square is simultaneously a cognitive act, a making visible, of absent causes, and by its very transitory nature a narrative moment in the unfolding of history. So, in effect, the complexities of virtual representation, so essential to rethinking our definition of ideology, are intertwined with a highly phenomenological vocabulary of symp-toms, brackets, visibilities, cultural texts, which the Althusserians set out to elimi-nate from critical theory with the help of poststructuralism.

The question then arises, What exactly is being determined by the logic of virtual representation? If we grant Jameson the ability to determine textual struc-tures to a very high level of specificity by adapting semiotics to a multiplicity of linguistic transformations, including the transformation of grammatical struc-tures into symbols of the human unconscious, what is being pointed to by the capturing of these transformations? My question sounds perhaps rather too Al-thusserian. But the answer I will offer unfolds the final arguments of this book. If the unconscious elements of Jameson's dialectic can be detached from his dialecti-cal transformation of textual principles, then perhaps we can talk more easily about what can be grasped and illuminated by Jameson's dialectic, without feeling that we are constantly being pointed back into unrealizable depths. The assump-tion of a totalized pattern of unconscious symbolism, which troubles humanists and fellow Marxists alike, may have more to do with the problems of *virtual representation* and how Jameson uses it than with the political and psycho-logical oppression of humankind. This question cannot be asked pragmatically. Undergoing the determination of the problem is part of the task of seeing its rele-vance to expressive language. In Jameson's case, determinations of dialectical textuality lead us back not to pragmatism but rather into the topic of deconstruc-tion.

When my reading of Jameson sent me back to look at the Lévi-Strauss text about the Caduveo I was quite amazed at its tone and authority. It struck me as a fantasy.

Here is a narrator, Lévi-Strauss, both exhausted and exhilarated by his difficult journey to Porto Esperança, experimenting with native foods and the ritual drinking of *mate* en route, encountering miniature colonialist economics at outward trading posts, where daily labor is bartered for sweets and alcohol in the evening. The ideological tone of a distaste for colonialism is clear until Lévi-Strauss arrives at Nalike and the Caduveo communities. Lévi-Strauss can no longer participate in or understand native peoples' social life. These natives are too arrogant, secretive, full of proud myths of their divine origin. In short, they are decadent aristocrats, lost in time, fixated by a slave economy, unable to procreate comfortably, and unwilling to raise infants, whom they often murder.

Lévi-Strauss's text raises a lot of suspicions. Has Lévi-Strauss cracked an ideological code previously kept secret by these natives or has he completely "transcoded" them in privileged epistemic terms, terms that reconcile sexuality and culture, meaning and appearance, decadence and hierarchy as if they were characters in a romantic novel? The ideological closure which is either being imposed or revealed by the Caduveo is at its most ambiguous in the body writing itself, the structuralist's key that will totally explain the history and meaning of this culture. As in this quotation from *Tristes Tropiques*:

> In the last resort the graphic art of the Caduveo women is to be interpreted, and its mysterious appeal and seemingly gratuitous complexity to be explained, as the phantasm of a society ardently and insatiably seeking a means of expressing symbolically the institutions it might have, if its interests and superstitions did not stand in the way. In this charming civilization, the female beauties trace the outlines of the collective dream with their make-up; their patterns are hieroglyphics describing an inaccessible golden age, which they extol in their ornamentation, since they have no code in which to express it, and whose mysteries they disclose as they reveal their nudity. (197)

The claim to perfect knowledge here is intertwined with a thoroughly aesthetic attraction toward these women. The trace, the hieroglyph, and the meaningless pattern are effaced under the beauty of the exposure, an exposure that is tactile and epistemological; and thoroughly and bizarrely ideological. The ideology *is* the aesthetic, the textual (and sexual) transformation of graph, line, signifier into symbol, mystery, and affect.

Strange as it may sound, the transformation this particular Caduveo woman undergoes is the same that Greimas's rectangle undergoes in Jameson's dialectic. What I am calling ideology in this charming conclusion to an analytical narrative is not an overt empirical distortion of the truth, not a stereotype; nor is it a mere projection of desire onto this particular Caduveo woman; it is not reification. It is perhaps something much more difficult to determine in the text of Lévi-Strauss's written words: the immediate substitution of the aesthetic for the linguistic, the polarity of manifest/hidden for the materiality of the signifier and *virtual* status of the trace.

This concluding glimpse of the Caduveo woman, yielding up unconsciously the coded secrets of her doomed tribe under the gaze of the anthropologist, has become a notorious fragment of modern structuralist theory. Feminist critics, among them Gayle Rubin and Christine Brooke-Rose, have been offended at the blatant gender-bias in Lévi-Strauss's account of this supposedly asexual lost culture.[11] The feminist rejection of woman as a semiotic object specifically protests against the mystery of the affect. Would this tribesperson, standing in opposition to the Western, male, knowing anthropologist be quite so mysterious in her symbolic decoration if she were not such an ignorant beauty? How far does the semiotic principle of reciprocal meaning extend? asks Christine Brook-Rose. Could man and woman, as axes of signification, exchange places in this moment of symbolic insight? The objection to an unconscious meaning that is being sharply determined by the method of dialectical semiotics, be it Lévi-Strauss joined to Marx, Greimas to Jameson, or Marcel Mauss to Gayle Rubin, lies in the continuing assumption that the material inscription on the surface of that woman's body is a virtual image of a cultural paradigm of some sort.

Only Jacques Derrida, to my knowledge, has offered a criticism of structuralist-Marxism based on the fact that those decorative reliefs traced upon the Brazilian natives are not virtual at all, but are as material in nature as writing can be. I will not trace in detail his attack on the ideology of the natural man living in an oral culture as it developed in *The Grammatology*. Instead, I return to Jameson's comments on Derrida in the *Prison-House*, where Derrida is criticized, from the perspective of Lévi-Strauss and Greimas, apparently for overestimating the material argument about writing, specifically, of all places, in his essay on Freud's figuration of unconsciousness as a writing machine. This takes us back to 1972 again. But as far as I know, Jameson's evaluation of the rather limited role deconstruction has to play in relation to dialectical criticism has not changed up to this writing. For Jameson, at first glance, Derrida's reading of Freud's essay on the Mystic Writing Pad leaves a place "open for Marxism" (*Prison-House* 177), primarily because the oblique tracing of consciousness upon the virtual surface of the unconscious harmonizes with the general attack on reification and with the establishment of a dynamic process of change and transformation. To this extent, Jameson welcomes Derrida as a member of the Tel Quel group of the early sixties. But as we read on, it becomes clearer and clearer that Derrida's affinity with the Left can be stated only in thematic terms: as a challenge to authority as the Absolute Signified, against hierarchy, authority, monopoly, and so forth. Libido, money, language; or, gold, the phallus, the father—all these terms crowd in upon each other in one analogical sweep of deadly, cultural symptoms. There is certainly none of the technically refined exposition such as we find in Jameson's discussion of Greimas, but the praise is sincere up to a point, since we are told that Derrida does indeed have a political ethic, which may be summarized as a "struggle against" forms of hypostatization. Soon, however, Derrida is left behind because he seems to fall into his own form of reified consciousness by giving written language priority over all other cultural, economic, and sexual practices.

I am following Jameson's assortment of terms very closely here because each does indeed stand for a Freudian category brought into relation with writing in Derrida's essay. But at the same time, Derrida attempts to downplay another set of psychoanalytical terms which are never put into question by Jameson: symptom, unconscious, symbolic, or hidden meaning—all the terms that govern the ideology of a culture and therefore are the total object of dialectical semiotics. As one reads Derrida's meticulous analysis of the necessity of writing to the elaboration of the doctrine of the Freudian unconscious, it becomes clear that the emergence of writing, *in its most material aspect,* is not at all easy to grasp.[12] Unlike the Caduveo woman covered in script, who becomes the object of competing ideological theories, the emergence of writing as a physical constituent in Freud's work is "irreducibly graphic," never easily translated into pleasure, pain, repression, or consciousness. Freud does not choose to represent the unconscious metaphorically as writing, any more than Derrida just chooses to make writing more important than metaphors about gold in the analysis of culture. Derrida follows Freud, prior to assessing his ideological worth, and the result is not to strengthen the link among unconsciousness, symptomatic behavior, and repression, but to discover each as function of the Freudian text. As Derrida puts it,

We shall let our reading [of Freud] be guided by this metaphoric investment [which makes the name of writing enigmatic]. Psychical *content* will
be *represented* by a text whose essence is irreducibly graphic. . . . We shall
not have to ask if a writing apparatus . . . is a *good* metaphor for repre-
senting the working of the psyche, but rather what apparatus we must
create in order to represent psychical writing. . . . Finally, what must be
the relationship between psyche, writing, and spacing for such a metaphoric transition to be possible, not only, nor primarily, within theoretical
discourse, but within the history of psyche, text, and technology?" (199)

From Freud's *Project for a Scientific Psychology,* through the *Interpretation
of Dreams,* and finally in the essay on the *Mystic Writing Pad,* writing imposes
itself as the only solution to the problem of elaborating memory as both infinitely
renewable to fresh sensation and fixed as a structure of recollection; to the problem of deciphering the dream work in a way that would not exhaust itself into
absurd pictograms if merely representations of thoughts; to the problem of stor-
age, information retrieval, and a screen against excessive stimulation. In each
case, memory inscriptions, neural pathways, instinctual drives simply cannot be
elaborated without a spatial structuring based on distinctions such as marked/
unmarked; spatial closeness or distance; nonmimetic, grammatical patterns more
akin to the hieroglyph than to the arbitrariness of the signifier.

I have been describing the characteristics of script, of writing, what philolo-
gists or codicologists are more likely to recognize than aestheticians or literary
historians. The hierarchy of levels or stages that Freud goes on to hypothesize is,
once again, virtual and metaphorical, but this is now a by-product of the original
graphic elements in the theory, not the other way round, as in the work of Jameson, Greimas, and Lévi-Strauss. Everything that Derrida writes on the subject of
our unconscious, the space that must be ever-restructured and then dissolved, that
makes psyche and text one productive act, goes against meaning as the product of
intuition. Perhaps from the perspective of ideology that is a good thing. Derrida
invokes allegorical images from Scripture in order to indicate the material status
of script within the history of culture: the parched woman drinking the inky dust
of the law (Numbers); the Son of man who fills his entrails with the scroll of the
law, which has become as sweet as honey in his mouth (Ezekiel). Compared to the
Caduveo woman decorated with writing, these scriptural enigmas cannot be
traced to some political unconscious. In fact they use the materiality of writing in a

particularly antiaesthetic way. They "write" the body as something quite literally written, broken up, spaced, graphically organized with no immediate suggestion that this is some repressed disfiguration of the body proper.

Derrida's counterreading of the relation between writing and unconsciousness, in the most literal terms possible, breaks Jameson's dialectical semiotics. It demonstrates that writing as a material form of language is not automatically in the service of a politically repressed unconsciousness. In fact it questions the resort to aesthetic features of language as a means of giving priority to the unconsciousness. But does the materiality of writing even deserve philosophical consideration? and how could it possibly be seen as a vehicle of a critical consciousness? Certainly as an absolute, the material properties of writing provide no answer to these questions. All that I would claim for Derrida's essay is a further determination of textuality.

The depth of the determination, which has been largely absent thus far in the philosophers I have examined, still requires a link to situatedness and human agency. Jameson's consideration of linguistic structure, history, and subjective totality gives a rough indication of how a highly determined concept of a text may be used to determine further crucial relationships between these very large, typically undetermined concepts. But in failing to analyze the material as opposed to the symbolic or virtual status of a text, in the final dialectical transformation of its internal structure, he finds himself positing unconscious meanings. To carry this sort of discussion about texts forward into a discourse of situatedness, we need to turn to deconstruction and the work of Paul de Man.

9 Paul de Man on the Hegelian Sublime

In previous chapters I have analyzed different concepts of language as they define the situatedness of human agents in a nonfoundationalist society. As the language of situatedness comes into focus, starting with the works of Taylor and Cavell, on through nonfoundationalist and poststructuralist literary theorists, I have called attention to the way basic concepts of language become highly determined by theories of textuality. Taylor's language of qualitative contrasts appears in retrospect to be an outline, a first orientation, into deeply situated expressions of human agency. Literary theorists do not necessarily see themselves making direct contributions to theories of human agency, but by connecting their distinctive discourse about textuality with philosophers' interest in expressivist forms of language, our entire grasp upon what matters about textual discourse is strengthened. Philosophical discourse also gains more refined insights into the highly expressive forms of language which it values in the name of symbolism and aesthetics.

The fusion of these different insights into one perfect synthesis is not possible, and to attempt such a synthesis in fact would be contrary to the arguments about pluralism put forward in this book. The function of a concept of textuality is to determine linguistic cruces which are comparable to moments of Taylorean choice. As I suggest in chapter 5, the actual task of determining these cruces is what leads to a determination of situatedness. But the whole point of situatedness, as a philosophical approach to personhood and literature, is to provide critical coherence and definition without relying upon universal principles or holistic assumptions. Pragmatically, universalist principles and holistic assumptions seem inadequate for coping with the plural interests and communities which inhabit the same public sphere. In turning, finally, to deconstruction and Paul de Man, my aim is to present the most highly determined theory of textuality thus far developed in the literary disciplines as the final instance of situatedness. But that does not mean that deconstruction englobes every other issue or that it cancels the writings of the philosophers who come before. Just the opposite. If determinacy is where we are led by discussions about nonholistic choice, plurality and incommensurability of values, and nonpropositional, nonparaphrastic uses of works of literature, then deconstruction is a name for the process of undergoing that sort of determination. In this book, the term *deconstruction* has no abstract meaning as the sheer negation of humanism. Its impact on the discourse of the social sciences and humanities is not global. But clearly it does not fit smoothly into certain specific humanistic assumptions, and it tends to meet the greatest resistance from critics who would identify themselves under the rubric of humanism.

Much of my effort in this book has gone into steering the connection, or apparent disconnection, between deconstruction and the philosophy of language away from broad and inaccurate assumptions about ontology, nihilism, relativism, and much of what the pragmatists would see as topics which have outlived their usefulness. In the case of de Man, I offer the most detailed textual analysis to be found in this book and attempt to draw out of de Man's approach the sort of language, agency, and situatedness which deconstruction contributes to my larger pattern of inquiry. That is not to say that de Man completes the inquiry in its final form, but only that his insights are as necessary as those of a Rorty or a Taylor or a Cavell. Further refinements are possible, and it is my hope that this book will set some of them in motion. I have chosen to focus this chapter on de Man's reading of Hegel for several reasons. First of all, de Man's essay on the Hegelian sublime completes an analysis of issues raised by Jameson's dialectic. We have seen that dialectical determinations of textuality are not easily reconciled with some of the best features of poststructuralist linguistic theory. Dialectical oppositions and inversions of meaning cannot be disentangled from aesthetic and phenomenological vocabularies, with the possible consequence that textuality once again becomes mysteriously symbolic and indeterminately unconscious. De Man's last essays are particularly concerned with disentangling these issues of language and aesthetics, and he aptly traces them back to their canonical source in the Hegelian dialectic and Hegel's writings on aesthetics.

As the canonical authority not only on the topic of aesthetics and critical theory but also on Taylorean situatedness, Hegel occupies a position of central importance. The way in which de Man takes up and analyzes issues arising from Hegel allows me to specify the limits and insights of deconstruction in the larger philosophical context of situatedness and language. De Man looks for a very specific determination of textuality in the Hegelian corpus rather than in Hegel's formulations about history, humanity, aesthetics, telos, and so forth. That very specific determination does not negate, refute, or diminish the canonical status of Hegel in any way. Perhaps it even could be seen to reestablish the canonical importance of Hegel, though I recognize that philosophers in the Hegelian tradition tend to find deconstruction very foreign to their concerns. The determination of a textual pattern within the Hegelian corpus is what is unique to deconstruction. Once I follow de Man's actual determination of that pattern, I will be able to comment on how it newly situates readers of Hegel in the context of nonfoundationalist and pluralist philosophies of language. Rather than assert a radical, revisionary appropriation of Hegelianism to the "nihilist" interests of deconstruction, I will assert a final blending of the insights of Taylor and de Man.

First, however, I must begin, as I did with Jameson, with a discussion of the issue of antihumanism. Crossing that bridge opens a consideration of what is properly textual in de Man's limited but crucial analysis of the Hegelian sublime.

In a recently published essay, Neil Hertz carefully defines one of the "characteristically unsettling" aspects of Paul de Man's writings: "his particular way of combining analysis and pathos, of blending technical operations of rhetoric . . . with language . . . whose recurrent figures are strongly marked."[1] There always seem to have been two de Manian voices in his deconstructionist writings, in the chronological sense of everything published after but including the essay on Derrida in *Blindness and Insight* (1st edition, 1971). One voice is dry and restrained to a degree that barely sustains its own forward discursive movement; the other bold and excited, on the verge of ever-more-powerful insights into the influence of figural language upon all human discourse, in philosophy, political theory, and ethics as well as literature. There is added pathos in the apparent lack of connection between these two voices. We can see the power of figural language but never hope to master it.

The pathos of de Man's writing deserves to be considered in detail as a first instance of the issue of humanism which it raises. Hertz rightly calls de Manian pathos idiosyncratic, since de Man uses the term *pathos* to define the whole category of rhetoric within language, but only if it can be purged of any affective overtones with regard to the human subject. Over and over, de Man's essays articulate a peculiar combination of surgically accurate linguistic analysis and human critical failure. The rhetorical contradictions and discontinuities in the meanings in many canonical Western texts (by Rousseau, Kant, Hegel, Wordsworth, and Proust) are strangely at odds with the sense that they are finally inconsequential, forgotten once we return to questions of immediate humanistic relevance. The rhetorical analysis claims to be truthful about language in general, but it suggests no concrete changes in discursive action. Where is the rhetorical force going? Does it just disappear back into a realm we have no other current word for except the *textual*? There certainly is a strong element of pathos in the very nature of deconstructionist argumentation. De Man recognizes a gap between the clearest, driest analytical formulation and its negative implications with regard to our whole sense of articulate being. The gap is rich in pathos, a combination of strongly achieved understanding and unmanageable human expression. Must deconstruction give up the *critical* features of Marxist and hermeneutical theory: human agency, decision making, and political empowerment?

To take one example: why does de Man object to the use of aesthetic terminology in the philosophy of language and in literary theory? *Aesthetics* is not a monolithic term of course. Traditionally valued as a pleasing articulation of an epistemologically stark conceptual order, and in its recent romantic phase as an expression of human autonomy, it is now perhaps looked upon, as in Jameson's writings, as a symptomatic expression of underlying social contradictions. But whether it is Schiller's aesthetics or Adorno's, Terry Eagleton's Marxism or

Christopher Norris's deconstructionism,[2] few would be prepared to follow de Man's complete reduction of aesthetic expression to the dryly rhetorical tropes of personification, parabasis, or prosopopeia, terms which are used to replace such human aesthetic faculties as imagination. Is the de Manian pathos that accompanies these figures a sign of critical weakness or strength? Is it implausibly wrapped up in the dreariest analytical language and irony or is it redefining the very terms of human expression in ways that should be further developed by contemporary philosophies of language? Most of the commentary on deconstruction favors the first option.

Two recent essays by Martin Jay serve as an economical illustration of where de Manian deconstruction seems to rest at the moment.[3] Jay is a tolerant critic of deconstruction. He wants to examine whether its contributions to the study of rhetoric are having an impact upon broader sociopolitical questions, for example, the legitimation of power in the *naming* of secular authorities like Marx or Freud or the shift from "ocularcentric" definitions of ideology (as a reflection or mirror of social contradictions) to linguistic definitions (which would treat the whole category of mimesis and representation as only one tropic possibility among many others). If deconstruction can be said to alter our basic understanding of authorship, citation, and specular models of knowledge, then its implications for the study of legitimation are very great. At least as a first step, Jay is willing to allow deconstruction its rather dehumanized picture of linguistic articulation on the grounds that its pathos may uncover a struggle for power and legitimacy hidden by the aesthetic ideology of mimesis, the phenomenality of meaning, and the trope of the mirror of the mind. Rather than return to a new, materialist aesthetics as an antidote to the deconstructionist reduction of human expression, Jay tries to work through some of the strictly linguistic arguments about apostrophe and personification to see if they support a critical investigation of the social construction of authority. That would give pathos a very different analytical edge.

Not surprisingly, Jay's essays argue the insufficiency of tropes as a primary medium of political criticism (while allowing for a politics of language along Habermasian lines). Nevertheless, his arguments focus our attention on some of deconstruction's strongest claims and on what continues to provoke the strongest resistance to it. On the positive side, deconstruction is important because it really does break with the "ocularcentric notion" of ideology as a "reversed and inverted" image of the underlying modes of production, which prevails even in Althusserian and recent Marxist-Freudian critiques like Jameson's:

> For [de Manian] deconstruction, the major mystifying ideologies of West-
> ern culture are the occlusion of the rhetorical moment in philosophy and
> science, the mistaken conflation of linguistic reference with the reality of
> an external object, the hypostatization of such categories as the Aesthetic
> or the Literary, the smoothing over of the mechanics of literariness in ev-
> ery text. ("Ideology and Ocularcentrism," MS 9)

Deconstruction's particular attention to the presence of tropological structures
pushes critical analysis well beyond the dialectical use of binary oppositions,
whether they be conceived hierarchically or through inversion. If the claim to
authority and value is structured more like a trope than a mirror, if it should be
separated altogether from symptomatic phenomena, then the whole notion of
ideology has to be recast in new terms. Although the argument is put in extremely
abstract terms, which makes its immediate relevance more difficult to see, Jay is
willing to concede that an advanced rhetorical approach to ideology may be
marking a crucial area of social inquiry thus far neglected. On the negative side,
however, Jay finds the same problem as Hertz: an apparent lack of connection
between the linguistic forces brought to the surface in the rhetorical analysis and a
sense of human agency. Jay writes, "To know that we have hitherto been confused
in our attempt to disentangle reference [the real state of affairs, such as class
exploitation or mystified power relations] from phenomenalism [the prevailing
view of ideology and aesthetics] may be an advance over blithely thinking we are
not, but it is not much of a step beyond ideology as an inevitable and irremediable
dimension of the human condition" (MS 10). Deconstruction "makes nothing
happen" and sees us "lapsing back into error." If all that rhetoric shows is that we
cannot rely on the "predicative function" of language to work our way out of our
false attachments, then it "provides very little basis for a workable concept of
ideology." Even worse, "deconstruction can be turned itself against many of the
values that oppressed groups have, perhaps in their benighted way, thought they
were fighting for, values like solidarity, community, universality, popular sover-
eignty, self-determination, agency and the like" (MS 13). Deconstruction is like
some universal solvent, "corrosive not only of mystifications, but also of any
positive alternative to them."

I think that Jay's remarks represent widely held attitudes about de Manian
deconstruction today. It seems fine to take a linguistic turn in order to dissolve the
link between ideology and aesthetics, to see that illusions about power may not be

graspable in phenomenal or specular terms, but unless we can rebuild norms, consensus, and legitimacy, we have not accomplished much. "Everything is an idealistic illusion" or "everything is a linguistic construct"—the difference is pragmatically null.

For deconstruction to count in the philosophy of language, it would need to be felt as a powerful shaper of our ability to articulate the issues Jay mentions. Its apparent pathos, its knowledge of its weakness, or its excessive concession of power to language itself is precisely what seems to get in the way of its adoption. Literary theories like neopragmatism and speech-act theory have questioned aesthetic terminology and the priority of the predicative function or seen them in conflict with rhetoric without abandoning human agency as the shaper of interpretive communities. The writings of Stanley Fish serve as one example in this book.

Hertz and Jay clarify some of the larger philosophical issues which de Man's writings must answer. The next step is to try some answers. It may be true that de Man failed to articulate the exact philosophical implications of his rhetorical analysis. I am relying on Hertz and Jay in order to draw out and assess some of these implications because I agree that de Man unsettles his readers. If deconstruction is really about the authority of certain linguistic forms, it cannot be just because it shows us that beliefs and values are implicated in our use of certain linguistic tropes. Furthermore, de Man's extraordinarily complex and precise reinterpretations of poems by Wordsworth, Shelley, and Yeats are not going to persuade literary humanists that an author is merely a personification of a figural mechanism. The gaps that Hertz and Jay identify need to be closed before the larger claims of deconstruction can be supported. I suggest we look again at the intersection of rhetoric, agency, and pathos in de Man's writings to see if this closure is possible.

One of de Man's last essays, "Hegel on the Sublime,"[4] is a condensation of many of the problems and topics I have sketched thus far. As I stated at the beginning of this chapter, de Man's focus upon Hegel is both strategic and necessary. Many canonical assumptions in the fields of aesthetics and political theory would be altered were deconstructive analysis able to redetermine (not radically negate) in contemporary terms Hegelian constructions of aesthetic symbolism, collective consciousness, historical periodization, and, most of all, what de Man calls "human autonomy as ethical self-determination" (HS 149).

In turning to this essay, I need to make clear right away what can and cannot be achieved by the deconstructive redetermination of key features of Hegelian philosophy. Even if de Man's (and Derrida's) interpretations of the Hegelian symbol/sign distinction and the end of art as a phase of human culture were to become widely accepted, a tremendous task of philosophical reconstruction would need to follow.[5] Any revisionary reading of Hegel is for today and belongs to multiple revisionary debates about the concept of law, of the subject, and the role of art in effecting political change. All that de Man's essay can show is the best case that deconstruction can make within this larger revisionary project.

The key deconstructive focus upon Hegel concerns a hitherto under-developed link between the human agent's power to negate natural relationships and the precise *linguistic* form through which this transformative power is articulated. Determining and developing this link is of vital importance, but what is equally striking about de Man's examination of this link is its precise location within the Hegelian corpus. Deciding where and how to analyze this link, *deciding upon a text for analysis* is as important as the link itself. De Man does not arbitrarily select any one of numerous passages in the Hegelian corpus in which negation and humanistic realization are articulated, for not all would be texts that force decisions about language in order to make that link work. Assuming the omnipresence of the link would commit a reader of Hegel to linguistic holism. Is the attachment to this link, even in committed Hegelians, worth rendering the multiplicity of social spheres that surround us in monolithically Hegelian terms? De Manian textuality is what links pathos, agency, and specific features of language in a closely determined form. It is this actual determination, rather than broad assumptions about the human speaking subject, which leads de Man to question Hegel's use of phenomenal or representational modes of articulating social structures in terms of the natural man.

From de Man's perspective, deconstruction's insights into a dehumanized linguistic structure (granting the possibility itself for the moment, which pragmatists might mistake for a radical separation of language from human agency) are extendable beyond their determination in a particular passage in the writings of Hegel. Nevertheless, and this is absolutely crucial, the insight into language cannot exist apart from its determination in the Hegelian text. The determination and philosophical articulation are inseparable, as we have seen in other chapters in this book. It is like Empson or Cavell determining a tragic utterance which reveals something about human speech activity but is neither imposed upon Shakespeare, nor entirely derived in the terms of one of his plays. Similarly, when de Man determines a passage of key significance in Hegel and gives it the status of a text, the nonarbitrary selection and determination is what finally brings the discussion around to the situatedness of an agent in Hegelian discourse. That is where de Man's essay returns to the concerns of Hertz and Jay.

Had de Man lived to respond to Jay, I feel certain he would have tried to show that Jay merely pays lip service to a trope like apostrophe, that he has not sufficiently engaged the possibility of rethinking the role of rhetoric in the discourse of the human sciences. It is one thing to say that politics and history appear to be contained by language (which makes deconstruction sound like idealism) and another to say that our ability to articulate solidarity must work through very highly determined and purposefully constructed linguistic forms, which may be captured best in the terminology of texts. For de Man, a trope like apostrophe is not an expression of solidarity with the traditions of the past, with the voices of the dead, or with the divine spark in us. The trope conveys a real effort to articulate the value of these beliefs. Its use needs to be authenticated and tested. In and of itself, it neither makes everything mere words nor serves as a secret weapon of ideology.

Through Hegel, de Man takes on directly the questions Jay raises about legitimacy, the critique of ideology without the use of specular and phenomenal models of meaning, and the possibility of a postaesthetic, strictly rhetorical analysis of literature. At the same time, de Man addresses Hertz's question about pathos; in fact, the essay is written as a quiet challenge to Neil Hertz, who is mentioned as the best of the non-Hegelian, Longinian readers of the sublime. De Man leaves answers for his critics in two very challenging passages from the essay on Hegel. But these passages also call attention to that highly complex connection between what is now emerging as the determination of texts via tropes and the dehumanization which needs to be disambiguated. These are the passages:

> When [in Hegel's chapter on the sublime in his lectures on aesthetics] we read of a hidden god who has "withdrawn into himself and thus asserted his autonomy against the finite world, as pure interiority and substantive power," or hear that in the sublime, the divine substance "becomes truly manifest" . . . against the weakness and the ephemerality of its creatures, then we easily understand the pathos of this servitude as praise of divine power. The language of negativity is then a dialectical and recuperative

moment, akin to similar terms that Neil Hertz has located in Longinus' treatise. Hegel's sublime may stress the distance between the human dis- course of the poets and the voice of the sacred even further than Longinus, but as long as this distance remains, as he puts it, a *relationship,* however negative, the fundamental analogy between poetic and divine creation is preserved. . . . The word speaks and the world is the transitive object of its utterance, but this implies that what is thus spoken, and which includes us, is not the subject of its speech act. . . . If the word is said to speak through us, then we speak only as a ventriloquist's dummy. . . . If we say that language speaks, that the grammatical subject of a proposition is lan- guage rather than a self, we are not fallaciously anthropomorphizing language but rigorously grammatizing the self. (HS 146)

When language functions as trope, and no longer as representation, the limits of the Longinian sublime as well as of its considerable powers of re- cuperation . . . are reached. As the section [on the sublime] develops, the divergence between Hegel and Longinus becomes nearly as absolute as the divergence between man and God that Hegel calls sublime. (HS 149)

The Hegelian sublime concerns the recognition of a supremely authoritative speech, belonging to the order of the divine, which enacts or posits human and historical events. It is therefore central in any discussion of human agency and phenomenalization and consequently of aesthetical and authoritative forms of language. In Longinus and Hegel, the perfectly sublime expression is the fiat, "Let there be light," God's positing of the creation. But our ability to recognize the authority behind those special expressions that deserve to be called sublime is always linked to our inability to represent or mentally image the power that speaks. That is what gives the sublime its special pathos and that is what the whole taboo on idolatry is about: the acceptance of God's word without a direct image of the creator. The sublime cannot be received other than verbally.

But this immediately entails a number of complications. First of all, why not just step pragmatically around the problem of divinity as a writer like Rorty or Fish might do at this juncture? Why not accept the separation of church and state, religious belief and civil politics, as separate spheres in a pluralized society? The problems of the sublime are perhaps matters for theologians and literary roman- ticists to settle. Surely it is not the sort of thing parliamentarians and sociologists need to worry over. Not so, for Hegel already makes it clear that the sublime is supposed to achieve precisely that separation; it marks the possible separation of the order of the divine and the secular in the first place! The deeper question it raises concerns the relation between the two orders: what are the limits of human power? how does it situate itself in strictly secular terms? what is the status of divine language if we are to allow it to have linguistic claims? The initial separation of two radically different orders of discourse is the beginning, not the end, of the analysis. The sublime separation of human and divine language is required even for the orthodox reading of Hegel that would see the two orders finally synthesized in spirit's self-knowledge. We come back to the initial questions: In taking human responsibility for the ability to posit laws, to enact our freedoms, do we gain or lose pathos?

The peculiar twist in de Man's approach, which meets the greatest resistance from scholars like Raymond Geuss, is saying that Hegel worked out these problems by treating human, nonsublime discourse as tropological and grammatical rather than symbolic and beautiful. De Man defies the interpretation of the Hegelian symbol as the realization of human rationality and freedom. Does de Man go too far in his deconstruction of humanity's sense of its own progressive strivings? Is it plausible to assert that Hegel's dialectic does not support the language of the symbol over the sign? The "grammatizing" of the self seems to deprive humanity of the sublime *and* the beautiful.

De Man wants to link the Hegelian sublime to tropological expression, a category of language generally neglected in the hermeneutical tradition. That seems a sound point of departure because the sublime is not definable as an image or an intuition. And the attempt to try to connect tropes to other issues associated with the sublime, like authority, the power to posit, and the negation of the natural, seems to be equally sound. But when de Man denies tropological expressions any "powers of recuperation" he sets the stage for a confrontation with theorists like Jay and Hertz who are willing to explore the use of tropes if it may enable, rather than disable, human agency.

The first de Manian topic that has to be disambiguated, therefore, is the dehumanization caused by the sublime. The claim that the sublime is divine is not particularly original. But what does divinity mean exactly? De Man follows carefully Hegel's history of the emergence of a monotheistic form of art. It starts with Indian and classical forms and leads to Mohammedan and Judeo-Christian ones, which is where the sublime begins. His real interest, however, is how monotheism forces Hegel into a definition of the symbol in nonrepresentational terms. From that moment on, the argument can cut two different ways. Divinity may separate itself from natural substance through its word, but by the same token the word separates itself from the human subject. Divinity is twisted around, against the explicit tenor of Hegel's argument, so as to mean the nonhuman. De Man likes the idea of wresting a particular concept of language out of the hands of a simple humanism and allows Hegel the necessity of that task, but he then out-Hegels Hegel by treating the divine as the necessity of the impersonal, generalized grammatical self—a very different matter, especially when this grammatical self can no longer serve as the dialectical vehicle of spirit.

De Man's underlying arguments provide a subtle blend of deconstructionist determination of what is really going on in the Hegelian text, genuine respect for Hegel's discovery of a real moment of an impersonal linguistic structure, and a serious philosophical challenge to secular humanism's effort to continue dialectical thinking by inverting the relation between the power called God and human agency. De Man treats the necessity for a moment of total dehumanization of language in order to argue on two fronts simultaneously: against theocracy (a relatively easy task in the wake of nineteenth-century European secularism) and against humanism.

De Man's is a somewhat bizarre philosophical strategy, akin in some ways to a work like Leo Strauss's *Persecution and the Art of Writing* (1952). He does not come out directly in favor of an antiaesthetic view of language, justifying it in open argument against aesthetic theory or semiotics or hermeneutics, as Jay does for example. Instead, he speaks of the philosophical tradition and even of Hegel himself as "censoring" the sublime insights into dehumanized language because we want to shelter ourselves from the sublime's implications. Sooner or later, however, the claim that the sublime can be determined only in impersonal, nondialectical form will need to be tested and debated. My own position is that the claim should be debated openly because some of what de Man says about tropes touches on how we reformulate the language of Hegel in an increasingly pluralized social discourse, where Hegel's authority does not, in any case, rest on foundationalist premises. At the conclusion of this essay, I shall try to indicate what I believe to be some of the limitations and the strengths of de Man's somewhat oblique position. For the moment, with some of the subtleties of de Man's reasoning kept in mind, I would like to consider how de Man establishes the grammatization of the self out of Hegel's sublime and how it pushes our discussion beyond the characterizations of deconstruction in Hertz and Jay.

The sublime belongs to a wider discussion of the concept of divinity as a singular but general form of consciousness. The "singularization" of spirit into some absolute generality is part of its progressive realization in history: in religion it is the movement from pantheism to monotheism, in art the postclassical emergence of the symbol, in epistemology the single field of unified knowledge, yielding "a deitic system of predication and determination in which we dwell more or less poetically on this earth" (HS 145). The ability to attach a *name* to this singular generality, be it Jahweh, Being, or I, is what attracts de Man's attention. De Man says that not one of these names is as yet sublime (*erhaben*), although they occur through a process of "sublation" (*aufgehoben*). They belong to the dialectical logic of mediation and negation, the interpenetration of the universal and the particular. All this, de Man says, is "in conformity with [Hegel's] tradition and with his place in the ongoing discourse of philosophy" (HS 145).

As soon as the naming of a mediation becomes sublime, the logic of mediation begins to break down. The important act of giving a name to singular generality remains, since without it there would be no definite critical position from which to predicate statements or negate natural attachments. What matters, however, is that the sublime name cannot function dialectically on all levels. How does this come about?

God is the model of singular generality, but when God speaks, as in the fiat, it is very unclear how the word stands in relation to humanity, as we could see in the long quotations I cited earlier (see above, pp. 166–67). The fiat, Hegel's own example of the sublimity of Logos, has the kind of positing, transformative power that normally moves the dialectic forward. The fact that it is strictly verbal, beyond phenomenalization *of the speaker,* is not in itself a problem, since one of the goals of the dialectic is to go beyond phenomenology. The problem lies in how the word is transmitted. In order to partake of the sublime transformative power of the fiat, humanity must quote it. Through quotation, humanity gains access to the properties associated with singular generality: a unity of knowledge; apparently autonomous positing power; freedom from emphemeral natural appearances—but all this is at the cost of a terrific pathos before God. Although humanity may quote God's sublimity and thus move beyond aesthetics altogether, humanity is robbed of its own agency. God is the subject of every predicate, even ones that make use of dummy human speakers. Quotation, therefore, is hardly a very dialectical process when it comes to the failed synthesis of the singular generality (only the first level of the dialectic) and human consciousness (which aspires toward Godhead on the second level). I repeat de Man's witticism: "To be *erhaben* . . . is not the same . . . as to be *erhoben* or *aufgehoben*."

The mimesis (de Man's rhetorical term for quotation) of the sublime situates us squarely in a linguistic problematic: it uneasily combines the sublime power of an originating, nonphenomenalized speaker with the pathos of human weakness. It is what Jay and Hertz see as de Manian deconstruction par excellence, but which de Man immediately treats as a secondary problem, not quite touching upon the question of tropes, which is his major concern. The play of the sublime against human pathos indicates a moment of disorder in the dialectic, which still has Longinian or Pascalian recuperative powers. The play of sublimity against pathos is the focus of many contemporary literary theorists—for example, Hertz, W. K. Wimsatt, Harold Bloom, and Thomas Weiskal (HS 144).

A brief look at de Man's commentary upon the mimetic sublime shows that its pathos can be written off once we realize that it performs perfectly well. Only at the next stage in the argument, when the performative power of the fiat runs up against the blockade of something deeply tropological in Hegel, will de Man begin to speculate about an irreversible shift in our capacity for linguistic articulation. He chooses to call it the emergence of the prosaic element in social discourse, by which he emphasizes its nonpathetic quality.

De Man states that as long as we are required to speak with sublime force, and we always *are* required to do so if we wish to advance consciousness toward singular generality, human expression is reduced to ventriloquism and muteness. To speak with sublimity is to speak only God's language. He continues,

> But none of these [sublime] utterances are mute in the sense of being merely passive or devoid of reflexive knowledge. Quotations can have considerable performative power; indeed, a case could be made that only quotations have such power. . . . They are, however, devoid of positional power: to quote the marriage vows allows one to perform a marriage but not to posit marriage as an institution. And quotations certainly carry a considerable cognitive weight: if, as Longinus implies, the sublime poet here is Moses himself, then the question of the veracity of Moses' testi-

monial is bound to arise, that is to say, a cognitive critical inquiry is inevitably linked to the assertion of linguistic positional force. This accounts for the fact that in a statement such as "Let there be . . . ," *light* is indeed the privileged object of predication, rather than life (Let there be life) or humanity (Let there be woman and man). (HS 147)

The pathos felt in human muteness, the becoming of a grammatical pronoun in the name of Jahweh, in no way implies a loss of fidelity to the truth value of the utterances or to their power to bind the speaker to the words uttered (to uphold the marital vow, for example). Our pathos, therefore, can be turned around to mean things like loyalty to a higher cognitive-performative system of legitimate knowledge. As long as the possibility of miming, or quoting, the sublime is in effect, interpreters may battle over who possesses the language of the sublime. And one of the ways of proving one speaker's legitimacy over another's may have to do with which speaker has the greater pathos or the better grasp of performatives or the cognitive restraint to attach the sublime only to valid statements. The loophole in this connection between a subject of singular generality and its predicative-performative power lies in de Man's passing remark that all these utterances are "devoid of positional power." This means that another, profoundly Hegelian issue is temporarily being elided: real autonomy. The linguistic extension of sublime force throughout human discourse, in the double mimesis of performative utterances and cognitively valid statements, nevertheless locks humanity into heteronomy. Pathos is one thing, but being robbed of the actual ability to posit is another. I am not suggesting that de Man wants absolute freedom over all utterances, like the magical ability to utter "light" and make it shine forth. But even in Hegel there can be no negation or dialectic without autonomy, not pure, unmediated autonomy, but a recognition of our own proper capacity to develop and become the agents of our institutions and communities. That is one of the primary meanings of situatedness and comes through in Taylor's effort to align individual acts of decision making with the highest social norms and values. Something must give way in the construction of the sublime for language to advance beyond heteronomy.

For de Man, that something is pathos. In seeking an even more dehumanized language than Hegel seems to allow, de Man hopes to go beyond the lesser autonomy of heteronomous mimesis. In taking that next step he parts company with Jay and Hertz. Or perhaps it is the other way round, since it seems counterintuitive to follow de Manian deconstruction into further dehumanization in search of greater linguistic agency.

Before I consider the final phase of de Man's argument, I would like to buttress my last point. I turn one more time to Jay and Hertz to indicate briefly how I think de Man's comments upon the Hegelian sublime answer the objections of two of his most charitable critics (in the hermeneutical sense of those who want to assimilate some of his arguments rather than dismiss them outright).

Jay believes that the whole issue of heteronomy marks the limits of the deconstructive project. But his idea of deconstructive heteronomy is borrowed from Wlad Godzich, who merely attempts to introduce the topic in de Man's writings without working through all the arguments. When Jay seizes upon the term, he fails to go back to de Man's own writing to test it. Godzich writes that deconstruction "permits the assertion of an equality between all human beings by virtue of their dispossession from the domain of meaning. The insistence on aporia [conveys] the same sort of human powerlessness that obtained within religious thought, without any of the latter's transcendent dimension" (quoted by Jay in "Name-Dropping or Dropping Names?" 25). Assuming the validity of this general characterization of powerlessness, Jay goes on to question whether universal heteronomy can serve as a ground for authorial identity. If we are all equal before language, then perhaps the names we attach to specific philosophical positions are nothing more than the side effects of tropes like parabasis, prosopopeia, and personification. Names like Descartes, Leibniz, Rousseau, and Hegel are merely indicators of tropological displacements. But if authors and the authority they lend to distinct claims about the self and about knowledge are dissolvable back into the universal heteronomy out of which they came in the first place, then deconstruction has "rather chilling implications" (28). Jay seeks a middle path, somewhere between the exposure of bad rhetorical forms of legitimation and a modified Habermasian program that continues to try to achieve a rational basis for legitimation. We should indeed try to demystify the aura of the author, Jay suggests, for it often conceals all sorts of political moves. But we cannot do without some principle of legitimation; not all philosophical claims can be equal.

What I find puzzling about Jay's summary of deconstruction is the immediate connection he draws between heteronomy and tropes. Thus far, as I read the essay on Hegel, de Man has not even begun to discuss the way apostrophe and prosopopeia will change the outcome of sublime. It is true that naming and heteronomy are linked in the discourse of the sublime and that to some extent they are linked rhetorically through the term *mimesis*. But that is only a first step and by no means de Man's own position; in fact, as I suggested, the analysis proceeds in order to overcome the problem with universal heteronomy. When Hegel gives a name to singular generality, like the *I* or *God,* he is trying to develop the logic of predication and verbal positing. He is already anticipating the possibility of a Habermasian structure of discourse by demanding cognitive and performative validity for the use of the sublime. The debts that must be paid to the sublime in order for this logicolinguistic system to work are the cause of heteronomy. We are all equal before the necessity of the sublime, but that is the problem! Is there some other way to conceive singular/general consciousness that would not result in the hierarchization of a legitimating authority? For de Man, the question requires us to look at what Hegel goes on to say about tropes. De Man does not argue for a leveling of all discourse or of every linguistic function under the general rubric of rhetoric. The great Hegelian effort to define a progressive critical stance in terms of a singular generality, which de Man in no way dismisses, needs a more, not a less, sophisticated textual determination for the concept to take hold.

Neil Hertz's view of de Manian pathos requires a lengthier response. Hertz is a very attentive reader; his subtlety is a match for de Man's. The fine but crucial difference between Hertz and de Man's views on pathos may be seen in one section of "Lurid Figures" (89–91). Hertz notes de Man's focus upon two particularly lurid figures in Yeats's poetry, one of matricide and the other of castration. The "gratuitous violence" in the poetry intrigues Hertz, especially when it seems to come primarily from de Man's readings rather than from Yeats's language. But then Hertz goes on to recoup this violence, particularly in what he calls a "transferential dynamics of reading and a conjuring up of what is, in one sense, an unmotivated pathos" (91). We already know from the Hegel essay that transferential dynamics are what de Man calls the Longinian sublime, and that he concedes that Hertz is an expert interpreter of it. Pathos, in this model of interpretation, is not exactly ordinary human feeling or suffering; it is already linked to some sort of linguistic force that is generating violent and mutilated anthropomorphic images. As long as the imagery of pathos is made up of *human* figures (of sexuality, of dismemberment, of violence and death) some interpretive dissonance is bound to occur.

The pathos, however linguistically motivated, lies squarely within the agent's lack of self-identity with the realm of language. The more complex the use of language, the more likely the agent will produce disfigurations. The recuperative moment, therefore, is defined in the intense struggle to master a language which we can never hope to master. I think that Hertz is right to characterize a good deal of de Man's work along these lines. It is not the same as saying we are completely dehumanized by language, but it keeps the focus on the pathos of human efforts to master the realm of language.

De Man's essay on the Hegelian sublime seems to me an attempt to work beyond Hertz's dynamics of reading, both technically and philosophically: technically in treating the Hegelian sublime as a nonspecular figure, which does work because in the first instance it avoids *disfiguration* of the human before God (although it certainly conveys pathos); philosophically, in attempting to exploit the Hegelian *nonspecular* surface of language in order to do away with a global definition of humanity as a product of its own linguistic disfigurations.

Hertz's presentation of Yeats's text on castration sets up the terms for the next phase of de Man's essay. What we see Hertz put together as the definition of de Man's position is what de Man takes apart in his final analysis of the Hegelian sublime. In Yeats's "Vacillation," we are given the image of a tree, half "glittering flame and half all green," which leads the reader to puzzle out its meaning as natural, or emblematic, meaning a poetic icon drawn from mythological traditions. Deciding the difference in meaning forms part of a discussion of Yeats's poetic project. De Man sees it as an effort to separate poetry from the "natural seduction of images," to make it all emblem. Hertz's "pathos of uncertain agency" emerges in the difficulty of making a clear transition from the natural to the emblematic in these lines:

> And he that Attis' image hangs between
> That staring fury and the blind lush leaf
> May not know what he knows, but knows not grief.

The castrated figure of Attis that hangs between the natural and the emblematic tree, a figure of immediate pathos on the first level of interpretation, does not assert an identification with the reader. The real question, one upon which Hertz and de Man cross, is, "Who is performing the verb 'to hang?'" An emblem can be posited only by a poet. Hertz writes,

> The poetic act of hanging [Attis's image on the tree] that makes the difference [between natural and emblematic images], prefigures de Man's later explicit . . . interest in the distinction between the meaning and the perfor-

mance of a text. But it also exhibits how slippery the category of performance is, how easily the "poetic act" can be displaced, by an anthropomorphizing gesture, into the poet's act. (90)

Are we rigorously grammatizing the poetic self or fallaciously anthropomorphizing language? to recall the question de Man raised earlier. Hertz asks, "Is the stanza about an image or an action or a poet, a figure or a performance or a 'figure?' " But no matter which answer we try, the result will be the same, for they equally support the specular model of reading Hertz upholds. As image, Attis is an ambiguous mixture of natural and emblematic elements. As the product of poetic agency, something posited and so closer to the emblematic than to the natural, it nevertheless takes on anthropomorphic form. Textual performance moves us beyond natural self-imagery but only as far as disfigured, or mutilated, self-imagery, a partial anthropomorphization of an alien linguistic structure. Hertz continues, "Once Attis's image, the poetic act, and the vacillating reader are thus aligned, it is possible for the 'threat' of Attis's castration to be communicated down the line to the poet and on to the reader, in this case de Man" (91). Only more violent pathos and disfiguration can free the reader from too close an identification with the horrible self-image, from treating the poetry as a natural seduction.

Powerful as this model of specular disfiguration may be, it begins to sound less and less de Manian. As long as disfiguration is treated as a mirror of human self-distortion, with all its accompanying pathos about our inability to know ourselves clearly, we are treating performatives and tropes in terms of transferential dynamics, passing the pathos of our distortions down the line from poetry to poet to reader. But in the Hegel essay, tropes and performatives are put together in order to get out of the specular/transferential mode of reading altogether. De Man takes into account the pathos of textual performance in one version of the Hegelian sublime, its mimetic passage from God to man. I suppose there is a trace of disfiguration as well in the necessity of man turning into a speaking dummy. But it is outweighed by the genuine philosophical gains in the Hegelian system, namely, the whole system of valid predications and speech-acts. There may be a strain of severe pathos in the entire deconstructive project, and Hertz correctly discovers it in de Man's efforts to detach language from the "seduction" and identification of the natural. Does that mean, philosophically, that once language detaches humanity from nature, it imposes a burden of disfiguration? That would indeed sound more like English romanticism than Hegelian negation.

The linguistic capacity to posit, negate, and transform images of the self is always present in de Man's writing. Disfiguration and specular understanding are not the only concepts he works with, though they do occur with great frequency and have received a great deal of comment. De Man wants to explore the possibility of a further dehumanization of linguistic agency, down to the practically absurd "grammatization" of the self, where there is nothing left to disfigure. And he uses the concept of textual performance to accomplish this. The goal of the analysis is not a complete deconstruction of the human subject, however. It is intimately bound up with the Hegelian issues of ethical autonomy seen in the clarity of a linguistic consciousness. That linguistic clarity is achieved with the assistance of tropes which allow de Man to determine the textual status of sublime language. Jay rightly sees in de Man a break with specular models for the sake of political negation but confuses tropes with the disenfranchisement of universal heteronomy. Hertz rightly sees a complex human dilemma within the play of tropes and textual performance but seems to feel that anthropomorphizing the disfigurations within this play is better than abandoning the self entirely to the realm of grammar. That brings us finally to the last set of questions about de Man. How does he use tropes to convey something positive about linguistic agency and human autonomy? Why does he try to merge a radically grammatized self, practically devoid of natural characteristics, with the thinking subject of Hegelian philosophy?

The first analysis of a trope in the Hegel essay occurs after the discussion of the mimetic sublime and the fiat; the trope is drawn directly from the Hegelian text. Juxtaposed to the fiat is an apostrophe to God from the Psalms: "Light is your garment, that you wear; you stretch out the heavens like a curtain." As another way of stating the nonrepresentation of the sublime, the apostrophe is not very interesting. It suggests that the sensory field of perception is nothing more than an external garment of spirit. It is another expression of man's weakness before the sublimity of the divine. But now de Man adds a very special twist to this reading, which renders the meaning of the sublime in new terms:

> Unlike the *logos*, [apostrophe] does not have the power to posit anything;
> its power, or only discourse, is the knowledge of its weakness. But since

this same spirit also, without mediation, *is* the light, the combination of the two quotations states that the spirit posits itself as that which is unable to posit, and this declaration is either meaningless or duplicitous. One can pretend to be weak when one is strong, but the power to pretend is decisive proof of one's strength. One can know oneself, as man does, as that which is unable to know, but by moving from knowledge to position, all is changed. Position is all of a piece, and moreover, unlike thought, it actually occurs. It becomes impossible to find a common ground for or between the two quotations, "Let there be light" and "Light is your garment." (HS 148)

The density of argument and the pregnancy of the vocabulary, especially when it is being used to pull the ground out from under us, make de Man's point about apostrophe all the more difficult to grasp. And yet he keeps suggesting that he is getting at something very simple, prosaic, not an especially deep (or sublime) figure of speech at all. It is more meaningless than meaningful. But why? To answer this basic question, we need to think broadly at the same time we are following the technicalities of de Man's reading.

In the earlier discussion of the mimetic sublime, de Man states that when singular consciousness gains cognition and performative power it strangely seems to lose the ability to posit. The fiat posits, but man merely quotes. For an apostrophe, or trope, to occur, it too must be posited; it has no other claim to existence as a piece of language. It cannot claim existence as language by virtue of its cognitive or performative power. It neither yields further knowledge of the divine nor enacts ceremonies or performative utterances, such as commanding, requesting, promising, or plighting one's troth. It is altogether a rather clumsy device, one that would not be of analytical interest except for the fact that it does repeatedly occur. As a specific product of speech, marking something unusual in the human discourse about singular consciousness, it "posits itself as the inability to posit"—a paradox that will need to be clarified.

But first I need to expand upon some other features of the trope. When apostrophe occurs within the field of singular consciousness's "light," it is not through mediation. The ability/inability to posit cannot be dialectically raised or sublated through a mimetic or phenomenal or pathetic recuperation. Its occurrence therefore is without grounds or cause. It neither brings singular consciousness into closer contact with a civil order nor raises humanity closer to the level of the divine. The light of apostrophe does not seem to illuminate anything more about the light of the fiat as a source of cognition and critical change.

So we have to make sense of two aspects of apostrophe as a trope: "Position [as trope] is all of a piece [it does not move up or down like the mimetic model], and, moreover, unlike thought, it actually occurs." It is simply there in the Hegelian text, without being in the service of singular consciousness's development. Here we touch upon the basic insight of de Man's deconstructive project. The occurrence of a trope must be accounted for in the Hegelian text, but it does not seem to fit into any of the basics of the Hegelian system of logical predication or symbolization.

The technicalities of de Man's argument take us only so far, but they must be given their due. I believe these technicalities stand up very well to critical scrutiny. Apostrophe is not a mimesis or a mediation of anything: "Apostrophe is not representation; it occurs independently of any report, be it as quotation or narration, and when it is put on a stage, it becomes ludicrous and cumbersome" (HS 148). Apostrophe's status as a trope needs to be recognized in all its specificity. The fact that it cannot be easily assimilated to predication or quotation or narration should not tempt us to write it off as a marginal linguistic device, of secondary or even tertiary importance. When philosophers of language either ignore or overvalue tropes, they are refusing to interpret them in their own irreducible terms. To some, they seem insignificant because they lack cognitive weight, while to others they are the hidden dimension that drives all the other features of language. But de Man never makes these sorts of claims, which are often associated with deconstruction. He never suggests that apostrophe's inability to convey the power of the sublime demonstrates universal heteronomy. And he never says that it is a disfiguration of the cognitive functions of the sublime. There is a core of valid knowledge in the Hegelian sublime. But the question remains, Why does human agency articulate itself in a language of tropes even in the midst of its most searching cognitive enterprise?

If we follow de Man on the irreducible presence of tropes in Hegel's discourse of singular/general consciousness, we can see that they occur with greater and greater frequency in the lectures on aesthetics, as in the postsublime discussions of the literary genres of fable, epigram, and allegory. The irreducible, unmediated occurrence of tropes, not as a disguised speech-act or as a mimesis of human pathos, calls attention to a complex moment in which agency and pure *linguistic surface* are intertwined. Why is this important? At first glance, it is important precisely because the agency that expresses itself as a trope rather than a mimesis is devoid of power and authority. A singular/generalized agency is expressing itself in tropes, but the expression cannot be turned around in the immediate service of the divine or even perhaps of some unconscious drive. In positing itself freely, without cognitive or performative necessity, agency recognizes only itself right on the *very surface of the trope's presence as a piece of language*. That peculiar surface, with all its clumsiness, is not a symbol, and it does not express a disfiguration of humanity. The more it is posited, the more it stays on the surface of linguistic expression. It posits nothing outside of itself as a trope. This rigorous attention to the surface quality of tropes, so easily and erroneously confused with the absurd claim that nothing exists outside the text, is intended to be a moment of clarity, the light that illuminates the material existence of the text as something staring back at us strictly on the surface of its own inscription. It does not represent anything except the moment of agency that brought it about. Even when the apostrophe undergoes transformation, as when Hegel says that the garment becomes a hidden face (see HS 149), it does not reflect anything more than a linguistic shift. We are not moved any closer to the divine through the transformation. At this point, de Man suggests that the more we follow the surface of tropological shifts, the more we come to see the grammatical side of language, by which he means a materialist view of language as marks, notations, and signs, actual inscriptions that abound on the surfaces of human societies. The deliberately superficial grasp of marks and notations on the absolute surface of the Hegelian page is an attempt to break with sublime and symbolic revelation, but also with human disfiguration and pathos. It is a very austere clarity, however. What can we gain by the truth of this absolute reduction?

I would suggest that what we gain is an insight into situatedness that, like the sublime itself, can be very highly determined in the manner of de Manian deconstruction but is beyond totalization, either by linguistic fiat, symbolic elevation, or "sublime" utterance—forms of language we have seen Cavell and Fish use precisely at the moment they would define a social position for their readers without resorting to foundationalism, or Taylor and Jameson use as the foundation for a symbolic totality of expression..

I do not think that de Man's austerity vindicates deconstruction over the insights of these other theorists and philosophers, for all that we have before us, following a detailed linguistic analysis of tropes, are grammatical links between the material inscriptions of language. The use we put this insight to will depend on a variety of interests, including those which have been articulated by Hertz, Jay, and Taylor. But de Man's determination of the text of sublime requires us to rework those interests in forms of language which are incommensurable, in the recognition that the sublime does not unite performative utterances with mimetic utterances or with rhetorical figures of expression. This pattern of incommensurable strands of language is the object of textual analysis; it is crucial to the location of which passages in Hegel are deemed to be of textual importance.

In determining the textual form of the sublime by the use of tropological structures and material inscriptions, de Man does not radically negate its value and significance. It would be a mistake to argue in favor of a direct connection between the arbitrary use of a rhetorical figure like apostrophe and Hegel's concept of human autonomy. Unlike some of de Man's most sophisticated followers, Cynthia Chase, for example, I see no reason for concluding that the clarity of language as a surface, which is made possible in the analysis of tropes, upholds the general position that meaning can be undone as arbitrary, free of signification, or fictional.[6] That begins to sound too much like Jay's universal heteronomy or what philosophers like Taylor identify as negative freedom, which works counter to situatedness.

De Man situates us in Hegel's philosophy in a new way. His aim is not to refute Hegel by reducing a complex philosophical body of writing to nothing but rhetorical shifts and semantics. De Man raises questions about recollection, symbolic meaning, and acts of positing meaning by showing that they do not reach dialectical unification in the name of the sublime. But that does not mean that something as important as a Hegelian concept of situatedness loses all philosophical value. Perhaps just the opposite. It needs to be reconstructed out of a greater recognition of pluralism and partial identification and in the recognition that sublime utterances place speakers between truly incommensurable spheres of language. Compare Charles Taylor's orthodox statement about the surface of language and critical philosophy. Taylor writes of art's final goal as the "presentation" of spirit as mere surface. He sounds a lot like de Man on apostrophe when he writes of Hegelian aesthetics that art "only bodies forth an awareness of [the absolute] which is non-representative. Hegel speaks of it not as '*Vorstellung*' (representation), but '*Darstellung*' (presentation), or as '*Scheinen*' (showing forth or manifesting) of the Idea in sensible form (Gestalt). The work of art has a certain inner luminosity, as it were. It manifests the spiritual at every point on its surface, through its whole extent."[7] After reading this quotation, I would ask, Who allows us the better grasp upon the meaning of a clear surface of thought? Taylor, in the aesthetic terminology used by Hegel, or de Man, in determining the intricate structure that links these aesthetic terms to a manifestation, in tropes, of a prosaic, nonteleological surface. I would have to say de Man because he shows his position to be consistent both with canonical insights into the Hegelian corpus and with a nonfoundationalist adaptation of it to current debates about the philosophy of language. There is one major consequence of de Man's approach, however, and that is a definite loss of the experience of elevation that attaches to the sublime. If the sublime may be reconstructed as a new language for incommensurability, which to some extent it always was, the starkly de Manian presentation of the end of aesthetical and dialectical expressions of human consciousness entails the loss of affect which Hertz has noted.

But it is possible to see opportunities for the development of plural vocabularies for self-expression in the deconstructionist project, as some pragmatists have. The problem with pragmatism is that it celebrates the splitting of language to the point that the concept of situatedness disappears completely. A philosopher like Rorty might suggest that we do not need a de Manian kind of textual determination, that Hegelianism will circulate in a plural society to the extent that people need the vocabulary of the sublime or the aesthetic to establish certain forms of solidarity with each other. But by the same token, without a careful redetermination of sublime language, none of the Rortyan vocabularies would ever provide a sufficient degree of situatedness or help a reader of Hegel to articulate certain vocabularies in relation to other ones that uphold different, or plural, values. For instance, how would Rorty help us to decide, past a certain point, whether to use Hegel as a public writer, still relevant to debates about modernity and the public sphere, or as a private writer, like Proust, more interesting for what he says about human recollection and large patterns of narrative development? If what I have been arguing about the need to determine a textual instance of strongly resonant language is accepted, then these sorts of questions ought not to arise any more than Rorty's mock questions about the molecular structure of a thought. Incommensurable language games give rise to the need for situated choices and speaking positions, not a celebration of the negative freedom to split oneself up into so many discontinuous vocabularies.

It is also true, however, that de Man goes on to make some very troubling statements about his work on Hegel, as when he says that the only way past the mere surface of language is to escape it, through uncertainty about our mastery of it or through a forgetting of what we now know about it. When uncertainty and forgetfulness combine, the outcome is a random shift on the level of grammatical motion, an effort to raise ourselves beyond the surface of inscriptions into the state of human introspection and phenomena. Something seems to be missing, however, in the construction of a dilemma that places us between extremely analytical rigor and extremely arbitrary agency. That is the troubling aspect of de Man's writings which Hertz has called its pathos.

The situatedness which I have been articulating in this book is closely linked to the determination of texts by contemporary literary theorists. For situatedness to occur, readers must determine a central, important moment of incommensurable meanings and values, and they must be active in the articulation of that moment. The Hegelian power to negate and transform as well as the necessity of conceptualizing this power in specifically linguistic terms can provide an important correction to the pathos of the deconstructive method. But Hegelianism would need to be shaped in turn by the realization of a material, nonphenomenal dimension of language, which Paul de Man has pointed us toward at perhaps the highest level of textual determination that may be found in contemporary literary theory.

AFTERWORD

This book concludes that the concept of textuality in contemporary literary theory complements the philosophical concept of a situated self. Just as texts emerge out of irreducibly plural forms of language, so a situated self emerges in our recognition of the irreducible plurality of values and beliefs in contemporary society and culture. But the connection is more than an analogy: textuality and situatedness actually shape, or realize, each other in the expressive sphere of language. Selves and texts are constitutive events, and a language that determines and shapes contrasting meanings and values is vital to that constitutive process.

This book argues, further, that textuality and situatedness make up a coherent, nonholistic response to the passing of foundationalist thinking. The emphasis on contrast and incommensurablity, which I have taken from the writings of Charles Taylor, is what gives a constitutive act of choice a coherent purpose. In a deeply plural society, where a multiplicity of language games and local forms of

community and identity weave in and out of each other, specific, nontotalizable moments of choice bind human agents around central, if nonuniversal, values and beliefs. That moment of choice does not support arguments in favor of relativism or interpretive holism, but neither is it grounded in an objectivist cluster of truth values, intrinsic realities, and essential properties, or any other terms from foundationalist discourse. We need to see our way past the opposition between interpretive holism, on one side, and foundationalism and objectivism, on the other. We can achieve that insight with the help of a strong theory of textually determined language, built upon highly determined and constitutive moments of choice. One controversial name for such a strong theory is deconstruction. I say controversial because to many users of the term it stands (ironically) for an immediate, underdetermined assault against foundationalist thinking. In my argument, a textual theory like deconstruction gives precision and linguistic specificity to the crucial, if nontotalizable, decisions which are necessary to the development of an expressivist philosophy of language. The links which I find between pragmatist nonfoundationalism, expressivism, and deconstruction answer the ethical need for personal resonance, communicative action, and the discovery of which values count in a society composed of plural interpretive communities.

But the task of apprehending textuality in situatedness and the reverse occurs by repetition. Only by repeating anew prior determinations of textual meanings and structures can the human agent grasp and perhaps alter those determinations. The multiple and highly particular connections between large concepts of literature, history, personhood must be articulated over and over again if they are to gain concrete substance and shape the language that bridges personhood and community. The strength of textual analysis is in the quality of its determination and precision, but the result is not one governing definition of textuality. Repetition begins in the knowledge that communal values and individual identities are mutually shaped and produced; they cannot be apprehended apart from the critical exercise by which they are formed.

I can illuminate and unpack the significance of repetition with a concluding reference to Charles Taylor: Why, he asks, must philosophers read canonical works by Descartes, Kant, Adam Smith (and I would add Simone de Beauvoir and Mary Wollstonecraft), which many other humanistic researchers do not need to do, in order to carry out their intellectual labors? What is it about philosophers, Taylor asks, that gives them a "notorious professional deformation which makes them compulsively engage in expositions and re-interpretations of the canonical texts?"[1] His answer: Philosophy is "creative redescription" of a particular kind. These special philosophical descriptions have tremendous cultural weight in the claim they have upon personal identities. Canonical works of philosophy do not formalize a certain view of things, but rather push us into the past for "paradigm statements of our formative articulations" (26). Taylor's paradigm statements involve taking a critical stance, shaping a vocabulary, and situating oneself in a social landscape—topics which I have elaborated elsewhere in this book. Not all expressions are paradigm statements; not all vocabularies push us into situated judgment. But those that do become canonical. In the emended Taylorean vocabulary which I have been inventing in this book, a paradigm statement has a claim upon personally resonant forms of language.

Where Taylor writes the words "compulsion" and "deformation," I would write, less polemically, "repetition." The need to repeat recognizes the fact that the paradigm statements function immanently in the traditions at work in the culture. As a matter of fact, the political and epistemological concepts of Hobbes, Descartes, and, in this book, the individualism of Shakespeare or the dialectical, aesthetic language of Hegel, cannot be discussed namelessly; reconstructing the articulations of each writer is part of the task of apprehending their meaning and significance. When I say reconstructing the articulations, I refer primarily to the determination of a set of crucial utterances that shape a specific language as much as the ideas which are embodied in it.

That is why de Man on Hegel is canonical, in the modified Taylorean sense of that term, without necessarily serving the agenda of a committed orthodox Hegelian like Taylor. The Hegelian concept of situatedness, which brings together the individual and the universal, remains in de Man's reading of the passages on the sublime, but situatedness is remade in the image of textual determination rather than symbolic uplifting. To some readers of Hegel, de Man would be a radical revisionist, his version of Hegel practically unrecognizable from the perspective of mainstream scholarship in aesthetics and political science. But consider this question within the task of canonical repetition. A mainstream Hegelian like Taylor is unable to further the articulation of a language of contrast in spite of his ability to use the concept of situatedness to criticize weaknesses in objectivist science, radical Marxism, and radical pragmatism—criticisms which I wholly endorse in this book. The revisionist moment in de Man occurs not as a dismissal of the importance of the proper name, of the effort to bring together an authoritative level of understanding and individual apprehension, but rather in the textually determined insight that this effort is, by definition, a repeated effort that fails to reach closure. The radical elements of de Man's reading attack the theory of dialectical progression, not situatedness. Radical postmodernist revisionists and conservatives who uphold the intrinsic value of the great canonical works of Western literature are the ones who talk about deconstruction as anticanonical, be it for good or for bad. But in de Man's work, the canonical importance of Hegel remains; only the mode of apprehending what is important in Hegel has shifted to the task of repetition through textual determination. In the next instance, the question would be, How do multiple repetitions further shape our own present-day expressivist sphere of language, where personal identities and interpretive communities are in flux? To answer that question fully would require another entire book, but it is a necessary question and one that I hope to pursue in the future. In this context, however, it is a matter of setting the question on the right path.

I have defined personally resonant language in terms of local knowledge, highly determined linguistic structures, and the articulation of their crucial junctures. I have opposed this approach to holism, dialectics, and abstract conceptual paraphrases of various philosophical positions. Nevertheless, the debates in this book have been conducted in very abstract language. I prefer to finish this afterword with a set of very concrete observations about canonical texts and values in the discourse of contemporary North American departments of literature in universities and colleges. The controversy about the canon is more than an example or illustration of my theoretical concerns, however. Although I cannot fully engage all issues about canon formation, I think that the concept of a canon has special importance in literary studies. Canonicity is linked to Taylor's paradigm statements and the issue of determination by repetition, which I have just outlined. Basic intuition tells us that interpretation by repetition and the formation of a canon of literary works are interdependent actions. The debate about the canon has special relevance to literary studies.

Concerns about the canon are endemic to the study of literature and philosophy, what Taylor calls that "notorious deformation." Even neighboring interpretive disciplines in the humanities and social sciences do not seem as divided as the discipline of literature when it comes to questioning the value, ideology, politics, and privileges of mainstream authors, works, and ideas in the canon of their respective disciplines. The hermeneutical nature of literary studies seems to draw out an entire set of concerns about canon formation: as a measure of value, a set of rules for deciding meaning, a source of tradition, or an institutionally approved set of texts.

In the context of this brief afterword, I cannot attempt a detailed analysis of each major concept of canonicity. But I can assert, as an extension of this book's arguments, that we need to specify what is central about the event of canonization. If we need to talk about texts rather than textuality, situated judgments rather than universal values and norms, webs of cultural and social connection rather than holistic frameworks, then we need to talk about canonical actions rather than an always operating, ever-present canon which pervades every setting in which works of literature are discussed or analyzed. A narrowing rather than a widening of the focus yields better insights into the connections between the interpretive actions by which a canon is constituted and the ideals of plurality and situatedness.

Not every reading of a work of literature will be governed by or will fundamentally challenge a canon of literary works. But it is also true that the study of literature, more than other humanistic disciplines, requires a definition of canonicity in order to function. At the center of literary debates about the canon there is a profound tension between a commitment to social pluralism and the recognition of paradigm statements that we are compelled to repeat in order to become expressive of central ethical values and concepts. To grasp and resolve this tension we need to ask questions like, Where does the canon in particular acts of reading come into focus? where is concern about the canon felt most deeply?

In response to these questions, I offer the following three observations about the canon:

1. The literary canon, as we know it today in the so-called great writers and their most widely read works, usually defines the credentials of a professor of literature. It also defines the legitimacy and originality of a professor's research, and the student's qualifications that attach to a degree in literature. But not one of these qualifications is a direct, unambiguous expression of canonicity. Interpretive practices can realize what counts as the canonical in the study of literature, but one is not the same as the other. They are closely connected, however; they illuminate each other.

2. If canonicity can be addressed through a more finely tuned discussion of interpretive practices, we should not expect the outcome of the discussion

to be a simple set of texts or a canon of rules of interpretation that govern or control or formalize the individual pedagogical situation. Imagine the consequences if the classroom were taken literally as a vessel for the canonical tradition of humanism or classicism or historicism, if every class in a literature department had to amount to some profound hermeneutical contact with the past or some fusion of modernity with the past. That is an unlivable ideal. Yet discussions of the canon do express anxieties about the purpose and value of the time we spend on the study of literary works.

3. From the perspective of this book's discussion of expressivism and textuality, the event of canon formation or canon response is a special occurrence based in the claim that a literary work has upon the vocabulary of an interpretive community and the expressions that become decisive for one's personal identity in the interpretive community. No doubt the moment of choice, when highly motivated readers of literature decide to invest a portion of their egos in the rearticulation of authors' words, has to do with all sorts of contingent circumstances: where an institutionalized literary space like a college or university literature department sits in the cultural landscape, which interpretive practices are emphasized by the institution's pedagogy, the contingency of personal relations. But these contingencies would not be decisive for sustaining interest in the rearticulation of an author's language over the course of many years of study and writing.

When I say that a special, more-than-contingent conjunction of influences is canonical, I am trying to be consistent with my earlier statement that a fixed canon, or a concept of canonicity, does not operate all the time in each and every interpretive event, be it a reading experience, a classroom meeting, or a learned society forum. The canon focuses interpretive practice on expressions which have a decisive claim, without governing method or performance. As a focus rather than a rule, the canon is dialogical rather than methodological. It functions in the same way that Stanley Cavell describes paraphrasing: like a needle on a compass, a pathway, an orientation. Which is not to say that it fixes the best that has been thought or said or that it is the central monument of the literary profession. A work of literature begins to sound canonical if it gains a strong influence over the vocabulary of an interpretive community. If the adoption of a certain vocabulary, which becomes authoritative for the identity of the group, does not occur, it does not imply failure. I am saying that canonical readings are a rare but decisive occurrence.

Harold Bloom has probably come closest to spelling out the meaning of canonical interpretations when he speaks of being chosen by the study of litera-ture or of writers trying to take over each other's words or of the apprentice situation of the poetic ephebe or graduate student as a mixture of excitement and profound loss (that is, loss as it is perhaps captured by Harry Frankfurt, when choice means having to give up an alternative one continues to recognize as outside the formation of one's identity). Entering canonical discourse is no easy matter, and it is not an all-at-once entry in any event but something more akin to the identification of which literary expressions seem to speak for one's own posi-tion in a discourse. What matters in the canon debate is finding out the role that decisive literary expressions play in speakers realizing their dialogical links to each other. These links are not total or universal ones. In Cavell's words, they are just the ones that count as more than ordinary. For the purposes of this book, a limited but crucial insight into canon formation gives the study of literature its expressive dimension in society at large, without, however, making literature into a false substitute for the study of history, politics, or psychology.

The present debate about the canon, which is so inescapable to the study of literature, indirectly recognizes the expressivist dimension within the study of literature. If that recognition can be strengthened and specified, then the study of literature gains central importance in our society and culture. Part of that recognition depends on acknowledging the repetitious, linguistically determined, and personally constituted links between specific texts and specific cultural groups in our plural culture. Debates about the canon go astray, by contrast, when they attempt to connect canon formation, social change, and cultural value either very tightly or very loosely. It is analogous to Taylor's point about nominalists who seek first principles that govern or master language. It is analogous, further, to the opposition between epistemologists, who devalue language completely as a mere repository of designations, a set of signs operated by grammatical rules, and interpretive holists, who see the world as a language, a plenitude of meanings, which humanity has the task of deciphering.

Two passages from E. D. Hirsch's recent writings provide an economical demonstration of the futility of debating the canon in general terms which miss the expressivist moment. I think it is fair to use Hirsch to signal this misapprehen-sion since he has done so much to fuel the debate about the canon in his work on cultural literacy, and he claims support for his position by invoking the writings of New Pragmatists like Knapp and Michaels and of hermeneuts like Gadamer. In his book on cultural literacy, he writes,

> Suppose we think of American public culture as existing in three segments. At one end is our civil religion, which is laden with definitive value traditions [freedom, equality, self-government]. . . . At the other end of the spectrum is the *vocabulary* of our national discourse, by no means empty of content but nonetheless value-neutral in the sense that it is used to support all the conflicting values that arise in public discourse [and is hospitable to God, mammon, pornography, prudery, Zen]. . . . Between these two extremes lies the vast middle domain of culture proper. Here are the concrete politics, customs, technologies, and legends that define and determine our current attitudes and actions and our institutions.[2]

Farther on, Hirsch makes one more crucial point: the term *vocabulary* is equated with literacy and is summarized as the pragmatic ability to use language to communicate *any* point of view effectively.

Hirsch's three segments attempt to keep values in their proper place as founding cultural ideals which cannot be negated, while allowing political and cultural articulation the greatest possible plurality. There is no apparent limit to the human agent's ability to practice any belief whatsoever, to add value to literacy in the middle domain of cultural participation, but all the agent gains is the raw ability to communicate a belief. What institutional or collective form do these beliefs take other than the dream of pure, unmediated communication? As the human agent inevitably moves toward expressions of value it is very unclear how speakers gain historical substance or exist in concrete practice. The most Hirsch's outline of the public sphere offers is the transformation of the linguistic subject into the narrative point of view, but into any point of view, as if identity were infinitely interchangeable, lacking precisely in Taylor's situatedness. Hirsch may concede the eventual mingling of value and vocabulary, but precisely so as to exclude stability. The instability of the middle domain could be taken as a sign of its dynamism and potential for development. More likely, however, the instability is posited as a sort of negative freedom, the inability to change cultural institutions through expressive behavior, which remains merely anybody's point of view.

Hirsch is addressing the issue of literacy, not canon formation. But what kind of literacy is it that instructs us to put aside our fear of prejudice by assuming that we can suspend values in language, that we can acquire shared meanings independently of shared values? Hirsch assumes that the underlying fear of bias and confrontation of values remains the real stumbling block to educational reform. It is as if Hirsch assumes that, notwithstanding all his open admiration of American cultural pluralism, speakers do not need to articulate values and beliefs in direct contrast with each other in the middle domain, occupied by all the major institutions of the public sphere, such as the universities, the press, and the courts. Literacy is not the basis of culture, out of which higher philosophical and political speculations can grow. Literacy is the collective neutrality of culture hidden by our imaginary biases.

Once we think of neutrality as the key to Hirsch's cultural pluralism, it becomes a noticeable feature of an entire philosophy of language, based supposedly in pragmatism and hermeneutics. Points of this philosophy include the following: there is no language as such, except as it is actualized by the intention of a speaker; intention is not a matter of total or global actualization, however, for the linguistic or speaking subject is separate from the historical, value-laden subject; intentional meaning is never alien or foreign or indeterminate—it always works and can be disambiguated. These points are necessarily crude because they abbreviate a vast network of argumentation in Hirsch's works, but they are commonly held opinions thanks to the work of the New Pragmatists. I quote Hirsch's reference to Knapp's and Michaels's article "Against Theory":

> [The intentionalist argument] holds that intention is formally necessary at every moment of interpretation and that there can be no construed meaning without intention. One basis for this claim of formal necessity is as follows: all sequences of phonemes or graphemes can sustain more than one type of construed meaning. For instance, they might sustain allusive or nonallusive, ironical or nonironical, literal or nonliteral construed meanings. But every type of construed meaning is what it is and not some other type of meaning that might have been construed. So terms like "intention," "speech-act," and "authorship" are needed to indicate the formally required agency that makes the construed meaning this type rather than that in any instance of interpretation.[3]

Agency determines linguistic meaning. Whenever we are talking about meaning we are talking about a particular speaker who has acted or intended or

authored that particular meaning, whose posited identity determines our interpretation of signs as words. Or, as Knapp and Michaels put it succinctly, "Pinning
down an interpretation of [a] sentence will not involve adding a speaker but
deciding among a range of speakers" (14). But Hirsch's terminology hedges the
Knapp and Michaels position: intention is "formally necessary" or a "formal
necessity," or agency is "formally required." "Formally" calls attention to our
consideration of words as lived speech without adding any content. The main
point is to collapse the distinctions among intention, agency, and vocabulary
without producing a notion of prejudice, as if the particular speaker had special
jurisdiction over linguistic meaning. This peculiar antiformalist formalism has
been noticed and commented upon by Frank Lentricchia and David Couzens
Hoy. Lentricchia observes of the Hirschian speaker, "Though Hirsch's allusions to
Saussure's *le sujet parlant* . . . and to the whole scholarly process of retrieving the
cultural forms of another time [or of our time] would appear to involve his
method deeply in history and the historical person . . . his actual intention is
almost the opposite. . . . The 'actual historical person' is not the author that
Hirsch would reinstate, because the 'actual historical person,' saturated as he is in
process and particularity, is inaccessible to a hermeneutical system [that depends
on types]" (266). Hoy quotes Hirsch's *Validity in Interpretation* on the distinction
to be drawn between the "biographical person" and the "speaking subject": " 'In
construing and verifying verbal meaning, only the speaking subject counts.' "[4]

Hirsch extends his principle of intentionality, the way we author our meanings, to argue for the complete disappearance of the alien perspective:

> It is an evasion at best to argue that the interpreter's alien perspective dis-
> torts meaning, for it is impossible to distort something that cannot even
> exist by means of an alien perspective. . . . When, for instance, H. G. Gad-
> amer speaks of a fusion of perspectives, a *Horizontverschmelzung*, he
> overlooks the paradox that this intermediate perspective can no longer
> possess the meaning it pretends to carry into the contemporary world. Of
> course, the words of a text can be respoken from a new perspective and a
> new meaning formulated. Of course, as some critics insist, the reader can
> become a self-imaging author. But a text cannot be *interpreted* from a per-
> spective different from the original author's. Meaning is understood from
> the perspective that lends existence to meaning. Any other procedure is
> not interpretation but authorship.[5]

Either the alien is really already known as the formally posited speaker, or we ourselves become the author of the meaning. In either case, language is rendered transparent, immediate, and what Hirsch's most recent writings call literate, leaving speakers to decide a text's contemporary value at a later point in time. At this stage, however, it is hard to see how we would ever decide against what we understand; it would be like dissolving our very place in the social world. David Couzens Hoy sums it up very nicely: Hirsch's author/interpreter "has nothing against which to criticize his own understanding. . . . Such an empty principle is dangerous because it can undercut the awareness of the limitations of . . . interpretation and lead to a forgetting of the need for self-criticism (33)."

The search for a transparent vocabulary of cultural instruction or interpretation is contrary to the expressivist moment which the canon debate illuminates. This book offers a philosophical account of expressivism that is compatible with pragmatic pluralism and contemporary textual analysis. My concluding remarks about the canon point to a specific role for literary studies in sustaining connections among pragmatism, expressivism, and deconstruction. Far from being transparent, these connections must be determined over and over again. That is what I take to be the importance of our contemporary discourse about textuality. The aim of this book has been to set in motion further determinations of a personally resonant language arising from the study of literary texts.

NOTES

Pragmatism, Expressivism, and Deconstruction 1

1 Peter Railton, "Pluralism, Determinacy, and Dilemma," *Ethics* 102 (1992): 720–42.

2 Susan Wolf, "Two Levels of Pluralism," *Ethics* 102 (1992): 785–98. Wolf's essay is published next to Railton's (see note 1). The two essays are presented in the context of an *Ethics* symposium called "Pluralism and Ethical Theory." When I conclude that Wolf sees the effort to determine in finer terms a pattern of plural values in social norms and conflicts, I am subscribing to what Railton calls the *accommodation* strategy of moral theory, whereby "recalcitrant phenomena . . . [are accommodated] through theory enrichment . . . by articulating basic moral principles into a less coarse-grained scheme through recognition of various distinctions" (723). Accommodation is opposed to *riding roughshod* in the name of theoretical simplicity, or *explaining away* apparent conflict or anomalies (which Bernard Williams would call relativism, as I explain in the next chapter). The point about accommodation needs to be underlined at the outset of this book, since finely grained articulations are, by my argument, the link that sustains comparisons among Rorty, Taylor, and de Man. The entire architecture of this book places the pragmatist's recognition of plurality into a nonrelativist, situated language of contrast, which, finally, connects with the finely grained insights into language found in a strong

textualist like de Man. My concern is the implication of pluralism for literary studies, and what insights into literature may give back to ethical insights into personhood. Railton and Wolf, as ethical philosophers, do not address the role of language or texts, but they do uphold a notion of core values and generalizable principles that may be determined in the midst of genuine plurality. An ethical theory that seeks to determine a core statement while allowing for plural and incommensurable values is analogous to the function of textual theories as I present them in this book.

3 For a good discussion of the problem of relativism within a commitment to pragmatism, see Barbara Herrnstein Smith, *Contingencies of Value: Alternative Perspectives for Critical Theory* (Cambridge: Harvard Univ. Press, 1988), 155–73. Pragmatists like Rorty and Smith state that relativism and subjectivism are problems for truth-seekers, but that pragmatists see relativism as part of discovering cultural solidarity and enthnocentric practice. Pragmatists like Smith seek out social practices that "compel" or "constrain" action and use the problem of relativism to detail combinations of constraints upon agents. In fact, for Smith, Rorty is, paradoxically, insufficiently "relativist" because his description of solidarity and constraint is not fine enough and ultimately apolitical. See 169–70. A conventionally negative assessment of the relativist strains within pragmatism and deconstruction is found in Carl Rapp, "Coming Out into the Corridor: Postmodern Fantasies of Pluralism," *Georgia Review* 41 (1987): 533–52. Rapp characterizes pragmatism and deconstruction as "specious pluralisms," unable to adjudicate between different schools of interpretation and methods, loosely committed to an ideal of plurality of meaning and value for its own sake. In Rapp's essay, words like "pluralism," "postmodernism" and "relativism" are synonymous when applied to pragmatism and deconstruction. I cite his essay as a typical instance of the intellectual resistance to pragmatism and deconstruction on ethical grounds. But if we compare Rapp's position to the position of ethicists like Railton and Wolf on pluralism, we see that the emphasis on particularity and highly determined forms of analysis is what makes pragmatism and deconstruction genuinely plural. The philosophical difficulties of pluralism are barely acknowledged by critics like Rapp when they avoid the issue of carefully determined, particularized expressions of personal value and social coherence.

4 The topics of legitimation, justification, and belief are treated extensively in their recent books: Richard Rorty, *Contingency, Irony, Solidarity* (Cambridge and New York: Cambridge Univ. Press, 1989), esp. chap. 3, "The Contingency of a Liberal Community" which addresses the social critiques of Jürgen Habermas and Michel Foucault. Rorty continues the discussion in various essays in his two most recent collections, *Objectivity, Relativism, and Truth* and *Essays on Heidegger and Others* (Cambridge and New York: Cambridge Univ. Press, 1991), especially "Habermas and Lyotard on Postmodernity" in the second collection (on Heidegger). Fish's position is expounded in *Doing What Comes Naturally: Change, Rhetoric, and the Practice of Theory in Literary and Legal Studies* (Durham and London: Duke Univ. Press, 1989), especially the essays in the section "Consequences" and the essay on Habermas entitled "Critical Self-Consciousness, Or Can We Know What We're Doing?" I discuss Fish's position in part II of this book.

5 Richard Shusterman, *Pragmatist Aesthetics. Living Beauty, Rethinking Art* (Cambridge, Mass.: Blackwell, 1992), 120. The quotation belongs to a chapter entitled "Beneath Interpretation," which was published originally as "Beneath Interpretation: Against

Hermeneutical Holism," in *The Monist* 73 (1990): 181–204. The republication is note-
worthy because the word "universalism" replaces the word "holism" in the book
version of the essay. All further references will be to *Pragmatist Aesthetics,* but I continue to use Shusterman's points as criticisms of hermeneutical holism.

6 Rorty makes this point succinctly in *Contingency, Irony, and Solidarity,* 47–48: "To say
that convictions are only 'relatively valid' might seem to mean that they can only be justified to people who hold certain other beliefs—not to anyone and everyone. But if this
were what was meant, they would have no contrastive force, for there would be no interesting statements which were *absolutely* valid. Absolute validity would be confined to
everyday platitudes, elementary mathematical truths, and the like: the sort of beliefs no-
body wants to argue about because they are neither controversial nor central to
anyone's sense of who she is or what she lives for. . . . A conviction which can be justified to *anyone* is of little interest."

7 Martha Minow, *Making All the Difference: Inclusion, Exclusion, and American Law*
(Ithaca and London: Cornell Univ. Press, 1990), 381.

8 See *Contingency, Irony, and Solidarity,* 13–17. For a full discussion of the pragmatist
criticism of representational theories of language, see Walter Benn Michaels, "Philosophy in Kinkanja: Eliot's Pragmatism," *Glyph* 8 (1981): 170–202. Michaels analyzes the
discussion of perception and experience in Eliot's dissertation on F. H. Bradley. The
pragmatist analysis of perception seeks a synthesis of mental intention, practical experi-
ential context, and the object world. The same synthesis carries over into the doctrine of
the simultaneity of word and object in language. Michaels makes the point that, contrary to some readings of Eliot's modernism, Eliot does not seek after some full presence
which lies behind all language. In pragmatic terms, words and objects cannot be separated. The larger issue which concerns Michaels is how the fusion of word, object, and
intention supports the notion of interpretation as "always and only local, a function of
the situation you happen to be in," with its own "particular constraints in effect at the
time the sentence is spoken or understood" (185). The articulation of this point is now
identified with Michaels's new pragmatism or antitheory, which I discuss with reference
to Stanley Fish in chapter 7. My concern with the radical side of new pragmatism is
anticipated by the conclusion of Michaels's essay. The practical identification of interpretation, intention, and language suggests that reality is "a system of arbitrary
conventions" (195). Like Rorty, Michaels recognizes that the implications of radical
conventionalism are "to acknowledge its contingency without undermining its validity,
its power over us" (196). But that also appears to exclude the possibility of deciding
between alternatives because we are so situated or embedded in our particular set of
contingently held beliefs. My criticism of pragmatism questions whether a strong emphasis on a situated speaker, which indeed owes something to an attack on representationalist theories of language, entails the radical elimination of an act of decision making. On that point, Taylor, who is equally antirepresentationalist, presents a powerful
alternative to pragmatist situatedness which does not cancel the human agent's construction of choices in language.

9 See Rorty's essay "Freud and Moral Reflection," in *Essays on Heidegger and Others,*
vol. 2, in which he compares Freud's mechanisms of personality with other, scientific an-
alogues between persons and physical phenomena.

10 The emphasis here on defining conviction qualifies this point. Convictions, I shall argue, require an account of language that limits the value of representations, but they do not rule out language's ability to represent things in other contexts. Pragmatists do not reject representations, but they do refuse to give them the privilege of being the ideal form of language, and they refuse to attach other properties like objectivity and realism to them. In Rorty's jargon, representations are not the "final vocabulary," and they are not the language spoken by the world. In the literary disciplines, a similar debate centers upon the term *mimesis*. I think Charles Taylor gets to the essence of the representationalist controversy within pragmatism when he writes of Rorty that, in spite of some post-modern tendencies to celebrate a variety of language games, pragmatists seem to think that debates about realism and representation can be dispensed with in one stroke by taking a new "Big Picture" approach to knowledge. Taylor prefers a more detailed "contrastive" approach, as close to actual practice as possible, in which the priorities of different language games, including representationalism, change through a "coming and going between detailed reading and over-all view." I shall elaborate on Taylor's views as a supplement to pragmatism throughout this book. In a similar spirit, however, I suggest that Taylor's views can be supplemented by the insights of deconstructionism. See Taylor, "Rorty in the Epistemological Tradition," in *Reading Rorty,* ed. Alan R. Malachowski (Cambridge, Mass., and Oxford: Basil Blackwell, 1990), 257–75.

11 Jeffrey Stout, "The Moral Consequences of Pragmatism," in *Ethics after Babel: The Languages of Morals and Their Discontents* (Boston: Beacon Press, 1988), 243–65.

12 For an elaboration of this point, see Michael Fischer, "Redefining Philosophy as Literature. Richard Rorty's 'Defence' of Literary Culture," in *Reading Rorty,* 233–43. Fischer welcomes Rorty's efforts to give literature and literary discourse in general a formative role in social theory, but he notes that Rorty "exaggerates the shapelessness of the literary culture that interests him . . . literary critics speak a more stable vocabulary and heed firmer rules than Rorty supposes" (237).

13 I borrow these comparisons from Rorty's essay "Inquiry as Recontextualization: An Anti-Dualist Account of Interpretation," in *Objectivity, Relativism, and Truth,* 94–95.

14 James Tully, "Wittgenstein and Political Philosophy: Understanding Practices of Critical Reflection," *Political Theory* 17 (1989): 172–204. For Shusterman, see note 5. My comparison of Shusterman and Tully focuses on how they narrow down the event of interpretation. In other respects, Tully is primarily concerned with rethinking the concept of foundations much more generally in the context of social history and post-Enlightenment political philosophy. See, for example, his "Progress and Scepticism 1789–1989," *Transactions of the Royal Society of Canada,* 5th ser., 4 (1989): 21–33. I think it would be fair to say that Tully is not a pragmatist antifoundationalist as much as an antitranscendentalist. He would shift the concept of foundational discourse from things like reason, objective representation, methodological inquiry, systematic doubt, dialectical critique to a Wittgensteinian acceptance and familiarization with the "multi-plicity of the world," "its irreducible diversity and our relations to it" (32).

15 Taylor follows Gadamer in giving interpretation an ontological place in the definition of humanity, history, and culture. In many respects, Gadamer's philosophy of language and Taylor's overlap: in their rejection of objectivism and instrumentalism, and in their op-

position to linguistic sign theories, like Saussure's, which they view as antihumanist. And the connection could be pursued further through the debt both philosophers pay to Heidegger. As David Couzens Hoy writes, "Gadamer . . . [and I would add Taylor] follows Heidegger in abandoning the foundationalist enterprise that looks for a pre-suppositionless starting point in the self-certainty of subjectivity, and in stressing instead the interpretive and historical character of all understanding, including philo-sophical self-understanding" (in *The Critical Circle* [Berkeley: Univ. of California Press, 1982], 5). But the ontological and holistic context of hermeneutics is exactly what I am attempting to avoid. The argument I am putting forward in this book is that Taylor differs from Gadamer because he offers certain concepts of language that may be devel-oped in conjunction with pragmatism and literary theory. Those concepts are focused on Taylor's "language of qualitative contrast" rather than on the "logocentric" topics that are found in philosophical hermeneutics. To pursue the connection to Gadamer would cloud rather than clarify the issues in Taylor's philosophy of language which are stake in this book.

The finest analysis of Gadamer in the context of literary theory is found in Joel Weinsheimer, *Philosophical Hermeneutics and Literary Theory* (New Haven: Yale Univ. Press, 1991). Weinsheimer provides excellent commentary on how Gadamer's philoso-phy of language enlarges the concept of metaphor, canonicity, and the aesthetic status of the literary work. Weinsheimer is particularly fine at elaborating how the Gadamerian gap between the symbolized and the symbol makes possible an unfolding of meaning, an interpretive space in tradition and history, that cannot be captured in theories of lin-guistic substitution or indication which now seem to prevail in literary theory (see 101–10). In effect, the unfolding of a self-divided identity in the symbolic offers a criticism of things like the arbitrariness of the sign, allegory, the detached perspective; that sort of criticism would seem to have pragmatism and deconstruction as its targets. One very great difference remains, however. Throughout Weinsheimer's careful analysis, and in-deed throughout *Truth and Method* itself, terms like *symbol, text, tradition, mimesis* cannot be broken down, no matter how rich the play between them, even unto the last pages of Weinsheimer's book, where "text" and "scripture" are placed in a highly dia-lectical relation to each other. My point is simply that this type of discourse for situating the interpreter is inconsistent with pragmatist and deconstructionist development of those terms through finer layers *within texts* of nontotalizable contrasts. This book ar-gues that Taylor's effort to situate the interpreter in language can be made consistent with elements of pragmatism and deconstruction, whereas Gadamer's philosophy of lan-guage would probably no longer resemble itself were it to undergo the same treatment. Weinsheimer traces the limits to which the Gadamerian vocabulary can be put.

Finally, I see no need to be drawn into a lengthy debate about presence and logo-centrism, which is unavoidable when Gadamer and hermeneutical philosophy encounter pragmatist and deconstructionist critics at a very high level of generalization. In order to carry over notions like situatedness from hermeneutics into pragmatism or deconstruc-tion, as I would attempt to do through the writings of Charles Taylor, abstract opposi-tions, at the level of logocentrism in general, need to be avoided and replaced by finer contrasts that do actually perform the work of situating the reader. For the general de-bate about Gadamer in the context of pragmatism and deconstruction, see *Dialogue and Deconstruction. The Gadamer-Derrida Encounter*, ed. Diane P. Michelfelder and Richard E. Palmer (Albany: State Univ. of New York Press, 1989).

16 See Taylor's essay "What Is Human Agency?" in his *Human Agency and Language* (Cambridge and New York: Cambridge Univ. Press, 1985), 21. This essay and several others concerning the philosophy of language are discussed in chapter 3.

17 Charles Altieri provides a good definition of Taylor's expressivism in his essay "From Expressivist Aesthetics to Expressivist Ethics," in *Literature and the Question of Philosophy,* ed. Anthony J. Cascardi (Baltimore: Johns Hopkins Univ. Press, 1987), 134–66. Commenting on Taylor, Altieri writes, "Second-order [morally important] choices are contrastive because they are choices of meanings, not objects. Thus, they are constrained by the network of public associations that establishes meaning. But those contraints are precisely what enables expressive activity. . . . Selves have public identity when they consistently maintain the contrastive schemes projected in their reasons for their actions. . . . There is no way to know a self apart from its expressions. So what matters is not whether they are true to some preexisting process but whether a person's way of making actual deeds intelligible earns the evaluative predicates one wants to attribute to them" (146–47).

18 The terms *commensurability, conflict,* and *comparison* are not completely interchangeable with one another, since each denotes a slightly different assumption about an initial common quality that is being sought through a comparative analysis. *Incommensurability* assumes a difference between an A and B in comparison that could never be completely eradicated, no matter how fine the analysis. In that sense, *incommensurability,* while not always able to stand apart from terms like *comparison* or *relative degree of conflict,* is most important to Taylor's definition of the terms of a genuine decision, which posits at some level irreconcilable differences. My exposition of these terms relies on an essay by Richard J. Bernstein, "Incommensurability and Otherness Revisited," in *The New Constellation: The Ethical-Political Horizons of Modernity/Postmodernity* (Cambridge: MIT Press, 1992), 57–78. For a discussion of the connection between pluralism and pragmatism, which supports some of the general arguments of this book, see also Bernstein's "Pragmatism, Pluralism, and the Healing of Wounds," 323–40. By pragmatism, Bernstein intends a discussion of the link between pluralism and nonfoundationalism.

Beyond Relativism and Holism   **2**

1 See, for example, an excellent essay by Robert Stecker, "Fish's Argument for the Relativity of Interpretive Truth," *The Journal of Aesthetics and Art Criticism* 48 (1990): 223–30. Fish has been one of the stronger critics of the relativist fallacy, arguing that the beliefs which uphold the interpretive community make a relativist fluctuation of opinion impossible. Stecker points out a blurring of two quite different assumptions behind Fish's claim. One is the innocuous assumption that we need to consider context in order to interpret the meaning of utterances that may vary in meaning. Relativism is trivial in that sense. But to make truth and all belief entirely dependent on social or communal context is to relativize meaning in a much more radical sense. Stecker claims that Fish uses cases of the first type of relativism to underwrite philosophical arguments about the second type. If the second type were upheld, the world might vary from one interpretive community to the next, without order or critical comparison. That would seem to be another instance of the utopian and radical undercurrents within the new pragmatism, which I alluded to in chapter 1. This utopianism challenges the new pragmatists' claim to be situated and stabilized by an ongoing set of interpretive practices.

2 See Williams, *Ethics and the Limits of Philosophy* (Cambridge: Harvard Univ. Press, 1985), 156–73. Further references to the essay on relativism and reflection will be made parenthetically in the text.

3 See Dreyfus's essay "Holism and Hermeneutics," *Review of Metaphysics* 34 (1980): 3–23, esp. 20–21. The essay is particularly relevant in its commentary on Rortyan pragmatism and in the exchange with Taylor that accompanies it. The debate on holism concerns the degree of hermeneutical background, pragmatic familiarity, or situatedness necessary for critical choice and reflection upon practice. Overextending theoretical reflection presents an overdetermined picture of cultural practice, but for Dreyfus the pragmatist position is too flexible and gives no account of the consistency of changing one's beliefs or practices through reflection.

4 See Harry G. Frankfurt, "Identification and Wholeheartedness," in *The Importance of What We Care About: Philosophical Essays* (New York: Cambridge Univ. Press, 1988), 159–76. Further references are made parenthetically in the text.

Taylor on Situatedness   **3**

1 Charles Altieri, "From Expressivist Aesthetics to Expressivist Ethics," in *Literature and the Question of Philosophy*, ed. Anthony J. Cascardi (Baltimore: Johns Hopkins Univ. Press, 1987), 134–66. Further references to this essay will be made parenthetically in the text. I have found only one other extensive commentary on Taylor by a philosopher who is now widely read by literary theorists: Martha C. Nussbaum, *Love's Knowledge: Essays on Philosophy and Literature* (New York: Oxford Univ. Press, 1990), which contains the chapter titled "Transcending Humanity," 365–90. Nussbaum's chapter was occasioned by Taylor's review of her book *The Fragility of Goodness: Luck and Ethics in Greek Tragedy and Philosophy*. So there is indeed a bit of luck in the manner in which Taylor suddenly appears in Nussbaum's new book. Nussbaum addresses the important issue of a transcendental approach to philosophical issues in Taylor's works, which she contrasts to her own Aristotelean approach. I shall refer in more detail to her essay when I attempt to disengage Taylor's insights into the philosophy of language from the ontology to which he is clearly committed.

2 Charles Taylor, *Sources of the Self: The Making of the Modern Identity* (Cambridge: Harvard Univ. Press, 1989). Further references to this work will be made parenthetically in the text.

3 Taylor, "What Is Human Agency?" in *Human Agency and Language* (Cambridge: Cambridge Univ. Press, 1985), 29–33.

4 This little point deserves to be underlined. It rests on the whole idea of acknowledgment that I attempt to develop through a commentary on some of Stanley Cavell's work. A truer description of a state of affairs or a counterfactually organized search for consensus leaves out the whole question of how social agents adopt certain beliefs as authoritative for themselves. As Raymond Geuss puts it, "Agents don't *generally* come

to think that their beliefs are false if they discover that they have been 'determined' by factors of which they were unaware" (61). Similarly, dispelling an illusion will not convince an agent to change a pattern of beliefs and habits. A deeper sort of conviction is required to bring about a change through critical reflection. See Geuss's *The Idea of a Critical Theory* (Cambridge: Cambridge Univ. Press, 1981), 60 ff. Much the same point comes through in Williams's concept of confidence, which I discussed earlier, and in Callinicos's criticism of hermeneutics as taking for granted the solicitation of understanding it seeks to illuminate. I discuss Callinicos on pp. 56–58.

5 The whole question of whether or not Taylor's insights into language and personhood are underwritten by a sophisticated ontology has been taken up by Nussbaum in *Love's Knowledge*. Nussbaum's reply to Taylor is really more self-directed than directed at Taylor. She attempts to answer his criticisms about her own work, specifically whether it is possible to uphold a morality of literature without a notion like hypergoods. Nussbaum replies by invoking Aristotle and the need to recognize the particularity and contingency of moral experience and relatedness. I think her reply makes it possible to take up notions of central good, like Taylor's hypergood, and unpack them through a detailed engagement with textual expressions from literary sources. Such an approach is obviously much more in line with my own, and my effort to include the pragmatists in the discussion. Taylor's best insights into language as contrastive should be detachable from the telos toward symbolic hypergoods which he attaches to these contrasts. Nussbaum's reply indicates one possible way of recognizing Taylor's powerful contribution to contemporary moral thought without subscribing to his ontological assumptions. I differ from Nussbaum in believing that the best way to answer Taylor is to start from within his position on language and work up to the point where it touches concerns about textual construction. Nussbaum and Taylor seem equally remote from theories of textuality in spite of their common respect for and interest in philosophy and literature as similar human endeavors.

6 Richard E. Flathman, *The Philosophy and Politics of Freedom* (Chicago: Univ. of Chicago Press, 1987), 43. In addition to the work of Flathman, good discussions of Taylor may be found in Alex Callinicos, *Making History: Agency, Structure, and Change in Social Theory* (Ithaca: Cornell Univ. Press, 1988), and Richard Bernstein, "Why Hegel Now?" in *Philosophical Profiles: Essays in a Pragmatic Mode* (Philadelphia: Univ. of Pennsylvania Press, 1986), 141–75.

7 See Callinicos's chapter "Reasons and Interests," 96–133.

8 See ibid., 111–12, on this point.

9 Charles Taylor, "The Hermeneutics of Conflict," in *Meaning and Context: Quentin Skinner and His Critics*, ed. James Tully (Princeton: Princeton Univ. Press, 1988), 218–28; the quotation is from 225–26.

10 *Human Agency and Language*, 215–47 and 248–92, respectively.

11 Taylor does not see his own philosophical treatment of language, the triple-H tradition, and expressivism as being about symbolism at all. Criticism of his literary style and his readings of romanticism or modernism has to be qualified when we use the term *sym-*

bolism. Taylor is not building up a picture of expressive agency by treating topics like beauty or literary form; like Hegel, he seeks an intellectualized linguistic medium that would be able to bear a good deal more reflective consciousness than is normally given over to aesthetical philosophy. Therefore, when I apply terms like *literary* or *symbolic* to his arguments, I refer to his nonproblematic reliance upon figurative language, his refusal to scrutinize linguistic structure, and a certain indefiniteness of meaning he would appreciate as symbolical. All these arguments are for a good cause, namely, the attack upon meaning as strictly controllable or upon the primacy of the designative properties of the linguistic sign. My point is simply that these arguments can be carried much further within contemporary literary theory and need not rely upon a romantic characterization of the expressive capacity of the human agent.

A complex account of the aesthetic characteristics of Taylor's expressivism is found in Altieri, "From Expressivist Aesthetics to Expressivist Ethics." Altieri picks up very well Taylor's view of the agent's self-realization through the use of contrastive language, which is not a simple representation of social reality. He underlines Taylor's sense of the agent as being embodied in language, which becomes a means of establishing identity within the community of speakers. But interestingly, Altieri sees Taylor as an *aesthetic* point of departure for a Kantian definition of agency, as finding the impersonal imperatives of morality in "indirect presentations" of the concept, or "*hypotyposis.*" The upshot of Altieri's reading is to take Taylor in the direction of the development of our capacity for aesthetic expressions, which in turn gives ethical substance to our lives through the play of perspectives and the exercise of our capacity for imaginative expressions. I believe that Altieri's effort to combine the aesthetic and the ethical under the rubric of expressivism distorts Taylor's position, since it underplays Taylor's main interest in the concept of situated freedom, not a very Kantian notion. Nevertheless, I also believe that Taylor invites, especially in sophisticated theorists like Altieri, an aesthetic reading of his work because he leaves so many aspects of the language of contrast undeveloped, in a state of "purposive expression without purpose."

Cavell and the Decision to Mean What We Say   **4**

1 Stanley Cavell, *Disowning Knowledge in Six Plays of Shakespeare* (New York: Cambridge Univ. Press, 1987), 29.

2 For Rorty's attack on skepticism as a nonissue in philosophy, and hence on the basis of Cavell's work, see his review essay of Cavell's *The Claim of Reason* (1968) in *Consequences of Pragmatism* (Minneapolis: Univ. of Minnesota Press, 1982), 179–90. In citing Rorty, I am trying to indicate some of the obstacles that Cavell must overcome in making the issue of skepticism a real problem in the philosophy of language. My view is much closer to Cavell's than to Rorty's, as the conclusion of Part I of this book tries to make clear.

3 Cavell, "Aesthetic Problems of Modern Philosophy," in *Must We Mean What We Say?* (Cambridge: Cambridge Univ. Press, 1976), 73–96.

4 Gerald Graff, *Poetic Statement and Critical Dogma* (Evanston: Northwestern Univ. Press, 1970).

5 For a detailed discussion of this topic, see my "Resistance and Pregnancy in Empsonian Metaphor," *British Journal of Aesthetics* 26 (1986): 48–56.

6 For a brilliant evaluation of the tensive theory of metaphor with reference to Empson, see Paul H. Fry, *William Empson: Prophet against Sacrifice* (London: Routledge, 1991), especially the chapter "Advancing Logical Disorder: Empson on Method," 55–87. Fry challenges the sort of approach I take to metaphor via Empson and Cavell because he sees the dislocations of meaning within metaphor as serving a much more immediate social function, as virtually a critique of social morality. In that sense, he and I are not in disagreement about the real significance of the tensive elements within a metaphor, so well illuminated by Empson and, following him, Cavell. We differ with respect to the number of steps deemed necessary to proceed from an awareness of contrast to a position of moral conviction.

7 "Being Odd, Getting Even: Threats to Individuality," in *Reconstructing Individualism: Autonomy, Individuality, and the Self in Western Thought,* ed. Thomas C. Heller, Morton Sosna, and David E. Wellbery (Stanford: Stanford Univ. Press, 1986), 312.

8 For an excellent discussion of Cavell's views on deconstruction, and de Man in particular, see Michael Fischer, *Stanley Cavell and Literary Skepticism* (Chicago: Univ. of Chicago Press, 1989), 125–41. Fischer focuses upon the same discussion of the infamous "Archie Bunker" text and the topic of grammar versus rhetoric. I differ from Fischer in looking for an analysis of claims and situatedness in this debate. Fischer is primarily concerned with the opposition between skepticism and ordinary language philosophy, in Cavell's sense of the terms. In that sense, he does not investigate whether a deconstructionist definition of a text extends Cavell's insights into the nature of metaphorical language, and whether this in turn provides another angle on the claims which overcome skepticism. I believe that Fischer's approach reflects the larger issues that interest Cavell himself. My reading of Cavell's comments on de Man is clearly more against the grain and for the sake of developing the arguments of this book, which has little to do with the general topics of skepticism and ordinary language philosophy. For a difficult but provocative analysis of de Man and Cavell, see Stephen W. Melville, *Philosophy Beside Itself: On Deconstruction and Modernism* (Minneapolis: Univ. of Minnesota Press, 1986). I think it is fair to say that Melville looks at Cavell from a more de Manian perspective than the reverse and sees Cavell's interest in skepticism as part of a testing of authenticity and other metaphysical issues. Deconstruction as an attack on metaphysics therefore lines up with Cavell's interests in skepticism. But again, I do not see a strong connection to the approach I take in this book, which attempts to put aside as much as possible comparisons of philosophers and critics in terms of broad definitions.

9 The simplest sort of antiskepticism is perhaps exemplified in Eugene Goodhart's attack on deconstruction and other theoretical excesses. For Goodhart, deconstruction simply contradicts the fact that people do communicate and manage to get things done. See his *The Skeptical Disposition* (Princeton: Princeton Univ. Press, 1984). A similar but more refined dismissal of the problem of skepticism is found in the work of Anthony Cascardi and Michael Fischer. My point here is not to argue for more skepticism as against more faith in basic intelligibility, but to indicate that the use of a normative communicative background as the testing ground for deconstruction or skepticism begs the whole question. Most of the time, the pragmatist view of communication holds. The real question is what to make of those moments when it does not. Are they merely aberrations, marginally significant cases? Perhaps some are. But the same could then be said about the vast bulk of poetic expressions or about psychoanalytical discourse—two languages that Cavell considers of the highest importance. Literature or psychoanalytical fantasies are not the essence of human expression, nor do they govern lesser expressions. They are simply unrecognizable, however, from the pragmatist background. Goodhart and Fisher repeat, in different terms, Graff or Fish when they substitute a background of linguistic intelligibility for the *critical* location of contrasts, incommensurables, discontinuities of expression that pinpoint and define the work of convictions.

10 "Politics as Opposed to What?" in *The Politics of Interpretation*, ed. W. J. T. Mitchell (Chicago: Univ. of Chicago Press, 1983), 181–202.

Determining a Literary Text   **5**

1 Nonetheless, Rorty and Cavell differ sharply on the importance of addressing skepticism as an issue about personal identity. See n. 2, chap. 4.

2 One of the limitations of Stanley Fish's pragmatism may be seen in his entrapment upon these poorly opposed meanings of the term *text,* meanings which poststructuralism supersedes. In a commentary upon a collection of New Historicist essays, Fish uses the word *textuality* to define the "denial that the writing of history could find its foundation in a substratum of unmediated fact" (303). In that sense *textuality* means nonfoundationalism. But that definition is practically indistinguishable from what Shusterman calls the reverse foundationalism of "hermeneutical holism," in which everything becomes textualized. While Fish, in a manner characteristic of new pragmatists, clearly indicates multiple embodiments of New Historicist writing and makes no attempt to homogenize their language of history writing, he is unable to free himself from an underdetermined definition of textuality, as when he writes, "The conviction of the textuality of fact is logically independent of the firmness with which any particular fact is experienced" (308). Thus Marxist texts produce one kind of fact, psychoanalysis another, and New Historicism yet another. All are facts in the sense of holding people to convictions and concrete practices, what I would define in terms of situatedness. But all are equally encompassed by an interchangeable, monolithic conviction that a practice is at some level of abstraction the production of a text. I would see the term *text* in nonopposition to a word like *fact*, since that sort of opposition is bound to run in epistemic circles. Rather, the term *text* should be reserved for the action of constructing and determining the contrast and the hold of one interpretive practice as against another. The determination of a text is partly the determination of the language for expressing this contrast. See Fish, "The Young and the Restless," in *The New Historicism*, ed. H. Aram Veeser (New York: Routledge, 1989), 303–16.

Cavell and Empson on *Othello*   **6**

1 A full consideration of Cavell's analysis of Shakespearean tragedy is beyond the scope of this book. For an excellent general analysis of Cavell on Shakespeare, see Gerald L. Bruns, "Stanley Cavell's Shakespeare," *Critical Inquiry* 16 (1990): 612–32. Bruns takes

up directly the most complex issues in Cavellean criticism: the definition of *acknowledg-ment* and the "answering" which occurs in our exposure to literature. He has a superb sense of the key issues behind Cavell's use of literature which Cavell does not always make clear to his readers. I would differ from Bruns in two respects, however. He tends to emphasize the "characterizational" aspect of tragic figures and imagines a dialogue between the image of a person and the reader. I tend to see Cavell's strongest insights into Shakespeare in rather more textual terms, in the interstices of language. Bruns also compares Cavell to Gadamer in terms of the "situatedness or conditioned character—the limits—of our hermeneutical situation" (629). That is fine, and obviously I too would like to connect Cavell's comments on skepticism to a philosophy of situatedness. But I do not think Gadamer is directly applicable to the issues in literary interpretation. One of the main arguments of this book is that a full-blown definition of situatedness needs to emerge out of a carefully specified theory of textuality. Gadamer offers a complex history and philosophy of language, but, like Taylor, he does not engage the differences and structures that contemporary literary theorists reveal to be constitutive of texts. For William Empson's discussion of *Othello,* see *The Structure of Complex Words,* ed. Jonathan Culler (1951; rpt. Cambridge: Harvard University Press, 1989). Further references to this text will be made parenthetically in the text.

2 Christopher Norris, *William Empson and the Philosophy of Literary Criticism* (London: Athlone Press, 1978), 86.

3 See Bernard Spivack, *Shakespeare and the Allegory of Evil: The History of a Metaphor in Relation to His Major Villains* (New York: Columbia Univ. Press, 1958).

4 For a fuller discussion of this point, see my discussion of Cavell in part I, pp. 68–69.

5 I would refer to the following exemplary and influential discussions of *Othello*:

a. G. K. Hunter's examination of the historical context of Elizabethan color prejudice, which results in a theory of Shakespearean articulation as the difference between appearance and reality. A historical reconstruction of cultural prejudice makes possible an understanding of language as a transparent "social organism" rather than as an officially sanctioned code of verbal commands and performances. The barely noticed organic surface of language contains a "multitude of tiny unnoticed assents" that someone like Iago can exploit.

b. Spivack's treatment of Iago as a personification, or allegory, of evil, an omnipotent force that the literary tradition seeks to naturalize. Literary expression reduces to a contest between literature's traditional allegorization of evil and the local, historically specific attempts to naturalize the allegory.

c. Wyndham Lewis's discussion of Iago as the emergence of the average man's power for revenge, which undercuts shallow, conventional morality. We are challenged to accept Iago as the manifestation of our own inner strength.

d. F. R. Leavis's condemnation of Othello's magniloquent, figurative language as a form of tragic egotism which is bound to destroy itself. In this interpretation language is self-consuming, charged with vanity; Othello's bombast fascinates us but it immediately suggests its own collapse.

e. The highly sophisticated criticism of Peter Stallybrass, who is able to synthesize class, color, gender, and tragedy in a complex view of transgressive symbolic, ideological structures and contradictions (Desdemona as pure, chaste, and noble but also foul, corrupt, and debasing). Desdemona is the key symbol of the play's ideological contradictions.

See G. K. Hunter, *Dramatic Identities and Cultural Tradition: Studies in Shakespeare and His Contemporaries* (New York: Barnes and Noble, 1978), 31–59; A. C. Bradley, *Shakespearean Tragedy: Lectures on Hamlet, Othello, King Lear, Macbeth* (London, 1905; reprint New York: St. Martin's, 1985); F. R. Leavis, *The Common Pursuit* (London: Chatto and Windus, 1952); Wyndham Lewis, *The Lion and the Fox: The Rôle of the Hero in the Plays of Shakespeare* (New York: Harper, 1927); Peter Stallybrass, "Patriarchal Territories: The Body Enclosed," in *Rewriting the Renaissance: The Discourses of Sexual Difference in Early Modern Europe*, ed. Margaret W. Ferguson, Maureen Quilligan, and Nancy J. Vickers (Chicago: Univ. of Chicago Press, 1986), 123–42. Further references to these critics will be made parenthetically in the text.

6 See Stephen Greenblatt's interpretation of *Othello* in *Renaissance Self-Fashioning: From More to Shakespeare* (Chicago: Univ. of Chicago Press, 1980), 232–54. For an excellent discussion of some of the problems of New Historicist literary history, see Lee Patterson, *Negotiating the Past: The Historical Understanding of Medieval Literature* (Madison: Univ. of Wisconsin Press, 1987), 41–74. Patterson argues that the fluctuation between symbolical meanings and materially determined historical conditions makes the critical effectiveness of New Historicism very difficult to assess. That type of fluctuation may be seen in Greenblatt's comments on Othello, who appears, alternately, as a textual fiction and as a representation of concrete authoritarian practices.

7 Descartes, quoted in Cavell, "Being Odd, Getting Even," 283.

Fish and Coriolanus   **7**

1 I take the term *New Pragmatism* from the subtitle of a collection of essays originally published in *Critical Inquiry: Against Theory: Literary Studies and the New Pragmatism*, ed. W. J. T. Mitchell (Chicago: Univ. of Chicago Press, 1985). For a recent extension of the new pragmatist position, see Stanley Fish, *Doing What Comes Naturally: Change, Rhetoric, and the Practice of Theory in Literary and Legal Studies* (Durham: Duke Univ. Press, 1989) [*DWCN*], and his essay "Being Interdisciplinary Is So Very Hard to Do," in *Profession 89*, 15–22. For Fish's characterization of his work as antiformalist, see the first chapter of *DWCN*.

2 This is not the place to rehearse the methods of New Criticism, which has been widely analyzed by now. On the basic point about intraverbal tension, however, see W. K. Wimsatt on denotation and connotation in "The Substantive Level," in *The Verbal Icon: Studies in the Meaning of Poetry* (Lexington: Univ. of Kentucky Press, 1954), 133–51; and Cleanth Brooks on the internal structure of poems, which distinguishes them from statements, in "The Heresy of Paraphrase" in *The Well-Wrought Urn: Studies in the Structure of Poetry* (New York: Harcourt, Brace, 1947), 192–214; and John Crowe Ransom on the difference between logical structure and poetic texture in "Criticism as Pure Speculation," in *The Intent of the Critic,* ed. Donald A. Stauffer (Princeton: Princeton Univ. Press, 1941), 91–124.

3   On Graff and New Criticism, see my discussion in part I, pp. 72–75.

4   For an elaboration of this argument, see Steven Knapp and Walter Benn Michaels, "Against Theory," in *Against Theory*, 11–30, which in fact contains a criticism of Fish's earlier work in *Is There a Text in This Class? The Authority of Interpretive Communities* (Cambridge: Harvard Univ. Press, 1980). They find too much room between belief and expression in the earlier book. Fish seems to hold that it is possible to "see our beliefs without really believing them. To be in this position would be to see the truth about beliefs without actually having any—to know without believing. In the moment in which he imagines this condition of knowledge outside belief, Fish has forgotten the point of his own earlier identification of knowledge and true belief" (27). Much of *Doing What Comes Naturally* closes this gap more tightly.

5   These topics are covered in specific chapters of *DWCN*. For a response to Habermas, see 450–57, which is part of a larger effort to dismantle the notion of critical consciousness as a distance from practice or a reflection upon practice. Fish argues that changes in discourse come about through the direct contest of one set of beliefs against another. There is no possibility of bracketing norms of behavior, nor is it possible to specify a separate referential linguistic function that would ground the validity of a particular interpretive consensus. Habermas tries to invoke some abstract definition of a speech situation, but for Fish one cannot talk about pragmatism by abstracting away from all "particular situations of use." Similarly, he denies a view of the peer review process that would look for the intrinsic merits of articles, since there is no pure, disembodied intellectual merit. The anonymity of the author means that readers invent their own image of the author, another example of the unity of intention and meaning. See his essay "No Bias, No Merit: The Case against Blind Submission," 163–79. Also see his discussion of a committee charged with investigating the status of women in the university, 460–63. For "gender" to displace some chairperson's attachment to the notion of the intrinsic merit of members of the faculty, regardless of gender, "gender" does not become a new form of consciousness but an engaged "political or social category," with a direct influence upon the deliberative process of peer evaluation.

6   As one example, see my discussion of the term *text* in n. 2, chap. 5.

7   See his remarks on relativism in the title essay "Is There a Text in This Class?" in *Is There a Text in This Class?*, 318–21. Further references to this book will be made parenthetically in the text.

8   An even more telling cancellation of the act of choice is found in an earlier passage in the same essay, in a discussion of an "interpretive crux" in one of Milton's sonnets (155–58). When Milton writes, "They also serve who only stand and wait" the poetic context makes it unclear whether this is an affirmation of faith in God's will, in spite of the sense of his servant being abandoned, or the voice of an allegorical figure chiding a servant for questioning the service of God. Has the speaker of the poem come to realize and internalize the allegorical message, and so regain peace of mind, or is the message outside the complaint against God which motivated the poem's opening? Fish rightly suggests that the question cannot be answered by anything in the poem's formal structure, that in fact it is difficult to pin down which speaker affirms and which questions God's ways. But to leave the whole matter up in the air merely as the experience of any reader confronted with the poem begs the larger question of this reader's own beliefs

and the purpose of reading literature in the first place. The poem becomes, ironically, a purely literary expression of indecision, which plays no role in shaping a reader's own articulation of poetry in relation to everyday belief, which seems to stand altogether outside the act of poetic interpretation. The term *experience* conveys reading as an act, but one that is void in expressive identification. I am not suggesting that the poem can be decided one way or another, but that indecision cannot be attached merely to one little fragment of poetic language. It must be seen to resonate against the reader's own capacities for articulating a response to the poem. A critic like William Empson, for example, is concerned with ambiguity or indecisiveness in certain forms of poetry but goes on to place ambiguous poetry in the context of its influence upon larger patterns of social discourse. For further discussion of this point, see my "Empson's Generalized Ambiguities," in *Literature and Ethics: Essays Presented to A. E. Malloch,* ed. Gary Wihl and David Williams (Montreal: McGill-Queen's Univ. Press, 1988), 3–17.

9 See Jonathan Culler, *The Pursuit of Signs* (Ithaca: Cornell Univ. Press, 1981), 119–31; Robert Scholes, *Textual Power* (New Haven: Yale Univ. Press, 1985), 149–65; William Ray, *Literary Meanings* (London: Basil Blackwell), 152–69.

10 J. L. Austin, *Philosophical Papers,* ed. J. O. Urmson and G. J. Warnock (Oxford: Oxford Univ. Press, 1979), 251.

11 See "*Coriolanus* and the Interpretations of Politics ('Who does the wolf love?')," in Cavell, *Disowning Knowledge in Six Plays of Shakespeare,* 143–77.

12 "The Relativity of Interpretation," *The Monist* 69 (1986): 103.

13 For Cavell's attack on C. L. Stevenson's *Language and Ethics* (1944), see his book *The Claim of Reason: Wittgenstein, Skepticism, Morality and Tragedy* (Oxford: Oxford Univ. Press, 1979), 274–91. Empson also offers a criticism of Stevenson, particularly of false imperatives, in *The Structure of Complex Words,* 414–29.

Jameson's Dialectical Semiotics   **8**

1 See, for example, chapter 1 of Bernard Harrison, *Inconvenient Fictions: Literature and the Limits of Theory* (New Haven: Yale Univ. Press, 1991), 19–70, entitled "How to Reconcile Humanism and Deconstruction." I elaborate on this point in my review of Harrison's book in *The Dalhousie Review* 72 (1992): 119–20.

2 Louis Althusser, *Lire le Capital,* vol. 1, (1965; new edition, Paris: François Maspero, 1968). References are to the new edition.

3 Pierre Macherey, *Theory of Literary Production,* trans. Geoffrey Wall (London: Routledge, 1978), 40.

4 In calling *The Political Unconscious* (Ithaca: Cornell Univ. Press, 1981) Jameson's most important work, I would not wish to diminish the importance of his numerous other studies of structuralism, Western Marxism, modern culture, and world literature. I do think, however, that Jameson's development of a theory of dialectical semiotics, in relation to Althusser and French structuralism, is at its most advanced in *The Political*

Unconscious. Even Jameson's most recent, prize-winning book, *Postmodernism, or, the Cultural Logic of Late Capitalism* (Durham: Duke Univ. Press, 1991), makes use of what I would call Jameson's "dialectical/semiotical" approach as it is most fully developed in *The Political Unconscious.* See, for example, the chapter entitled "Ideology: Theories of Postmodernism," which deploys the Greimassian scheme of a fourfold opposition of cultural values. In other chapters, Jameson invokes the terminology of unconsciousness and aestheticism, two of his most problematical insights, as I argue in this chapter. Of particular interest, however, is his thoughtful and relatively generous engagement with the deconstructionism of Paul de Man (217–59) in his chapter on theory. Several points he makes in this context clarify the kind of contrast I am drawing between Jameson and de Man in this chapter and the next. Jameson has always looked to poststructuralism as a positive influence on the development of Marxism, and in de Man he finds an attempt to break down cultural "homologies" (239). In that respect, deconstruction provides fresh fuel for Marxian dialectics. Yet the entire tenor of Jameson's comments on de Man goes back to an effort to put the terminology of deconstruction into the form of dialectical insights into language and agency (see 244 and 245).

5 I refer to Dominick LaCapra's review essay entitled "Marxism in the Textual Maelstrom: Fredric Jameson's *The Political Unconscious,*" in his *Rethinking Intellectual History: Texts, Contexts, Language* (Ithaca: Cornell Univ. Press, 1983), 234–67; and to Paul Smith, *Discerning the Subject.* Theory and History of Literature, vol. 55 (Minneapolis: Univ. of Minnesota Press, 1988), which discusses Jameson's work at various points.

6 For added commentary on the Caduveo example in Jameson's work as a whole, see William C. Dowling, *Jameson, Althusser, Marx: An Introduction to the Political Unconscious* (Ithaca: Cornell Univ. Press, 1984), 119–22. Dowling says that the contradictions uncovered in Caduveo art are crucial for "Jameson's entire system." He continues, "The Caduveo example contains the essence of Jameson's theory and method." I cite these remarks to lend support to my own focus on the Caduveo example in this chapter.

7 In addition to *The Political Unconscious,* see *The Prison-House of Language* (Princeton: Princeton Univ. Press, 1972); and A. J. Greimas, *On Meaning,* Theory and History of Literature, vol. 38, trans. Paul J. Perron and Frank H. Collins with a foreword by Fredric Jameson (Minneapolis: Univ. of Minnesota Press, 1987).

8 See Claude Lévi-Strauss, *Tristes Tropiques,* trans. John and Doreen Weightman (New York: Atheneum, 1974), 151–97, the chapter on the Caduveo. All further references to this text will be given in parentheses in the text.

9 A. J. Greimas and François Rastier, "The Interaction of Semiotic Constraints," *Yale French Studies* 41 (1968): 86–105.

10 A. J. Greimas, *Structural Semantics: An Attempt at a Method,* ed. Ronald Schleifer, trans. Daniele McDowell, Ronald Schleifer, and Alan Velie (Lincoln: Univ. of Nebraska Press, 1983), xxxiii.

11 See Christine Brooke-Rose, "Woman as a Semiotic Object," in *The Female Body in Western Culture: Contemporary Perspectives,* ed. Susan Rubin Suleiman (Cambridge: Harvard Univ. Press, 1986), 305–16. Brooke-Rose is especially effective at pointing out the social absurdities that can arise from Greimassian semiotics if the logical validity of the rectangle is taken on faith. For a commentary that questions why women seem to illustrate best the mechanics of the sign, see Gayle Rubin, "The Traffic in Women: Notes on the 'Political Economy' of Sex," in *Toward an Anthropology of Women,* ed. Rayna Rapp Reiter (New York: Monthly Review Press, 1975), 157–210. Rubin focuses on Lévi-Strauss's anthropology.

12 See Jacques Derrida, "Freud and the Scene of Writing," in *Writing and Difference,* trans. Alan Bass (Chicago: Univ. of Chicago Press, 1978), 196–231.

De Man on the Hegelian Sublime   **9**

1 Neil Hertz, "Lurid Figures," in *Reading de Man Reading,* ed. Lindsay Waters and Wlad Godzich (Minneapolis: Univ. of Minnesota Press, 1989), 82–104.

2 Compare Terry Eagleton, "The Ideology of the Aesthetic," *Poetics Today* 9 (1988): 327–38, and Christopher Norris, *Paul de Man: Deconstruction and the Critique of Aesthetic Ideology* (London: Routledge, 1988), esp. the first section of chapter 2, "De Man and the Critique of Romantic Ideology," 28–38. Eagleton praises Hegel's "heroic eleventh-hour attempt" to make a direct connection between theoretical reason and the development of civil society. But the effort was too great, too full of "convoluted discursivity" once it attempted to free reason from the aesthetic. In Kierkegaard's terms, Hegel's system cannot be "lived." For Eagleton, aesthetic philosophy today should be seen as part of a tactile, affective materialism of the body. It helps us to feel our ideological repression once wrested away from the philosophy of the fine arts. Deconstruction, if it is Hegelian, is similarly too abstract, too unlivable in Eagleton's view. Norris, by contrast, sees de Man working against Hegel in order to upset the entire romantic tradition. Hegel is the foundational author for the models of interiorization, communion with the natural world, and recollection that we identify with romantic aesthetics. Hegel is a source of literary ideology in the sense of false consciousness about the linguistic structures really at work in the great romantic texts.

Neither of these views quite captures de Man's reading of Hegel, though they are certainly representative of widely held views about deconstruction and about whether or not it has anything to say about ideology. De Man rejects a return to a sensory connection between ideology and aesthetics, like Eagleton's, but only after he has recast the topic of political agency by emphasizing Hegelian negation's break with the idea of interiorizing the natural world. That is where the crux of the debate lies and where de Man would separate Hegel from the English romantics.

3 The essays are Martin Jay, "Name-Dropping or Dropping Names? Modes of Legitimation in the Humanities," in *Theory between the Disciplines,* ed. Martin Kreiswirth and Mark A. Cheetham (Ann Arbor: Univ. of Michigan Press, 1990), 19–34, and id., "Ideology and Ocularcentrism: Is There Anything behind the Mirror's Tain?" I am very

grateful to Martin Jay for providing me with the manuscript of the second essay and for his comments on an early version of this chapter.

4 Paul de Man, "Hegel on the Sublime," in *Displacement: Derrida and After,* ed. Mark Krupnick (Bloomington: Indiana Univ. Press, 1983), 139–53. Hereafter HS.

5 For Jacques Derrida's discussion of the sign in Hegel, see "Le puits et la pyramide: Introduction à la sémiologie de Hegel" in *Marges de la philosophie* (Paris: Les Editions de Minuit, 1972), 79–127. Two very forceful expansions upon the work of Derrida and de Man are Andrzej Warminski, *Readings in Interpretation: Hölderlin, Hegel, Heidegger* (Minneapolis: Univ. of Minnesota Press, 1987), and Cynthia Chase, "Giving a Face to a Name: De Man's Figures," in her *Decomposing Figures: Rhetorical Readings in the Romantic Tradition* (Baltimore: Johns Hopkins Univ. Press, 1986), 82–112. Warminski and Chase offer extremely detailed and complex discussions of how meaning may be dephenomenalized and of the figure of apostrophe and its relation to the authority of citations in Hegel, Derrida, and de Man. But their work is entirely within deconstruction, an elaboration upon the de Man/Derrida position, which to my mind already takes for granted the big questions of how far authorship and agency can be treated as an essentially rhetorical problem. I have learned much from Chase's essay in particular but find that some of the broader philosophical questions about deconstruction emerge in its more resistant critics, like Jay. For example, see the exchange between de Man and Raymond Geuss in *Critical Inquiry* 10 (1983): 375–90. Although the exchange is very technical, involving disputes over the precise meaning of various terms in Hegel's corpus, it is clear that Geuss challenges de Man's fundamental attempt to "grammatize the self." In his response to Geuss, de Man begins to make explicit how the whole question of language would alter basic procedures in social philosophy.

6 See her discussion of the text on apostrophe and the sublime in "Giving a Face to a Name," 95–97.

7 Taylor, *Hegel* (Cambridge: Cambridge Univ. Press, 1975), 472.

Afterword

1 Charles Taylor, "Philosophy and Its History," in *Philosophy in History,* ed. R. Rorty, J. B. Schneewind, and Q. Skinner (New York: Cambridge University Press, 1984), 19.

2 E. D. Hirsch, *Cultural Literacy: What Every American Needs to Know* (Boston: Houghton, 1987), 102–03.

3 E. D. Hirsch, "Against Theory?" in *Against Theory,* ed. Mitchell, 48–49.

4 See Lentricchia's discussion of Hirsch in *After the New Criticism* (Chicago: Univ. of Chicago Press, 1980), 256–80 and David Couzens Hoy, *The Critical Circle* (Berkeley: Univ. of California Press, 1982), 31, quoting Hirsch. For a fuller discussion of this point, see pp. 30-35.

5 E. D. Hirsch, "Faulty Perspectives," in *Modern Criticism and Theory,* ed. David Lodge (London: Longworth, 1980), 262.

INDEX

"Analytic Lyric" —

Curiously, conjoins the
development of a new "critical"
mode with development of a new
poetic (lyric) stance or concern.

— Poetry as criticism?

— cf. G. Ulmer on Anti-Aesthetic: A way of getting
around merely descriptive or explanatory (instrumental?)
language, of "learning by doing."